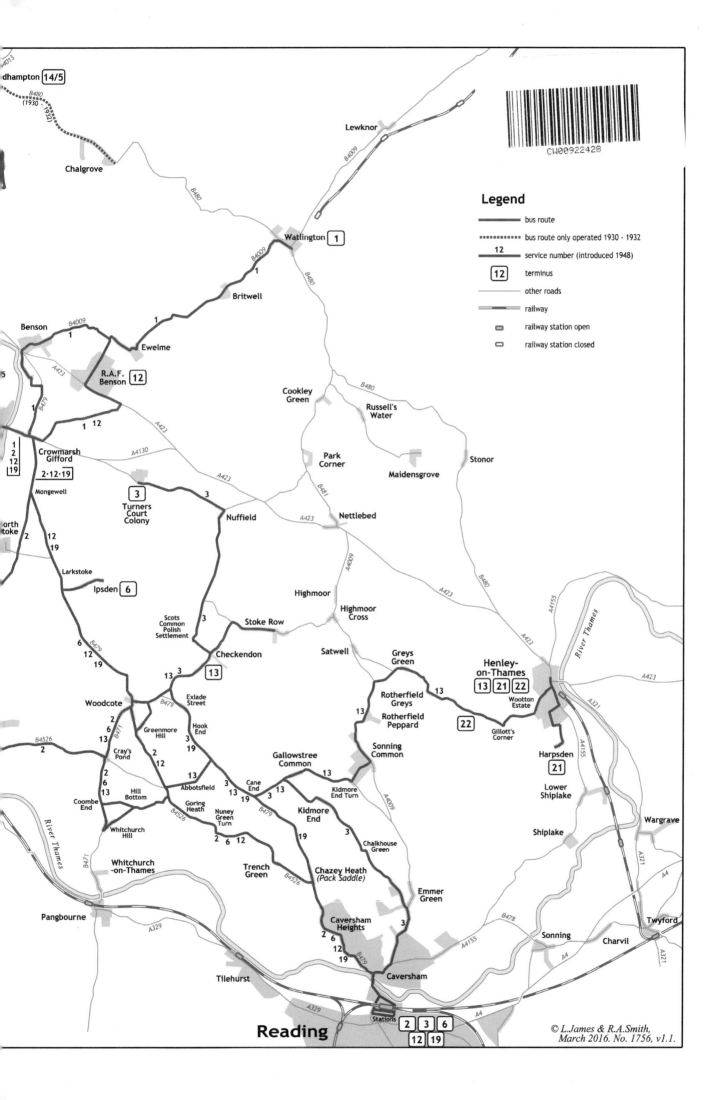

KEMP'S
and
CHILTERN QUEENS

1929-2002

Seventy-three years of buses trundling the lanes of rural South Oxfordshire

Laurie James & John Whitehead

Venture *publications*

CONTENTS

TITLE PAGE: Kemp's Motor Services Ltd perhaps reached its zenith at the beginning of the 1950s. Two post-war vehicles, Dennis Lancet J3 CBW 864 new 1947 and Commer Avenger EBW 838 new May 1950 flank former Green Line coach BRD 922, perhaps the most famous Kemp's (and, later, Chiltern Queens) vehicle. They are seen here in Baylis Road Coach Park, near Waterloo Station, on 19th July 1952, presumably on layover during a Weekend Forces Leave Contract from RAF Benson. (AB Cross)

PREFACE

This book has been a long time coming, for John Whitehead had been researching the history of the locally-based bus operators in south Oxfordshire for nearly 40 years. There are probably very few archive or reference sources that he has not explored and to supplement what he gleaned, he interviewed some of those who owned the buses and coaches, are related to them, worked for them or used their services; some of those people are no longer with us. More recently, Laurie James had, separately, been researching well-known operator Chiltern Queens and has now worked with John to assemble the information, to undertake further research and interviews and to write this text, some of it based on John's earlier essays. John also selected the illustrations and wrote the captions.

The wooded south-western Chiltern Hills are not the most promising territory for running profitable bus services and until the First World War, passenger transport, such as existed, was largely the province of the village carrier with his (or her) horse-drawn van. The area was deeply rural and somewhat remote, despite being situated only about 40 miles from London. The inhabitants mainly worked locally and never travelled very far for work or pleasure. However, their horizons were broadened with the coming of the motor bus, enabling shopping trips and the occasional outing on Sunday to the far-away seaside, eagerly anticipated and long-remembered afterwards, if one could afford the fare, in view of the very low wages then earned by most people.

Our story is centred on an area known by the ancient name of Langtree Hundred, around the village of Woodcote in Oxfordshire. It is more than just about bus routes and vehicles as the tale is bound up with the social history of the district. Part 1 recalls the carriers and the small-scale bus operations of various local proprietors, mainly in the period up to 1930. Some of the bus services evolved from, or were in addition to, a carrier service. There was also short-lived experimentation during the formative years of a much larger local operator – The Thames Valley Traction Co Ltd. Then came a man originally from Essex, with bus operating experience in Leicestershire, who in a few years swept away the opposition and established a network of services which effectively revolutionised the travel opportunity for working class families in the district, making it convenient, reliable and affordable. His name was Harry Kemp. After another World War, that brought great social change in south Oxfordshire, his business expanded to cope with new demand and opportunities, before falling on hard times in the difficult early 1950s. All is explained in Part 2.

The successor to Kemp's Motor Services Ltd was headed by two Reading-based businessmen of means. Their new company, Chiltern Queens Ltd, described in Part 3, was to be a local household name for 47 years as well as of great interest to the bus enthusiast fraternity due to the noteworthy and immaculately-presented fleet. The epitome of the friendly, reliable rural independent bus operator, Chiltern Queens was known well beyond the south Oxfordshire Chilterns until its sad and undeserved demise in 2002.

The authors hope that this book does justice to the history of these concerns and past efforts of all the proprietors, their families and staff, in serving the inhabitants of the area and that it is a suitable tribute to an era of rural public transport endeavour now gone.

Laurie James, Walton-on-Thames 2016
John Whitehead, Reading

These three Plaxton-bodied Leyland Leopards on a private hire to Epsom Races in the early 1980s show off the very best and most modern that Chiltern Queens could offer as the firm's coach hire business moved up-market while still retaining the original smart dark green and grey coach livery. Each served the business well, two of them, UUD 623T and SFC 32P, latterly being given ageless (or cherished) registrations. *(PM Moth)*

INTRODUCTION

We should begin by trying to select a boundary for the area on which our account is mainly focussed. It has to be defined largely by the River Thames to the south and west, a line from Crowmarsh Gifford through Nuffield and Stoke Row to Rotherfield Peppard in the north and the road from Peppard to Caversham through Sonning Common and Emmer Green in the east. However, by necessity, our interest extends beyond this chosen boundary to places such as Benson, Ewelme, Watlington and Henley-on-Thames in Oxfordshire and across the Thames to Wallingford, Didcot, Abingdon and the intervening villages in what was once Berkshire, but transferred to Oxfordshire on 1 April 1974. Thus, the Thames north of Goring Gap is no longer a county divide. The County Borough of Reading, within the ceremonial county of Berkshire, is also highly relevant and to this was annexed Caversham, on the north bank of the Thames, from Oxfordshire in 1911. The County Borough status of Reading was lost in 1974. To clarify, we are concerned with the westernmost side of the most southerly part of the Chiltern Hills, where the soil contains flints set in clay, overlying chalk.

With a landscape shaped by the Ice Age, featuring many small valleys and 'bottoms', the southern Chilterns were once extensive heath-lands, with wooded escarpments. After the Enclosure Acts at the beginning of the nineteenth century, much of the land was cleared for agriculture, but a fair amount remained wooded, including the famous beech woods. At the exposed southern end, there is open arable land, similar to the Berkshire Downs.

The River Thames cuts its way through the chalk hills, so separating the Berkshire Downs from the Chilterns. Continuing eastwards, the river follows the edge of the Chilterns and into the Thames Valley, then onwards towards London and the sea. Reading is the largest town served by the bus operators described and the most important commercial and shopping centre for a large hinterland. It became a key stopping and resting point on the London to Bath and Bristol road in the days of horse-drawn coaches and it was also a junction with a road to Oxford, which passed through Goring Gap and over the Thames at Wallingford. The opening of the Kennet & Avon Canal in the eighteenth century, linking Reading to Bristol, brought additional trade. Accessibility was revolutionised with the coming of the Great Western Railway in the nineteenth century, which established its main lines from London to Bath, Bristol, Somerset, Devon, Cornwall, Oxford, Birmingham and South Wales. Road and rail links brought trade and prosperity, thus the town grew over the years to its current considerable size. Once a small village, another place to grow with the coming of the railway, was Didcot, where the Great Western Railway provided a fair amount of employment,

with an important junction station and an engine shed. Later, Didcot was noted for its large army camp and later the construction of two adjacent power stations. The cooling towers were visible for miles across a considerable area of the Vale of Oxford, although those of the Didcot 'A' power station were demolished a short time ago, following its decommissioning.

An alternative road route to Oxford left the London to Bath road at Maidenhead and then proceeded by way of Henley-on-Thames, Bix and Nettlebed to Crowmarsh Gifford and Benson, thence northwards to Oxford. However, the area between the Thames and this route witnessed little in terms of the establishment of good roads, so that it remained a somewhat remote, very rural backwater. The main purpose of a trackway that developed between Caversham and Crowmarsh Gifford, through Chazey Heath, Cane End and Exlade Street, is revealed in the name of Inns either along it or close by – The Pack Horse and The Pack Saddle at Chazey Heath and The Four Horseshoes at nearby Checkendon.

The railways never entered our main area of interest, the nearest stations being some distance away at Reading, Henley, Wallingford and Goring & Streatley. A branch line was built from Cholsey & Moulsford station on the main line, (which replaced a previous station three quarters of a mile away, originally named Wallingford Road and then Moulsford) to Wallingford. This was opened in July 1866 by the Wallingford & Watlington Railway Co, with the original intention of continuing to Watlington and beyond. The independent owners sold out in 1872 to the Great Western Railway, which had actually been operating the line. When it was realised that the line would never cross the Thames and continue to Watlington, plans being abandoned in 1868, the locally-promoted Watlington & Princes Risborough Railway was built, opening in August 1872.

So, with poor road and rail communications, the Industrial Revolution passed the area by. Life was quite simple and basic up to the end of the First World War. The indifferent water supply, with most houses relying on wells, hampered development even after the South Oxfordshire Water & Gas Co built a reservoir in 1905 near The Black Lion inn on Greenmore in Woodcote, enabling a piped supply to some houses in the district. Mains electricity arrived as late as 1934, but a few affluent families had their own generating engines. Unless one was in an occupation, such as a blacksmith, baker, shopkeeper, builder, miller, teacher or carrier, the main form of employment was in agriculture or in woodland-related trades, such as charcoal burning or making pegs, pit props or chair legs for the furniture industry which was centred on High Wycombe and Stokenchurch. There were a few brickworks where clay was workable, such as that run by the Woodcote Brick

& Tile Works Ltd until the Second World War, at the top of Long Toll. After the First World War, a farm worker's wage had only reached 30 shillings (£1.50) a week and it could be said that there was real local poverty until the Second World War. Families would supplement their income during lean times by finding casual work as stone pickers. Stones and flints were picked from the fields and sold to the County Council for repairing roads. The roads in the southern Chilterns were largely surfaced with consolidated stones and many were not sealed with tar until the early 1930s. People either worked near their homes within walking distance, or at most a cycle ride away. The concept of daily commuting from the south Chiltern villages to a town for employment was extremely rare.

The location of the premises of two of the bus operators about to be described – Kemp's Motor Services and Chiltern Queens – was the village of Woodcote (meaning 'a cottage in the wood'), situated about seven miles north-west of Reading and five miles south-east of Wallingford. With part of the village at five to six hundred feet above sea level, Woodcote is the highest point in the Chilterns locally. Until 1952, it was part of the Parish of South Stoke. The church of St Leonard originated in mediaeval times, although subsequently much-rebuilt and there are a few cottages from the Tudor and Georgian periods. However, at the start of the twentieth century, there were little more than 20 dwellings and a few farms, although a new school building was opened in 1899. Even at the end of the First World War, Woodcote was no more than a hamlet and real growth did not start until the 1920s. Some local authority housing was constructed from 1947 but from then on right up to the present day numerous private houses have been built including several estates, serving what is largely a dormitory residential cohort. The population today is probably around the 3,000 mark – in 1951 it was only around 700. The village has Langtree Secondary school, which draws in students from the surrounding area. Of interest is a one hundred feet high steel transmitter mast at Greenmore Hill, originally constructed after the Second World War to enable radio and television broadcasting experiments. A notable local person was Maggie Beeson, an aunt of Chiltern Queens driver Phillip Smith, who retired as the village Postmistress in 1945 and lived until 1990 to the age of one hundred and four years. She was apparently the oldest bell ringer in Britain at the time she had to give up in 1985, having started ringing in 1902!

In the second half of the nineteenth century and predominantly in the first 30 years of the twentieth century, most villages had their own carrier, in some cases two, who would usually operate on different days. Their function was to take local goods to market in the towns or to the nearest railway station and to bring back all manner of commodities from the town traders to the village inhabitants or shopkeepers. Goods carried included parcels of groceries, sides of meat, clothing,

timber, livestock, bicycles – in fact whatever might be needed and ordered from suppliers. They operated to set routes and times, concentrating especially on Market Day and having taken orders from customers in advance, the carrier or his assistant would visit the shops in town and deliver the items in late afternoon or early evening on return to their home area, on a commission or fixed-fee basis. Quite often, it was the custom to put out a sign, such as a piece of cloth or paper on a stick at one's garden gate, to signal the carrier to stop and collect an order. Usually, a wagon or a van with a canvas top would be used, drawn by one or two horses and on arrival in town, the vans were parked conveniently close to the market or main shopping area, whilst the horses were taken to stabling at various inns until it was time for the return journey – an activity known as ostlering. For the south Chiltern villages, the destination inevitably meant Reading, where carriers would congregate at Abbey Walk outside the Shire Hall, adjacent to Forbury Gardens.

In some cases, passengers were also carried but this was subsidiary to the transport of goods. However, the journey and time away from home took up much of the day, a period of time that the lady of the house from a working class family could ill-afford and the fixed fare was often not sustainable on rural household income at that time, unless there was a special reason for going to town. Even the gradual transition from horse power to motor van from the First World War onwards did little to improve patronage as it was still cheaper to have the carrier collect one's shopping rather than go to Reading, Wallingford, Henley or wherever oneself in the carriers van, with the added discomfort of sharing it with all manner of goods being transported. As we shall see, some of the carriers later acquired motor vehicles which were more suitable for carrying passengers, perhaps up to fourteen people at one time, so fares could be lowered. These vehicles could provide more trips per day than the horse-drawn vans and it was these early 'omnibus' services which began to enable more outward travel for village-dwellers and reduce the problem of rural isolation.

Prior to 1931, the licensing of omnibus drivers, conductors, vehicles and in some cases services, was the province of various local authorities, acting under powers contained in the Town Police Clauses Act 1889 regarding the regulation of hackney carriages and omnibuses – horse drawn at first and later motor buses. The provisions of the legislation were mainly exercised in the larger towns, usually to reduce congestion in the streets and at terminal points, but sometimes, in the competitive era of the 1920s, to avoid wasteful duplication if it was felt a particular route into town was already adequately served. The County Borough of Reading was active in this respect, but smaller towns such as Wallingford, Henley and Didcot were not, as presumably the local Councils regarded it as unnecessary. However, matters changed significantly with the enactment of the standardised national licensing system within the Road Traffic Act 1930, which was designed to introduce coordination and quantity control of omnibus services and to regulate the competitive nature of service provision that was rife in many areas.

From 1 April 1931, only the licensing of taxi cabs and other vehicles with less than 8 seats and hired as a whole, was undertaken by local authorities. In relation to public service vehicles, parts of the Town Police Clauses Act were repealed and bus operators had to apply to an area Traffic Commissioner for a Road Service Licence; normal bus services were termed Stage Carriage services, whilst the term 'Express' was used for those with a more limited number of stops – mainly longer distance services. A programme of Excursions and Tours also required a licence, but Private Hire work did not. The Commissioners decided which services would run, at what level and by whom. When competing applications were received, they would hold a Hearing in the 'Traffic Court', where operators could be legally represented to promote and protect their interests and were able to object to even a minor proposed amendment to a route or timings put forward by another operator if it was felt to be a commercial threat. Having heard all the evidence, the Commissioner would make a decision and a Road Service Licence issued, renewed, amended or refused. The Commissioner also regulated and approved the fares to be charged.

If, at the outset, an operator could prove that they ran an established service which was in the public interest and met a need, they generally received permission to continue. Due to often weighty objections in a formal courtroom setting, getting a licence for a new or extended service was far more difficult for operators than when they dealt (if at all) with local authorities. Public Service Vehicles had to undergo close scrutiny by a Ministry of Transport vehicle examiner to ensure they were fit for use under more stringent national criteria.

For some of the small local operators in our story, the new regulations and associated paperwork were very unwelcome and some soon left the industry, being unwilling or unable to adjust and find the time and money attached to the extra administrative burden or vehicle certification and maintenance costs. The provisions of the Road Traffic Act 1930 were in force until 1980, although somewhat differently administered during the Second World War. The subsequent effect of 'Deregulation' after 1980, which continues today, is discussed in Part 3.

ACKNOWLEDGEMENTS

Whilst gathering information for this book, the authors have received information, memories, documents and photographs from many people over many years. Grateful thanks are offered for considerable assistance and enthusiasm from Michael Allen, Trevor Back, Colin Barrett, Philip Battersby, John Bennett (Loughborough), John Bennett (Checkendon), June Cope, the late Ernie Cox, John Davies, Ian Dyer, Kathleen Kemp, Martin Iredale, Peter Jaques, Paul Jenkins, Vicky Jordan, Paul Lacey, Jack Passey, Michael Plunkett, Tony Sears, Tom Shaw, Philip Smith, Mike Stephens, Gillian Stokes, Pat Walsh, Mary Weller and the late Harold Wynn. Particularly useful photographic contributions came from Graham Geoghegan, Graham Low, Ray Smith, Chris Spencer and the late Mike Dare.

We must also acknowledge the PSV Circle, the Omnibus Society's library, Reading Central Library, Berkshire Record Office, Oxford Library and the Reading Transport Society (later the British Trolleybus Society), as well as various websites – particularly Census 1911, Polish Settlement Camps in the UK and History of RAF Woodcote.

Relevant parts of the manuscript were read by Michael Allen, Colin Barrett, Jack Passey, Tony Sears and Gillian Stokes, to whom we are grateful for their helpful comments.

Efforts have been made to ensure correct attribution of the images within, but the origination of some is unknown, hence they are credited as part of the collection of the person who supplied them. Apologies are sincerely offered for any error in this respect. When dealing with events of long ago, there are always likely to be gaps in documented material and personal memories that are hard to verify, so some matters have been recounted in good faith. Some detail ideally sought has been lost in the mists of time and now we are unlikely to ever know for sure. Any error of interpretation or omission is ours alone and we apologise if we have inadvertently conveyed or perpetuated a falsehood.

Finally, in no way least, love and gratitude to our wives for their support and forbearance.

Laurie James, Walton-on-Thames
John Whitehead, Reading

PART I
VILLAGE CARRIERS and EARLY MOTOR BUS SERVICES

Woodcote and Checkendon Carriers

The character of the road to Reading from the Woodcote and Checkendon direction, through Exlade Street, Cane End, Chazey Heath and Caversham, has changed considerably since the start of the twentieth century. At that time there were only four houses between St Peter's church at Caversham and The Pack Saddle inn at Chazey Heath, together with Toots Farm at the top of what is now St Peter's Hill. Beyond the Caversham boundary, the road was bordered by high, tree-lined banks as far as Shepherds Lane. The Pack Saddle, which the road today bypasses, was on the Reading side of a sharp bend and a forked road junction in a tree-clad cutting. This was the route to town of several of the village carriers, with their horse-drawn vans.

At least by the turn of the 19th century, there were two carriers from Woodcote listed in Kelly's Directory. One was Thomas Cox, also a Poultry Dealer and the other was Solomon Joseph Havell, who lived at The Bungalow, Whitehouse Road, Woodcote; he ran to Reading on Monday, Thursday and Saturday. The Havells were a large and long-established Woodcote family and by 1911, the business was in the name of Solomon's wife – Laura Ann Havell, who had been born in Gloucester around 1869 as Laura Rogers and had married in October 1889. She was also operating on Tuesday, but passengers were apparently not carried on any day. Havell was then listed as a farm labourer, possibly at Hammond's Estate in Checkendon, although his cousin, Joseph Watts, was assisting Mrs Havell with the carrier business, which was still in existence after the end of the First World War. Solomon died in 1939, whilst Laura passed away in 1945.

Performing a similar function from Checkendon, was George Harwood who with his wife Marrey, lived at Emmens Fields in that village. He ran to Reading on Tuesday, Thursday and Saturday, possibly serving Woodcote as well, whilst concurrently, James King ran on Monday, Wednesday and Friday and carried passengers too, at a fare of one shilling each way. Later, a carrier from Checkendon was Bill Packham, probably

with a motor van and by the early nineteen thirties (by when motor bus services were well-established) it was a Mr Cottrell, running to The Boars Head in Friar Street in Reading on Tuesday, Thursday and Saturday.

Pat Walsh recalls that his Great Grandmother's father, Dennis Higgs was, until the First World War, a goods carrier based in Checkendon at Bradley Street. He would take loads of chair legs produced by the wood turners in the beech woods, to the furniture factories at High Wycombe and Stokenchurch, in a horse-drawn covered heavy van. He would also deliver wood for fuel to local houses and around Caversham. Later, another van was used for general goods carrier activities and on trips to Reading his daughter Lizzy would purchase goods for village customers that would be taken back to Checkendon. Dennis enjoyed a tipple of whisky and on occasions when Lizzy was not with him, he stopped at The Pack Horse inn. On setting off home, he would fall asleep at the reins, but the horse would find its own way through Cane End and Exlade Street until it was back in Checkendon, with its master still asleep on the seat at the front of the van. Coincidently, Lizzy's future husband, Harry Wells, was distantly related to Ted Page of Cleeve, who we will meet later.

For an eye-witness account of travelling with the carrier, it is fortunate that Miss Kitty Hope wrote down her memories for the Checkendon News-Letter, about 30 years ago, when she was over 90 years of age:

A typical carrier's covered wagon, thought to be Paddick's, from Cane End, and seen here at Kidmore End Well c1907, was the type which might convey passengers as well as goods in fairly cramped conditions. *(Commercial post card)*

"In the days before mechanised transport, the only way most of us in Checkendon had for shopping was the carrier's van. It had seats each side and a canvas hood. It went to Reading two or three times a week. If you wished the carrier to call, you put a card in your window and he would come and take your shopping orders – grocery, shoes, clothes or whatever you wanted. You paid the carrier a fee for each order (2d or 3d) and shops would send goods on approval.

Dennis and Emma Higgs, of Bradley Street, Checkendon, on the occasion of the wedding of their daughter Eliza to Arthur Ashly, with proud Dennis driving the family to church using Albert Salmon, of Stoke Row's carriers wagon with the canvas tilt removed c1905. *(PJ Walsh)*

If you were making the journey yourself, you waited by the road and took your place in the van. At about 9am the van started the journey, picking up more passengers and parcels on the outskirts of the village. When all were aboard, you set off for Reading surrounded by parcels, packages and perhaps some chickens in a crate for the market, chatting pleasantly to your fellow travellers as the van made its way along the wooded roads.

At The Pack Horse, a stop was made to rest the horses and for the travellers to have refreshment, then on through Chazey Heath to Caversham and down St Peter's Hill into Reading. The carrier would go to the hostelry of his choice, usually The Boar's Head or The Duke of Edinburgh, where the ostler stabled the horse. The passengers went to their favourite shops and the carrier took the orders he had been given to the various suppliers, which delivered the goods to the van later.

At the appointed hour, the passengers returned to the van and the homeward journey began. If the load was heavy, you would be asked to walk up some of the hills. There was further rest at The Pack Saddle and then on into Checkendon, with the carrier delivering the parcels and collecting his fees. In winter through the dark lanes, the only light was a candle lantern on each side of the van. Arriving home about 5pm, you gathered up your shopping, said goodbye to your fellow travellers and paid the fare of one shilling for your day's outing."

Dennis and Emma Higgs out for a jaunt aboard Albert Salmon's carrier's wagon, in Bradley Street, Checkendon c1905. *(PJ Walsh)*

Goring-On-Thames Carriers

A plethora of proprietors has been recorded as providing a carrier service to Reading from Goring-on-Thames via Crays Pond, Goring Heath, Trench Green, Chazey Heath and Caversham. By 1883 there was Stephen Swaine on Wednesday and Saturday. By 1887 it was Edward Tillen and in 1895 by a Mr Wall on Friday, Alfred Bacon on Tuesday and Saturday and Alfred Hazell on Tuesday, Thursday and Saturday. Bacon had given up by 1899 in favour of Joseph Pope, running the same days as Hazell, but by 1903 Pope had been replaced by William Hales, from Cleeve. Around 1907, Hazell dropped out, leaving Wall and Hales to continue until about 1915. Hales also served Whitchurch Hill and had a two-horse van.

Shortly afterwards, William Hales was replaced by Harry Smith, who initially also relied on horse power. On Saturdays, at least, it is understood that Smith took passengers to Reading and charged 6d each way. Having obtained a motor van, he projected his service to start from Wallingford via North Stoke, South Stoke and Cleeve. Information collected for Kelly's Directory indicated that by 1923, he also ran what was described as an omnibus from South Stoke to Wallingford on Fridays – quite likely the same vehicle used on other days for the trip to Reading. However, by the middle of that year, he had sold out to AJ Muggeridge, apparently a very 'laid back' fellow. The latter ran a Ford Model T station bus named 'Skylark', possibly the same one used previously by Smith, in which he carried passengers on the same services as formerly run by Smith. During the space of one year, Muggeridge made a poor show of running his business and developed a reputation for unreliability. However, in the early nineteen twenties, country folk in the vicinity of Woodcote would walk down to Crays Pond or down Long Toll to the bottom of College Woods, to catch Smith's or Muggeridge's vehicle for a trip to Reading.

Although Thames Valley started a bus service from Reading to Woodcote in June 1921, the timetable was not helpful in allowing a convenient shopping trip to town for Woodcote residents, so the Goring carrier had to suffice until Charles Wilkinson came on the scene. Around mid-1924, Muggeridge disposed of his business to Edward Page.

Edward Page

Edward George Page was one of the five offspring of a farmer, as a young child living at Rose Farm in Rocky Lane, Bix, according to the 1911 census, later moving to Highmoor Farm at the village of that name on the Reading to Nettlebed road. By 1924, Ted Page was not much more than 20 years of age and had already married Annie Howard-Watson, moving to live at a house named 'High View' in Cleeve, near Goring. He established a haulage business and acquired Muggeridge's carrier/bus activities as well. The service to Reading was curtailed to start at South Stoke and as the old cast iron Caversham Bridge was closed at that time for replacement by the current ferro-concrete structure, it meant that a detour to Reading town centre was required via Reading Bridge and Vastern Road. It was not long before Page replaced Muggeridge's Ford, with another Ford T – a 14-seat bus, registered as MO 3808, on 11 September 1924.

It may have been the closure of Caversham Bridge that prompted Page to re-route his Reading service by way of Goring Bridge, Streatley Bridge and the 'valley' road through Pangbourne, Purley and Tilehurst, but this is not yet proven. However, between 23 May and 1 October 1924, the Thames Valley Traction Co Ltd extended some weekday journeys on their Reading-

Ted Page with UD 2594, his 1929 Brockway JBF with Duple dual-door 20-seat body and full complement of male passengers – thought to be on a local Goring British Legion outing in the early-1930s. *(Goring Gap Local History Society)*

Another view of Ted Page with Brockway UD 2594, which was a particularly rare make in Britain. It appears to carry a maple leaf type of radiator badge, rather suited to the north-American origin of the chassis. *(Paul Jenkins)*

Wallingford service 5, which turned short at Streatley, to continue over the river to Goring on Thames and Cleeve Crossroads. Although this speculative experiment was of short duration, it may have been a warning to Ted Page to vacate 'their road'. If indeed he had changed his route, on restoring his service to run through south Oxfordshire, Page found that he was now suffering competition from Charles Wilkinson. Ted continued driving the bus himself, whilst employing Tommy Coles to drive a Ford truck on haulage work.

On days when the bus services did not run, the vehicle could be used for private hire work or the occasional excursion. On Saturdays, the South Stoke to Reading bus service increased to three round trips. To provide a better vehicle for excursions and private hire, Ted Page took delivery of an American-built Brockway JBF coach with 20-seat bodywork by Duple, first-registered on 9 January 1929 as UD 2594. Brockways were a fairly rare import into the United Kingdom, not least for use as passenger vehicles.

The introduction of a regular bus service by Harry Kemp in 1929 between Wallingford, Goring and Reading, at cheaper fares, was a serious competitive threat to Ted Page. Consequently, he withdrew the Friday South Stoke to Wallingford service and reduced the Reading service to Saturdays only, concentrating on coaching work for the rest of the week. His Ford T

bus, MO 3808, was last licensed to 31 December 1929 and seems to have been replaced by a dark red-liveried Ford AA, which had a 14-seat bus body of unknown make, registered on 22 November 1929 as UD 3431.

In accordance with the requirements of the Road Traffic Act 1930, Page applied for Road Service Licences in April 1931. These were for the South Stoke to Reading service via Goring-on-Thames, Crays Pond, Whitchurch Hill and Goring Heath on Saturdays and for excursions starting at Cleeve ('High View') to Aldershot Tattoo, Southsea and Windsor, as well as other destinations on special occasions. Objections were lodged by Harry Kemp and Thames Valley and the application for excursions was also objected to by the Southern Railway, as the latter had established a policy of doing so in regard to any excursion licence applications which covered areas served by their trains. At a hearing at Maidenhead in May 1931, the licences were granted.

In February 1932 it was necessary to seek renewal of the excursions and tours licence, with various additional destinations being applied for, including Ascot Races, London, Brighton, Bognor Regis and Whipsnade Zoo. The requested start point was Goring-on-Thames (The Garage), as Page had had one constructed on some land in Wallingford Road, Goring. Picking up points were sought at South Stoke, Streatley, Whitchurch Hill and Pangbourne.

Although the application was granted, the Great Western Railway had lodged an objection to a pick-up point at Pangbourne. On appeal, the Minister of Transport instructed the deletion of Pangbourne from the licence.

Harry Kemp's new bus service seems to have had such a marked effect on Page's Saturday Reading service, that discussions concluded in March 1932 between the parties, resulted in Page agreeing to make the licence over to Kemp; Page's last day of operation may well have been 26 June 1932. This left him with his coaching and haulage work, whilst competition from Ernie Cox and regular bus services had rendered the need for a carrier service largely redundant, as people could now easily visit Reading themselves to do their shopping.

Page decided to sell his carrier work about 1932/3 to a Mr Vincent. The latter thought that the haulage activities were included in the deal and was somewhat aggrieved to discover, too late, that they were not. It is thought that expensive litigation ensued, although Page won the case and continued to operate a lorry. Soon after, Ted Page built a new house named 'Sunniways', adjacent to his garage.

Around 1933, the Brockway coach was replaced by a REO 20-seat coach, probably a Gold Crown model. This was painted dark red, lined out in cream and sign-written by local man Eric Taylor across the rear in gold. It had a hard roof, was luxuriously appointed, with curtains, navy-blue check wool rugs to each seat and a silver-plated flower vase behind the windscreens. When spares were required, Ted had to go to the REO agent in Goldhawk Road, London. After being stored in the garage for a time, the Brockway passed to J Meadows & Son of Barton Seagrave, Northants and then to Mr J Haywood of Sileby, Leicestershire by December 1935.

Following the death of his wife, Ted Page was able to employ Vera Stratton from Goring Heath (bus operator Ernie Cox's cousin) to keep house and look after his four-year-old daughter, Audrey. Vera also restored order to the paperwork for the coach and haulage business, as Ted detested dealing with it. At whatever time a coach arrived back at night, Vera would always hand wash the outside and sweep out and clean inside, finishing with a cloth dipped in eau de cologne.

In due course, a haulage business had to be licensed for the type of work it undertook. At one point, Ted Page forgot to renew his 'B' licence for general haulage duties and had to re-apply. In order to trade in the interim, he had to operate under the more restrictive trader's 'C' licence. This meant he had to buy the load he was carrying and then re-sell it to the consignee on delivery! Work he undertook included transporting coal from Goring station to the gasworks and tent pegs made in the woods around Highmoor, for he still had contacts in that area and still owned two cottages at Stoke Row.

On occasion, Page would undertake work for Butler's Coaches of Henley-on-Thames and Smith's Coaches of Reading. He also maintained his excursion and private work until the outbreak of the Second World War and conveyed children from Goring School to the County School at Sonning Common, fortnightly, for woodwork lessons. Although quite illegal after the implementation of the Road Traffic Act 1930, he would fit wooden boards across the coach gangway between the seats so as to accommodate more children. Whilst Page had no worries about occasionally bending the rules, it is said that visits from Mr Jackson – the Traffic Commissioner's Inspecting Officer – filled him with terror. Ted's daughter remembered being taken regularly to the seaside, to the extent that her father came into conflict with the Schools Attendance Officer. She had vivid memories of sing-songs on the way home and the summer Sunday evening mystery tours inevitably included a stop at a country public house. Many had beer gardens and Ted's rockery at 'Sunniways' is said to have benefitted from plants 'acquired' on these occasions. Vera Stratton would prepare blackboards advertising the excursions and place them by the gate at 'Sunniways'. No tickets were issued but Vera took the money at the house and read out a list of names before the coach departed. Vera always had her special seat at the front, next to the driver.

As Page had never actively sought contract work, he was quite hard hit when leisure travel had to cease in September 1939. However, he was fortunate in being able to secure some work for his REO coach (without driver) from Mr Crowe who ran Peggy's Coaches in Reading, and who was transporting war workers every day from Reading to the Maintenance Depot at RAF Milton, near Didcot. When the coach was parked in a street in Reading overnight, petrol was siphoned on more than one occasion, causing failure whilst en route to Milton. Ted or Vera would make sure that the full quota of petrol was received when the tank was filled at Jacob's Garage in Streatley.

By the time the RAF Milton work had finished – possibly after the end of the war – the condition of the REO had deteriorated and it was stored unlicensed in the garage at 'Sunniways'. It was still there around 1950 and it is thought that it was finally dispatched to Harold Goodey's scrap yard at Twyford. Meanwhile, due to increased haulage work, the Ford AA bus UD 3431 was converted into a lorry around May 1945. The carriage of goods was to continue for a considerable time. Ted passed away in the late nineteen seventies, followed a few years later by his second wife. Audrey Page, who became Mrs Jenkins, inherited 'Sunniways' on her father's death. Her son, Paul Jenkins, lived there for a time. The garage was later demolished, followed by the sale and demolition of the house for redevelopment.

Charles Wilkinson ('Woodcote & District')

After the Great War, Charles Wilkinson and his wife were butler/chauffeur and cook respectively to the Wallis family at 'Querns', Goring Heath. By 1921, Charles had already considered that introducing a bus service might be quite remunerative and the subject was often discussed in the servant's quarters. The Wallis family moved away and the Wilkinsons took a cottage on the Hardwick Estate, owned by Lady Rose, in an orchard next to Goring Heath Post Office. So, Charles bought a bus and commenced his service in August 1923. By all accounts, he was a likeable man and had been encouraged and aided in his venture in a significant way by Edward Mullard, who lived nearby at 'Ladygrove' and was the Goring Rural District Council surveyor. Mullard is said to have been one of the first owners of a motor car in this part of Oxfordshire.

The bus was first registered on 2 August 1923 as BW 6918 – a Fiat (possibly a type 2B) which had been ordered by the Italian army but never used. It came from the well-known motor vehicle agents Vincents of Reading Ltd and was fitted with a 14-seat general purpose body built by them at their Castle Street workshops. Constructed of timber, with plywood side panels, it was finished externally in a grained and varnished livery. It had a fully-enclosed passenger compartment, with boarded roof and glazed windows. Entry was by a pair of doors and a tailboard at the rear. There was inward facing seating for six along each side, which could be easily removed when needed for the carriage of goods. There was a tip-up seat fixed to the inside of one of the doors and the remaining passenger could sit next to the driver. The rear and front side lamps were oil, whilst the two large front head lamps were powered by acetylene, which apparently were next to useless after being alight for more than about ten minutes. Although reliable mechanically, it had pneumatic tyres with twin rear wheels, which were rather close together and rubbed under load, got hot and burst, not aided by the fact that the local roads were unsealed, with frequent pot-holes.

Wilkinson's service started at Woodcote Crossroads, by the War Memorial dedicated to the Fallen in June 1920, proceeding by way of Crays Pond, Whitchurch Hill, Goring Heath, Trench Green, Chazey Heath and Caversham, to terminate in Vincent's Yard, opposite Reading General Station, a location also used at that time by House Bros for their service from Watlington. If a heavy load was being carried on the return journey, the normal route out of Caversham via the steep and narrow St Peter's Hill would be forsaken for the easier route via Priest Hill, Kidmore Road and Highmoor Road.

It is thought that originally, a flat fare of one shilling was charged, which caused passengers making shorter journeys to complain about paying the same as those from Woodcote. On Mondays to Fridays the bus left Woodcote at 9am, returning from Reading at 12.30pm on Monday and Wednesday and at 4pm on Tuesday, Thursday and Friday. Before refrigerators were available, very little food shopping was done on Mondays (wash day!) and Wednesday was Early Closing for shops in Reading. On Saturday, the little bus performed no fewer than 8 round trips, culminating in a 10.30pm departure from Reading, or at whatever time all the patrons had exited the Palace and Royal County Theatres.

During the week, the time spent in Reading was linked to the requirements for carrying goods as well. Lengths of timber for local carpenters supplied by Warwick Bros in Oxford Road were commonly transported, also new bicycles from R Watts & Co for Brown & Cox's cycle shop in Woodcote, items of furniture ordered by local residents, one and a quarter hundredweight bags of flour for Cecil Lee, the Woodcote baker and meat for Crays Pond butcher, Fred Pointer. Jacksons, an outfitter in Reading, sent a man round the villages every six weeks and orders were dispatched by Wilkinson's bus and delivered to customers. The driver would be given shopping lists by housewives along the route and for a 3d carriage charge, packets of groceries from Baylis, the Co-op, Liptons etc were delivered to customers by bus. The last Saturday evening trip from Reading was invariably full to bursting with humanity and it was not uncommon for two or three people to sit on the tailboard and more than once one brave soul went home lying on the roof.

Originally, Charles kept his bus in the orchard next to his cottage, but later obtained the use of a barn at Charity Farm in Goring Heath, by courtesy of Frank Chapman. His bus service was the first to offer a convenient link to and from Reading for the Woodcote district, with a degree of comfort and good reliability, notwithstanding some earlier operations by the Thames Valley Traction Co. It became very successful and in June 1924 a Sunday afternoon and evening service was added, which as well as allowing time in Reading, was advertised in the local newspapers to promote a travel opportunity for townspeople to spend an afternoon in the countryside. Originally referred to as 'Wilkinson's Bus', the service was later branded as 'Woodcote & District'. Another Fiat vehicle was obtained from Vincents, registered BW 8275 on 26 November 1924, fitted with magneto ignition, pneumatic tyres and a dynamo for the provision of electric lighting. The body built for it by Vincents was more like a bus as we know it, with 20 forward facing seats, opening saloon windows, a rear emergency door and a front entrance on the nearside, operated by the driver. The livery was brown and cream.

The success of the service allowed an increase on Friday to two round trips, whilst the number on Saturday was reduced to five; both the Fiats were needed on that day. Wilkinson bought some land in Whitehouse Road, Woodcote around 1924 and built a garage large enough for the two buses. He may have built it slowly himself in his spare time, as the concrete floor was not laid or the doors hung until sometime in 1925.

During the week when the bus service was run with BW 8275, the first Fiat was used for some private hire work and, occasionally, the odd haulage or household removal job. Milk churns were taken from farms to Theale Station in 1924 during the railway workers' strike and a load of eggs was once taken up to London, with three punctures and two tyre bursts being suffered on the one trip! Wilkinson's vehicles took cricket, football and darts teams to away matches and there were excursions to Ascot Races and the Aldershot Military Tattoo. Such was the number of people and vehicles attending the Tattoo, it took a long time to exit the bus park and the driver was often not home for bed until 1am or 2am for the whole of the week.

Maintenance work could take all night to complete so that the buses were ready for use the next day. Wilkinson only ever employed one other person, who drove and did the maintenance. For most of the time, this was Ernie Cox, who had worked with Wilkinson at 'Querns'. When the bus service started, Ernie was working as a driver for Goring Rural District Council but was later employed by Wilkinson at weekends and subsequently full-time. Around 1925, Ernie was not happy that he was not being paid for all the extra hours worked, so he left to drive a four ton Peerless lorry for Smallbones, who were building contractors in Streatley. Ernie's replacement was found lacking, so after six months he was begged to return. Ernie was often requested to be the driver by private hire customers. One of these was Mrs Woolfall, headmistress of Mapledurham Elementary School at Trench Green, who organised a trip to the Aldershot Tattoo.

In 1926, Wilkinson was asked to also serve Checkendon, to which he responded by trying a new service, starting in Woodcote and then running into Reading via Checkendon, Exlade Street, Cane End, Gallowstree Common, Kidmore End, Chalkhouse Green, Emmer Green and Caversham. However, other proprietors were already established on that route, so the experiment was quickly abandoned. It seems, however, that he did extend his original service from Woodcote to Checkendon on Sundays. There was also a short-lived attempt to run a service into Reading from the Thames-side village of Mapledurham, with one round trip on Fridays, but the patronage did not cover the cost of provision.

Conversely, another venture had proved more lucrative, perhaps since the 1924 rail strike. When the bus from Reading had arrived at Woodcote and the passengers had alighted, the vehicle would run on to Goring-on-Thames as a parcel delivery service. This also enabled parcels to be collected from Goring & Streatley Station for delivery to Crays Pond and Woodcote.

Around 1926, Vincents started to develop their premises in Station Approach, Reading, in order to consolidate their activities onto one site. A modern garage, workshop, filling station and showroom complex was completed in 1928 and became a Reading landmark for the next 50 years or so. This meant that Wilkinson and House Bros were obliged to relocate their bus terminus to outside Shire Hall in The Forbury, which was actually closer to the town centre. The new terminus point had been used for many years by the carriers as there was only two hundred yards to walk one's horses to The Elephant public house in the Market Place, for stabling prior to the return journey.

The Royal Agricultural Society of England's Annual Show in July 1926 was held on farm land on the north side of Henley Road, at the top of Donkin Hill, in Caversham. The new Caversham Bridge had just opened and to alleviate traffic delays, the Borough Council initiated a temporary one-way system involving the two Thames crossings, as well as co-ordinating a shuttle bus service from Reading General Station to the showground at a fixed fare of 6d (2½d) each way. Charles Wilkinson identified a revenue opportunity, so drove the original Fiat on the shuttle service, with his wife as conductress. On the Saturday, the larger Fiat driven by Ernie Cox operated 8 excursion trips from the surrounding districts, so the normal operation of the bus service on that day must be open to question. Returning the excursion passengers home took until 1am on the Sunday morning.

While Wilkinson had been rapidly successful with his business in various ways, his demise, probably in late 1927, was just as fast. It has been suggested that he turned to alcohol, got into debt and was possibly adjudged as bankrupt. Ernie Cox was never paid for the last three weeks and three days of his employment. Wilkinson's buses were 'taken from him', presumably repossessed if he had defaulted on hire-purchase payments or seized as assets to be sold to cover a debt. The 20-seat Fiat BW 8275 materialised with House Bros of Watlington and was recorded as 'scrapped' in August 1933, but the smaller Fiat's fate is less clear. However, there is a suggestion that House Bros had a new REO chassis fitted with a second hand 14-seat bus body with a rear doorway, which was to hand. The fate of the Wilkinson family is uncertain; the only Charles Wilkinson listed in the 1931 Kelly's Directory for Berks, Bucks and Oxon, is for a miller at Watlington. Whether this was the same person, whether there were any family links with that town, or whether a vehicle dealer like Vincents found a suitable customer for Wilkinson's buses in the form of House Bros, is waiting to be discovered.

Woodcote, therefore, lost its pioneer bus service, but not for long . . .

Ernest Cox

Ernest William Cox was born at Goring Heath in 1902 and at the age of fourteen went to work at 'Abbotsfield' in Deadman's Lane, where his duties involved looking after a pony and washing and polishing cars, including a Renault, a Bugatti, a Rolls Royce and a Daimler. The chauffeur taught him how to look after the Hornsby 8hp stationary paraffin engine, which produced electric light in the house and pumped water from a 226ft deep well that his future father-in-law helped to dig. The training was invaluable as in 1917 the chauffeur was called-up for military service and fifteen years old Ernie was left to cope on his own. Having learnt to drive cars on the premises, he asked for a pay rise in 1919 and was promptly sacked! With knowledge of the stationary engine, he also serviced one used for charging batteries at the Wallis residence at 'Querns'. When he was sacked from 'Abbotsfield', the owner of 'Querns' gave him a job as footman, where he worked with Mr and Mrs Charles Wilkinson, whom we met previously and who later gave Ernie a job as a bus driver.

When Wilkinson's 'Woodcote & District' bus activities collapsed, many people were bereft of public transport, so Ernie received a fair amount of local encouragement when he considered entering the bus business for himself, not least from the aforementioned Mr Mullard. With no small amount of courage, Ernie decided that as he knew what to do, he would try and emulate Wilkinson's previous success. He did so largely by himself, although his mother helped as much as possible and he had to sell a brand new BSA motor cycle that he had only just bought, in order to raise enough finance to buy a bus.

Cox's first vehicle was a 21.7hp Oldsmobile, a forerunner of the REO marque, obtained through Easter Bros who were charabanc operators and garage proprietors of Queens Road in Reading. Ernie recalled that knowing of a charabanc about to become available, Easter Bros obtained the vehicle on his behalf, removed the charabanc body and fitted a second hand 14-seat saloon bus body of unconfirmed origin. This had a yellow livery, with a name in an oval on the side which had been painted out. There is an unproven possibility that this body came from a Ford Model T (registered MO 2060) which had been sold by Tuck & Furlong of Touchen End, near Holyport, who operated a service from Maidenhead to Bracknell under the name 'Yellowbus', although this operator did not sell out to the Road Motor Department of the Great Western Railway until June 1928. The origin of the Oldsmobile chassis is also speculative; Cox suggested it came from George Ford at Silchester, but research shows that another operator from Silchester – Lovegrove & Lovegrove – had a 1921 Oldsmobile 14-seat charabanc about due for replacement around 1927/8, registered HO 7958 and once used on their bus service from Silchester into Reading. Whatever, Ernie had the bus repainted yellow and recalled that it had windows all round, a boarded roof, a front entrance, perimeter seating, electric lighting and pneumatic tyres, being thoroughly reliable.

It is not clear what period elapsed between the demise of Wilkinson's service and Cox's replacement, but Ernie estimated that it was only about three weeks. He replicated Wilkinson's route, timetable and fares and also carried goods. Householders wishing Ernie to 'call' would put a paper on a stick and put it out over their gate. When he started his venture, Ernie was living at home at Rag Farm, Goring Heath but the bus was kept at Martin Alright's Westholme Farm. On 17 June 1928 he married a girl from Checkendon who was the grand-daughter of another local bus proprietor – Sam Hall. Mr and Mrs Alright made available three rooms at Westholme Farm for Ernie and his new wife, but after the birth of a son they moved to Copyhold Farm on the Whitchurch Hill to Goring Heath road.

At some stage, Cox acquired through Easter Bros a so-far unidentified Wallace 20-seat charabanc, with canvas roof and side curtains. The Wallace was a rare make produced in very small numbers between 1919 and 1922 by Richmond Motor Lorries Ltd of London W12 using American components and a four cylinder 'Red Seal' petrol engine. Ernie's had pneumatic tyres, electric lighting and was painted brown. It was intended for private hire work, which was not too plentiful owing to the worldwide recession evident after the Wall Street Crash in 1929. However, there was some work available transporting cricket or football teams to away matches at weekends or occasionally a darts team in the evening during the week. At weekends, the services of Mr Alright were enlisted to drive it when Ernie was running the bus service. Later, a Morris 20-seat bus apparently replaced both the Oldsmobile and the Wallace. It carried a blue livery with white window frames and the only good thing about it according to Ernie, was the lights, as the engine gave trouble and the fairly long chassis cracked and had to be strengthened by Girdlers Ltd of Reading, the steel stock holders. The Morris apparently came from Chelsea in London, which suggests perhaps the Lots Road disposal yard of the London General Omnibus Co or maybe the firm of bus dealers, H Lane.

From 6 July 1928, the Thames Valley Traction Co made one of their periodic short-lived incursions into the part of south Oxfordshire which forms the focus of our story. Their service 7A linked Reading with Cane End via Caversham and Chazey Heath, with some journeys extended to run from and to Goring Heath, Woodcote and Checkendon, with first inward to town and last outward further projected to Stoke Row, where the bus was kept. Fortunately, this competition had little effect on Ernie Cox's fortunes, despite the fact that it paralleled his service, but a new, regular service at cheaper fares started by Harry Kemp in August 1929 between Reading and Woodcote, soon extended to Wallingford and Didcot, was a significant threat.

However, the event that really shaped Ernie's future was the implementation of the regime of control, licensing, record-keeping and form-filling required by the Road Traffic Act 1930. For owner-drivers such as Ernie, this was seen by many as valuable time spent in an unproductive way, instead of being out earning a living. Not having that sort of mind and in view of the all-embracing competition from Kemp, Ernie considered that it was just not worth the bother of carrying what few passengers there were and opted instead to be a goods carrier only. The bus service, therefore, ceased in late 1930 or early 1931 before applications had to be made for Road Service Licences. The Oldsmobile had previously entered the fleet of House Bros, whilst the disposal of the Wallace and the Morris are unknown.

For a few more years, Ernie was a goods carrier, having bought a van and a piece of ground at Whitchurch Hill on which to keep it, to which was added a new bungalow for the family in February 1932, named 'Sunny Home'. From 1933, goods hauliers were required to be licensed and Ernie obtained an 'A' licence allowing him to carry goods for hire and reward anywhere in the UK. Under arduous wartime circumstances and with poor financial reward, he ceased trading in 1941 and instead drove lorries for the Royal Ordnance Factory at Theale, carrying bomb parts and sten guns. After the war, he sought to reinstate his goods vehicle licence but this was refused, as the Labour Government was restricting new issues in advance of impending legislation to nationalise the road haulage industry. Ernie then sold the pantechnicon that he had stored for the duration and went to work at the RAF Woodcote stores depot. In later life he lived with one of his daughters in Dorset and died there in October 1994, aged 92.

Samuel Hall & Sons 'Red Bus Service'

Samuel Hall was born into a farming family around 1857 in Kineton, Gloucestershire. His working life started early – bird scaring at seven, leading plough horses at eight and driving the plough at twelve years of age. Five years later he was living-in as a groom, on a wage of eight pounds a year plus a pair of new boots at Michaelmas. Some of his spare time was spent weeding fields at 3d an hour. Around 1874, aged nineteen, he moved to Oxfordshire to work on farms and in due course actually rented one from Christchurch College, Oxford, which he farmed for many years. Over the years, he and his wife Bessie produced eleven children. It is thought that this was the same Sam Hall who had a rest from farming by 1895, being recorded as a shopkeeper in Checkendon in Kelly's Directory. By 1911 he was a farmer again at Fullbrook's Farm on the Checkendon side of Boundary Road, just outside Woodcote. By the time he enters our story he was already into his sixties and was 83 when he passed on in 1939.

Samuel and his two youngest sons, Reginald (born c1895 and Albert, born early 1901, (there just must be an Albert Hall) started a motorised carters and haulage business in late 1919, after the Armistice. Halls are said to have owned an American-built Kelly-Springfield lorry with 'coal scuttle'-style bonnet and canvas full-tilt. With no passenger transport into Reading from Woodcote and Checkendon at that time, the Halls organised some trips into town on certain Saturday evenings, so the locals could enjoy the Palace or County Theatres. Although the fare was half-a-crown (twelve and a half pence in decimal currency), the trips were very popular, especially with courting couples who enjoyed the darkness on the return journey when the rear canvas flaps were tied down. However, Halls had a second vehicle for carrying passengers. Early Reading motor vehicle records state that in 1920, a new Halford, painted green (DP 3335), was registered to Samuel Hall; quite possibly it had bodywork constructed by Vincents in that town.

The Kelly's Directory compiled in 1923 advises that S Hall & Son were running a 'motor carrier's' service into Reading on Tuesday, Thursday and Saturday from Checkendon. A contemporary source from Woodcote referred to a carrier's lorry going twice-weekly to Reading, that it was partially fitted with seats and that the return fare was 2/6d (12½p), without specifically mentioning Halls, although they could have been the operator being recalled. Also, a resident of Woodcote at the time, one C Cotterhill (or Cotterill) purchased a new 14-seat van-bus in June 1924. It was a Ford model TT registered BW 7872; nothing else is yet known, including how Mr Cotterhill fits into our story, although the funeral of one Christopher Cotterill, aged 63 years, took place at Woodcote on 26 May 1937.

Talking about the period after the Great War, one of Sam Hall's daughters – Mrs Benwell – reminisced in the book Our Farm that, "with one covered lorry my father and brothers re-started a carrier's service to Reading (years before it had been done by covered van) on two days a week for passengers and goods. Then a larger lorry with seats went to Reading twice a day, the fare being 2/6d. For a short while a bus service was run by another man. Our lorries were sold and a bus service started. Still the fare was 2/6d". It is unclear as to which vehicles (possibly the Kelly-Springfield or the Halford which may both have been a lorry-cum-bus) that Mrs Benwell was describing, or who 'another man' might have been.

Around 1923/4, it is estimated, Reginald Hall left the business to become a chauffeur at Hammonds Estate in Checkendon. About that time, the Hall family moved to Horne's Farm in Tidmore Lane, Woodcote.

Hall's bus service started at Checkendon (Whitehall), running presumably via Tidmore Lane and Red Lane to Woodcote Memorial, continuing along Whitehouse Road, Greenmore and Reading Road to Exlade Street, thence to Cane End, Gallowstree Common, Kidmore End, Chalkhouse Green, Emmer Green and Caversham into Reading, initially probably via Reading Bridge, as Caversham Bridge was being rebuilt. In between journeys, the bus is known to have been parked at The

Duke of Edinburgh public house in Caversham Road, opposite the end of Tudor Road. The name for the business seems to have been The Red Bus Service, although later it seems it was referred to as just Hall's Bus Service.

Of the buses used, there is some uncertainty. One is thought to have been a Dennis, fully-enclosed, fitted with bench seats down each side for twelve or fourteen passengers and thought to have been Indian red in colour. There is an outside chance that it was DP 4860, a 14-seat bus used for a short period by Matilda Watts for her 'Rapide Motor Bus Service', whom we will meet later.

In due course there were two round trips on Monday-Friday, more on Saturday and two on Sunday. Win Hall once remarked that when she married in 1925 to become Win Minchin, Saturday operation had definitely been established as her younger brother Bert was unable to attend the ceremony as he had to drive the bus. There is a suggestion that by 1927 or 1928, certain journeys, possibly on Saturdays only, were routed between Cane End and Caversham via the more direct Chazey Heath option. An alternative theory is that the latter occurred slightly later, in 1929, in order to counter competition from Thames Valley's service 7A, which may have abstracted some revenue from Halls' service in terms of passengers from Woodcote.

In due course, Halls acquired another vehicle, thought to have been a Commer with 20 forward-facing seats, not first-registered in Oxfordshire. By then, another driver may have been employed in the person of Frank 'Rusty' Thatcher from Woodcote, who had learned to drive a lorry for Bishops, the local coal merchant, at The Black Lion public house. The original Dennis is thought to have been traded in for a new Dennis G, registered RD 1094, with a 20-seat body possibly built by Vincents. Dennis records state that chassis no. 70579 was delivered to CH Stout, Reading, on 1 January 1930. However, Stout's garage was at Shalbourne on the Berkshire/Wiltshire border and seems to have been involved as the supplying dealer. The reference to Reading is taken to mean that the chassis was destined for bodying in the Reading area, hence the suggestion of a body by Vincents. Other sources indicate that the vehicle was first-registered in Reading on 13 September 1929 and passed to an Oxfordshire operator on the 24th of that month.

The 1928 Kelly's Directory, compiled in 1927, suggests that Halls were possibly still running a separate carrier's service at that time on Tuesday, Thursday and Saturday. The daily carrier service listed in the 1931 and 1935 editions of the Directory should be treated with caution as the compilers were not always precise in their definition of a 'carrier' and an 'omnibus proprietor', especially if the named person had evolved from the former to the latter. There is also a possibility that carrier activities may have been sub-contracted to Ernie Cox, who was by then married into the Hall family.

In any case, Bert Hall, Ernie Cox and George Shaw (from WR Jackman & Son), were the best of friends and would often meet up for lunch together in a cafe in Cross Street, Reading.

In places such as Reading, where local by-laws relating to the operation of hackney carriages had been in force, local authorities were authorised to make recommendation to the new Traffic Commissioners, in the lead-in to the practical implementation of the Road Traffic Act 1930. In March 1931, the County Borough of Reading's Watch Committee authorised the Town Clerk to request the Southern Area Traffic Commissioners to grant a licence for Halls' Checkendon to Reading service, by which time any Saturday variation via Chazey Heath seems to have ceased. S Hall & Son therefore submitted their application for a Road Service Licence for their service, which received objections from Thames Valley, Harry Kemp and WR Jackman & Son. At the Hearing in May 1931, no decision was announced. As stated above, Thames Valley had decided not to apply for a licence for their service 7A and it was withdrawn from 1 January 1931. This left three contestants, two of whom were good friends. Licences were eventually granted in July to all three, but Kemp was not permitted to serve Checkendon and Hall could not serve Woodcote en-route. A condition seems to have been introduced whereby different operators were required to charge the same fare between common points. As a result, Hall and Jackman were required to reduce their fares to come into line with Kemp's cheaper rates.

Halls also applied to licence a small series of excursions starting from Checkendon. These were to run from April to September to Sonning and Ascot Races, Aldershot Military Tattoo and Southsea, the licence being granted in May 1931. As it was probably thought that coaching work may well have a better long-term future for the Hall business, the following month they took delivery of a Commer 6TK with luxuriously-appointed 24-seat coach bodywork by Willmotts and first-registered as GP 4326 to an S Smith of London E17. The following year, additional excursions and tours were authorised when the licence came up for renewal, whilst in 1933, additional picking up points were sanctioned at Exlade Street, Cane End, Stoke Row, Gallowstree Common and Kidmore End, but not Woodcote as applied for.

When the bus service licence was renewed in 1932, the service was obliged to terminate at The Duke of Edinburgh public house in Reading, rather than near Reading Stations, the fares were to be co-ordinated with Thames Valley and no passengers could be picked up or set down between Hall's garage and the junction of Exlade Street with the Checkendon road. The change of Reading terminus and the picking up restrictions may have resulted from an objection from Kemp. The next licence renewal application was granted in October 1933, which allowed reinstatement of Reading Stations as a terminal point.

Sam Hall, on the Checkendon side of Woodcote, operated GP 4326, a 1931 Commer 6TK with Willmott dual-door 24-seat coach body, which, it is believed, was usually used on private hire and excursion work. *(Museum of English Rural Life, University of Reading)*

When Jackman gave up running his Stoke Row-Reading service in autumn 1932, Kemp successfully applied to extend his Reading-Woodcote service to Checkendon, thus largely duplicating and competing with that of Halls. It is possible that Jackman offered the licence to Halls, but it could have been declined for financial reasons.

Feelings between Hall and Kemp were probably running very high. However, the Halls carried on for a short time and no doubt reluctantly, approached Kemp around autumn 1933, regarding him taking over their bus service. Kemp applied to integrate the Halls service with his own, with a December 1933 application eventually being granted in April 1934 by the East Midlands Traffic Commissioners, which body was now covering a larger area after the abolition of the Southern Traffic Area. However, Hall may have ceased operation before then.

Ensuring that Kemp could not benefit in any greater way by also acquiring a surplus vehicle, Hall sold his Dennis (RD 1094) in autumn 1933, which by 14 October had turned up in the fleet of Ongar & District Motor Services (EA Curtis), in Essex. It may have been replaced (but perhaps not until 1934) by a Gilford LL15SD normal control coach, registered OT 7917, with a dual-door 20-seat body by Strachan & Brown. It was new in March 1928 to the Aldershot & District Traction Co Ltd, was sold to the East Kent Road Car Co in 1930 and reached Hall via a dealer, probably still painted in the East Kent maroon and cream livery. By 1934, the fleet therefore comprised two Commers – one bus and one coach – and the Gilford. This information was confirmed many years ago by Cecil Allen to his son Michael. Cecil ran a garage in Woodcote and carried out maintenance work on Hall's vehicles at that time.

In due course, S Hall & Son decided to cease operations entirely. Samuel Hall passed away in December 1939; Frank Thatcher got a job with Kemp's, but Bert Hall went to work for AC Cox (Silver Grey Coaches) of Reading, taking the Gilford and quite possibly one or both of the Commers with him, although there is also a suggestion that Commer GP 4326 had been sold prior to that. Cox sold out on 28 February 1939 to Smiths Coaches, also of Reading, by whom Bert Hall was subsequently employed for the rest of his working life. During the war he drove an ENSA party around as well as undertaking works contracts. He died in retirement around 1980, being remembered as a particularly nice person, liked by all.

Bert Hall, Sam Hall's son, who later took over running the business, on ceasing the operations and selling up the bus and coach business at Checkendon, moved into Reading and went to work with Silver Grey Coaches, where he is seen (front left, in dark uniform) with colleagues during a private hire job to Wantage c1938. *(John Whitehead Colln)*

17

The Thames Valley Traction Co Ltd in South Oxfordshire

During the early 1900s, the tramway-owning British Electric Traction Co Ltd (BET) recognised that the motor bus was going to have a bright future as a cost-effective way of feeding people into tram systems from outlying areas and as a way of developing services in more rural parts. Thus, a number of fledgling territorial bus operations were initiated or bought into, which by 1912 were co-ordinated by the subsidiary British Automobile Traction Co Ltd (BAT). Although the Reading tramway system was controlled municipally rather than by BET, an opportunity for a motor bus operation in the area was identified by Sidney Garcke, son of the founder of BET, Emile Garcke. The family lived at Pinkneys Green, near Maidenhead.

Passenger transport using the internal combustion engine was virtually non-existent locally, so Sidney Garcke invited an acquaintance, T Graham Homer, to return to England from Canada. Together they established the Reading branch of BAT, despite the difficulties one would expect from wartime conditions. The first service (from Maidenhead, through Twyford, Sonning, Caversham, Reading and Pangbourne to Streatley) commenced on 31 July 1915. The name on the side of the vehicles was 'British', with a saxon green and white livery. In October 1915 Wallingford was reached, with later a further extension to Abingdon for a short period.

Further 'British' services were initiated, including experimentally one from Reading northwards to Peppard Common via Caversham, Emmer Green and Sonning Common, which commenced in April 1918. However, this was discontinued the following month due a wartime shortage of manpower and fuel. With the war over, the service was reinstated 'by popular demand'

from 8 March 1919, with three return journeys per day worked from the company's Reading depot. In October that year, the service was diverted from Peppard Common to the village of Peppard and on past Peppard Sanatorium and Borocourt Hospital to Stoke Row.

Prior to the arrival of 'British' on the Peppard route, various carriers were active in the area. For example, in 1911, Kelly's Directory records the existence of Charles William Brown of Kingwood Common, whilst running from the small town of Watlington to Reading was Edwin Matthews on Tuesday, Thursday and Saturday and CE Jackson on Tuesday and Saturday. These probably ran through Peppard en-route. Jackson also ran to Henley on Thursday, Oxford via Stadhampton on Monday, Wednesday, Friday and Saturday, to Thame on Tuesday and to Wallingford on Tuesday and Friday. In the 1920s, the elderly Bill Smith was still running his horse van carrier's service from Stoke Row to Reading ('Boar's Head' in Friar Street) via Peppard, Sonning Common, Emmer Green and Caversham.

Probably the very first passenger/carrier motor bus service into Reading from a neighbouring town was one started by House Bros of Watlington around 1912, via Nettlebed, Highmoor, Peppard Common, Sonning Common, Emmer Green and Caversham. This had to cease when the House brothers were called to the Forces but was re-started after the Great War, continuing until the business closed in 1987. Similarly, Albert C Butler started a bus service from Peppard Sanatorium into Reading in July 1914 under the title 'Peppard & District', having taken over a jobmaster's business on Gravel Hill, Sonning Common. This also ceased during the war and the vehicle, of Star manufacture registered BL 029, was sold. When Bert Butler restarted his business after the conflict, he concentrated on charabanc operation.

By 1920, 'British' had a fleet of 34 Thornycroft J-type vehicles and BAT decided that operations should be

British Automobile Traction, whose green buses carried the fleetname 'British' were the forerunners of the Thames Valley Traction Company. A new operating area centred on Reading, later Maidenhead, started on 31 July 1915 and in April 1918 a new 7 mile route commenced from Reading to Peppard Common, possibly to replace services by two operators which closed because their owners had been enlisted. The 'British' service itself had to close a month later due to petrol shortage but was re-introduced on 8 March 1919 and extended by 2 miles to Stoke Row during October 1919. DP 1826 was a 1916 Belsize 3-ton with Brush 26-seat body, seen here at Peppard in April 1918. *(Paul Lacey Colln)*

reconstituted in a new company. The Thames Valley Traction Co Ltd came into being on 10 July 1920, owned 86 per cent by BAT and the remainder by Tillings, another bus-owning conglomerate, which decided to work in partnership with BAT, rather than competitively. The detailed history of 'British' and Thames Valley has been written and published already, so we confine attention to the company's few northward forays from Reading, over the Thames into that part of south Oxfordshire relevant to our story.

From 1 August 1920, Thames Valley gave the number 8 to their Stoke Row service; this was changed to 7 on 1 May 1922 remaining thus for over 58 years. Apart from some limited competition, some of it short-lived and described later, Thames Valley was to have the route largely to itself and it was the company's only one of longevity within our main area of interest. Some journeys were extended on Monday to Saturday from Stoke Row to Highmoor and Nettlebed from 23 May 1924. Perhaps to discourage any temptation by potential competitors, it was decided to provide earlier journeys in the morning into Reading and later journeys back in the evening. A cost-effective way to facilitate this was to 'outstation' a Thornycroft J-type single-deck bus at The Cherry Tree public house in Main Street, Stoke Row. This saved dead mileage, although on Sundays service 7 was still worked by a Reading-based vehicle and crew.

In order to find work for his charabanc in the lean winter period, Reg Bragg of Reading proposed to run a bus service thence to Peppard. However, in December 1925, the Hackney Carriage Sub-Committee of the Reading Watch Committee refused to issue a licence as they felt that the route was already sufficiently provided-for.

In April 1928, the Board of Thames Valley gave approval for the purchase of some land in Main Street,

Probably taken outside the Stoke Row village post office c1932-5, these are the Stoke Row men who ran the Thames Valley Traction Co operation from the dormy shed. The identity of the driver on the left is uncertain but may be Sid Bishop, while the one in the middle is Charlie Butler (killed in the war). The conductor on the right is George Shaw, who was previously actively involved in operating the WR Jackman & Son bus service from Stoke Row into Reading. *(June Cope)*

Stoke Row, near the church. This was for a small garage, or 'dormy shed', capable of housing three buses. Construction was rapid and new schedules required the use of two buses from Stoke Row on service 7 from 25 May 1928. This was reduced to one in May 1933 and finally ceased in May 1940, after which all journeys were operated by Reading depot. The 'dormy shed' was sold around spring 1946, subsequently being destroyed by fire.

Thames Valley indulged in some experimentation with its service development in the early 1920s. Three services operated by the same Reading-based vehicle were started in June 1921, including one numbered 15 with two round trips on Monday, Tuesday, Thursday and Saturday. Starting in Reading at St Mary's Butts, it ran to Woodcote via Chazey Heath, Trench Green, Goring Heath, Whitchurch Hill and Crays Pond. Monday operation was suspended after three months, presumably due to poor patronage on what was traditionally an unpopular day for going to town. However, in October 1921, the service was renumbered 16 and diverted between Reading and Whitchurch Hill via Tilehurst, Purley and Pangbourne, then over the toll bridge across the Thames to Whitchurch-on-Thames. Passengers had to disembark whilst the bus crossed the bridge and also pay the toll fee for pedestrians. The change in routing was to strengthen the company's offering between Reading and Pangbourne and to gain more patronage than that offered by the old route. Monday

Thames Valley's Stoke Row dormy shed, in Main Road, was first proposed in early 1928 and land was purchased next to the church, opposite the Maharaja's Well and the building had been erected and commissioned by 25 May 1928, when new schedules were introduced on service 7 (Reading – Stoke Row – Nettlebed) and two single-deckers were the initial allocation. *(Paul Lacey Colln)*

operation was reinstated and a Sunday service of three journeys each way was added.

Further adjustments came during 1922 – Monday and Thursday operation was deleted in January, Thursday journeys reinstated from 1 May with a renumbering back to 15 and final withdrawal in October. In terms of convenient travel opportunities for Woodcote residents, the morning departure time for Reading and the late afternoon return was never going to be popular as it required too long a time for a housewife to be away from home and it offered no improvement from the previous carrier services. The 2/10d (14p) return fare was nearly 42 per cent more expensive than the carrier and country folk on a low income had better ways of spending the extra 10d.

The availability of the Stoke Row 'outstation' shed resulted in a later attempt by Thames Valley to penetrate the Woodcote district. A third vehicle was allocated from 6 July 1928 in order to commence new service 7A, which ran into Reading daily from Checkendon, Woodcote, Goring Heath, Chazey Heath and Caversham. The first journey each day and the last back was projected from and to Stoke Row respectively. Some of Thames Valley's services that carried few passengers were operated with 20-seat Leyland Z7-types, with bodywork by Ransomes, Sims & Jeffries. Seven of these arrived from Barnsley & District in May 1929 and were unofficially referred to as 'Pups', on account of their size. One was allocated to Stoke Row for service 7A.

The emergence of Harry Kemp in 1929 caused serious competition for Thames Valley as well as other local operators as already described. In an attempt to improve their position, Thames Valley re-timed and strengthened service 7A and diverted it via Whitchurch Hill from 16 May 1930 in order to combat Kemp and for the same reason also introduced a variation numbered 7B which meandered between Checkendon and Reading

Thames Valley 192 (HE 2323) was a Leyland Z7 with 20-seat body by Ransomes, Sims & Jefferies, new to Barnsley & District in June 1925 and transferred to Thames Valley in May 1929. This vehicle (or one of its sisters) was of the type sent to Stoke Row dormy shed, being ideal for operating through the narrow lanes of the southern Chilterns. (Paul Lacey Colln)

via Exlade Street, Cane End, Gallowstree Common, Kidmore End, Tokers Green and Caversham. The latter service only lasted until 1 September 1930, whilst a new Kemp service from Checkendon to Reading started in November that year, causing a strategic withdrawal by Thames Valley, which abandoned service 7A after 31 December 1930. Their timetable dated 1 January 1931 stated that the service was 'temporarily suspended' – probably a bluff, as it never returned. Having failed to make any appreciable inroads in the area south of the Henley-Nettlebed-Crowmarsh road (apart from service 7), Thames Valley capitulated in advance of the need to make applications for licences under the provisions of the Road Traffic Act 1930, in order to concentrate on other, more-established, operations elsewhere.

Frederick Simmonds

Apart from the Watlington to Reading service of House Bros, with whom Thames Valley may well have reached an understanding, the latter received no challenge to their service 8 (later 7) until April 1922, when a rival appeared on the road between Reading and Peppard, most likely in parallel. Competition came in the form of Frederick Simmonds of 11 Blenheim Gardens, Reading, using a Ford Model T, with a 14-seat bus body constructed by local builders/carpenters Russell & Paddick of Sonning and Woodley, who apparently were personal acquaintances of Simmonds. It was registered in April 1922 as DP 4400, although at that stage it may not have been bodied, but was so during that month, so it is possible that the service commenced at that time. However, Reading's Hackney Carriage Licensing Sub-Committee did not issue a Hackney Carriage Licence Plate or a driver's licence to Simmonds until 19 September 1922! Information probably collected in autumn 1922 for the 1923 Smith's Directory for Reading indicated that the service ran daily and that the Reading terminus was at the Sorting Office in Blagrave Street, behind the new General Post Office.

Thames Valley were not pleased as the newcomer was a potential threat to the viability of their service, but failed to take positive action for some months. In early 1923 they deployed two of their 'Scarlet Runners', which could be used to 'chase' a competitor by attempting to keep in front of them in order to reach intending passengers first. Thames Valley by then had changed their fleet colours to red and white. Specially built for the purpose, the vehicles were two Ford Model Ts with 14-seat Vincent bodies, registered MO 773/4 and with fleet numbers 54 and 55. The aggressive retaliation worked, as in April 1923 Simmonds sold out to Thames Valley, no doubt after an offer had been made and he is believed to have gone to work for them as a driver. His bus became No. 56 in the Thames Valley fleet, becoming a 'Scarlet Runner' itself for the summer, but in November 1923 it was sold to Yorkshire Woollen District, another British Automobile Traction subsidiary.

THE THAMES · VALLEY
TRACTION COMPANY, LIMITED.

READING, CANE END, WOODCOTE & STOKE ROW.

COMMENCING APRIL 1st, 1929,
The
Following Service of Omnibuses
WILL BE IN OPERATION.

TIME TABLE and FARES.
WEEK-DAYS AND SUNDAYS.

		a m	a m	p m	p m	p m	p m	p m	p m
READING (St. Mary's Butts)	dep.	9a45	10 55	12 15	2 50	...	5 15	7 35	8b45
" (G.W. & S.R. Stns.)		9a48	10 58	12 18	2 53	...	5 18	7 38	8b48
Caversham (Bridge Street)		9a54	11 4	12 24	2 59	...	5 24	7 44	8b54
The Pack Saddle		10a 5	11 16	12 36	3 11	...	5 36	7 56	9b 6
Cane End (The Fox)		10a15	11 25	12 45	3 20	...	5 45	8 5	9b15
Goring Heath (P.O.)				12 55	...	...	5 55	8*15	9b25
Woodcote (War Memorial)				1 5	...	...	6 5	8*25	9b35
Checkendon (P.O.)				1 12	...	...		8*32	9b42
STOKE ROW (P.O.)	arr.			....	...	...		8*40	9b50

		a m	a m	a m	p m	p m	p m	p m	p m
STOKE ROW (P.O.)	dep.	8s25	9s45	....	...	...	...	p m	p m
Checkendon (P.O.)		8s33	9s53	....	1 48	...	...	...	...
Woodcote (War Memorial)		8s40	10s 0	....	1 55	...	...	6 10	...
Goring Heath (P.O.)		8s50	10s10	....	2 5	...	...	6 20	...
Cane End (The Fox)		9a 0	10 20	11 30	2 15	3 25	...	6 30	8b10
The Pack Saddle		9a 9	10 29	11 39	2 24	3 34	...	6 39	8b19
Caversham (Bridge Street)		9a21	10 41	11 51	2 36	3 46	...	6 51	8b31
READING (G.W. & S.R. Stns.)		9a27	10 47	11 57	2 42	3 52	...	6 57	8b37
" (St. Mary's Butts)	arr.	9a30	10 50	12 0	2 45	3 55	...	7 0	8b40

s Sundays only.   b Saturdays and Sundays only.   * NOT Saturdays or Sundays.
a Not Sundays.

FARES. READING-CANE END-WOODCOTE-STOKE ROW.

Reading (St. Mary's Butts)
— Caversham (Highmoor Road)
4 — Farthingworth Green Turn
6 3 2 The Pack Horse
8 5 4 2 Cane End (The Fox)
8 6 4 3 2 Littlehourne Kennels
10 8 6 5 3 2 Goring Heath (P.O.)
1/- 10 8 7 5 4 2 Woodcote (Brick and Tile Works)
1/1 11 9 8 6 5 3 — Woodcote (War Memorial)
1/2 11 10 8 7 6 4 2 — Exlade Street Turn
1/3 1/- 11 10 8 7 5 3 2 2 Checkendon (P.O.)
1/4 1/2 1/- 11 9 8 6 5 4 3 2 Uxmore Farm (for Brush Works)
1/5 1/3 1/1 1/- 10 9 7 5 5 4 3 2 Stoke Row (P.O.)

RETURN FARES.

Reading and Farthingworth Green Turn	..	..	..	7d.
" " The Pack Horse	..	..	..	9d.
" " Cane End	..	..	..	1/-
" " Goring Heath (P.O.)	..	..	..	1/4
" " Woodcote	..	..	..	1/8
" " Checkendon	..	..	..	1/8
" " Stoke Row	..	..	..	2/3

This Notice is issued subject to the printed regulations contained in the Company's Official Time Tables.

LOWER THORN STREET, READING.   T. GRAHAM HOMER,
19/3/29.   General Manager.

BRADLEY & SON, LTD., PRINTERS, READING

Thames Valley tried hard to get into our area of interest on 1 April 1929, just prior to Harry Kemp commencing operations during August 1929. *(Paul Lacey Colln)*

Mrs Matilda Watts (The Rapide Motor Bus Service)

Only a short time after Thames Valley had dealt with Frederick Simmonds, a Hackney Carriage Licence was granted on 19 June 1923 to Mrs Matilda Sophia Watts, of 30 Westfield Road, Caversham, for a new 14-seat omnibus. This was registered as DP 4860, but further details are unknown, except that it was in a dull red livery. It is also not known if Mrs Watts drove it herself. The route was again Reading to Peppard, but beyond Emmer Green (Mrs Watts' birthplace in 1876) it left Thames Valley's route and ran via Chalkhouse Green and Kidmore End to Sonning Common village and then via Brind's Corner and Gravel Hill to Peppard. The service also partially competed with Sam Hall's bus into Reading. Advertising in local Reading newspapers in summer 1923 showed that the fare from Reading to Peppard was 1d less than Thames Valley's 10d rate. In those days a difference of as little as 1d was an important consideration for most bus passengers, although the end-to-end journey was more circuitous. The terminus point in Reading was given as Reading Stations (probably in Blagrave Street) but that at Peppard is unknown.

MOTOR SERVICE.

THE "RAPIDE"
MOTOR BUS SERVICE
is now running between
READING and PEPPARD
VIA
Kidmore End and Sonning Common.

FARES from Reading to
Emmer Green 4d.,   Kidmore End Pond 7d.,
Tanner's Farm T. 5d.,   Sonning Common 8d.,
Kidmore House 6d.,   Peppard 9d.

The Rapide Motor Bus Service was advertised in local papers. This one is from The Reading Observer for Friday, 28 September 1923. *(Paul Lacey Colln)*

Mrs Watts' son William, aged around 25 years, was licensed by Reading Borough Council as a driver on 22 January 1924. However, press advertising of the service ceased after that month and there was no application to renew the vehicle's licence plate in spring 1924. It is likely therefore that the service ceased in the first quarter of 1924, for an unknown reason. It may have been poor viability due to insufficient custom or change in the personal circumstances or health of Mrs Watts. It may also be that William took over due to her incapacity, but decided to cease operations quite quickly. Surviving motor taxation data indicates that the records for DP 4860 were transferred from the County Borough of Reading to Berkshire County Council (a separate licensing authority) on 29 August 1924, but there is no note of a subsequent owner or the vehicle's eventual fate. Matilda Watts was certainly deceased by 1928, whilst William Watts was to become employed by Thames Valley as a driver.

WR Jackman & Son

Ellen Greenaway was the sister of William Greenaway, who ran a business in Stoke Row hiring out horses and farm carts and, later, agricultural engines and threshing machines. Ellen married Horace Shaw and lived at 1

William and Ellen Jackman (formerly Shaw, nee Greenaway). (June Cope)

School Lane, Stoke Row. The Shaws had a daughter Alice (born 1902) and a son George, born 1910. Sadly, Horace Shaw developed tuberculosis and was unable to work, so Ellen Shaw started a carriers business, to provide a livelihood. She ran to Reading (Abbey Walk) from Stoke Row via Checkendon, Woodcote, Exlade Street, Cane End, Gallowstree Common, Kidmore End, Chalkhouse Green, Emmer Green and Caversham.

Following the death of Horace Shaw in the early 1920s, Ellen married for a second time, to William Richard Jackman, who worked for Bill Greenaway. Jackman therefore took his part in the family carrier operation. Around the mid-1920s, the horse-drawn van was replaced with a motor vehicle. Perhaps recognising the success in neighbouring villages of the bus services being run by Charles Wilkinson and Sam Hall, the Jackmans decided to better cater for the increasing number of passengers that they were carrying to Reading.

Also based in Stoke Row was Edwin John Stallwood of The Cherry Tree public house, who, on 30 January 1925, took delivery of BW 8476, a Ford 1-ton 'van-bus' with 14-seats. It has not been possible to determine its use or whether Stallwood and his Ford had any connection with the Jackman story.

An application by Jackman for a licence from Reading's Watch Committee in June 1927 was refused as 'the present service is considered satisfactory'. However, there may have been a misunderstanding about the route to be followed, which, of course, was not the same as Thames Valley's service 7. However, Jackmans' motor bus service did receive a licence, perhaps after a successful appeal involving clarification of the route. At least initially, operations were conducted under the name The Triumphant Bus Co.

Although confirmatory documentary evidence is not available, based on information gleaned from local sources it is thought that Jackman's first bus (replacing the motor van) was a fourteen-seat Dodge, which was said to be a smart little vehicle, with polished chrome radiator and a light blue and cream livery. Bill Jackman used it to run one round trip to Reading on weekdays, using The Forbury as his terminus.

George Shaw, on leaving school, had gained employment at the Hamilton Star Brush Company's factory at Stoke Row. He lost the tops of two fingers due to an accident on the saw bench and it has been suggested that the financial compensation of about £15 that he received may have been used towards a deposit for a second bus. This is thought to have been a new Chevrolet, with four cylinder petrol engine and a fourteen-seat 'country bus' body painted dark blue and white, having what was described as a somewhat unattractive design. It had small windows, a passenger doorway at the front nearside and double van-type doors at the rear. Alice Shaw is understood to have collected the bus from Great Western Motors Ltd, paying cash for it with money she took with her in the brown leather satchel her mother had worn round her waist when collecting fares and commission on the carrier runs. She then drove the bus back to Stoke Row.

George Shaw's part in financing the Chevrolet may be how he came to join the business, which became known as WR Jackman & Son. He took over the running of the Reading service, generally with the Chevrolet, whilst Bill Jackman used the Dodge on local private hire duties, for the inevitable village sports teams or pub darts teams. By 1928, the Reading service consisted of one round trip each day Monday to Friday, no less than five on Saturday and also one on Sunday.

Although Thames Valley had started a low frequency service to Woodcote and Checkendon in July 1928 and Harry Kemp had started serving Woodcote in August 1929, it was Kemp's new service from Checkendon to Reading initiated in November 1930 that presented a more serious competitive threat to the Jackman business. The latter's Stoke Row to Reading service was, therefore, reduced to run only on Tuesday, Thursday and Saturday and in all probability it was around this time that it was decided to try something new, with a Friday service between Woodcote and Henley-on-Thames via Checkendon, Stoke Row, Highmoor, Satwell and Greys Green.

Applications were made in April 1931 for Road Service Licences under the provisions of the Road Traffic Act 1930. Objections were lodged by Thames Valley and also by Harry Kemp and Hall & Son with regard to the Reading service. At the hearing at Maidenhead on 11 May, no decision was reached but subsequently, the Thames Valley objections were discounted and a licence granted for the Henley service on 22 May. On 3 July 1931, the Jackman application for the Reading service was granted as applied for, but conditions were placed on the grant of rival applications from Kemp and S Hall & Son. Quite possibly, both Jackman and Hall had been obliged to reduce their fares in order to 'come into line' from common points with the lower rates of Kemp. In view of his small vehicles, limited patronage and service level, Jackman was probably the most adversely-affected. Therefore, it was decided to cease operating the Reading service, whereupon Harry Kemp applied for a licence in September 1932 to continue operating it, but to a revised timetable. The grant for the transfer of the licence was made on 9 December 1932.

Meanwhile, the Henley service continued and an application for an additional round trip on Saturday evenings from Stoke Row to Henley for cinema-goers, was granted on 2 December 1932. An application for a round trip from Stoke Row to Henley on Tuesday afternoons was granted on 14 July 1933. It is thought that the Chevrolet maintained the Henley service and that the Dodge became a 'carrier's van', carrying goods only between Reading and Stoke Row and vice versa, possibly as late as September 1939 on the outbreak of war.

George Shaw seems to have left the business in the late 1930s and worked for Thames Valley from the Stoke Row 'outstation' shed, subsequently driving one of their Leyland 'Beaver' petrol tankers. He had signed up with the army as a reservist in 1939, so was called-up when war broke out. After the conflict, he worked for Cope & Cope Ltd, who were general agricultural engineers in Reading and became a travelling representative for the firm.

The ending of the Henley service is uncertain. It may have been withdrawn as non-essential in September 1939, when stringent petrol rationing was brought into effect. Alternatively, it and the carrier business may have struggled on under wartime operating constraints and decreasing viability until around mid-1940. It has been advised from within the family that Bill Jackman had turned to drink, sometimes leaving his passengers in the bus whilst he disappeared into a public house for 'a quick one'. Kemp's Motor Services Ltd did provide a replacement service from Woodcote to Henley on Thursdays by February 1947, but whether this had commenced at some time during the war, operating on a Defence Permit (as normal Road Service licensing had been suspended) is unclear – it was not in the Kemp printed timetable folder in 1941 or 1944.

The Dodge is thought to have been disposed of during the war to JRA House of Watlington, where by all accounts it was used for collecting and delivering washing in the Watlington area, which was then taken to and from the Caversham & Reading Steam Laundry Co in Caversham.

As for the Chevrolet, its actual fate and the date cannot be substantiated. Local legend has it that the villagers of Highmoor obtained the use of it for an outing which ended with an evening at the local pub. After much imbibing, the revellers decided that it would be a good idea to push the bus into the village pond, where it apparently remained. A pond-cleaning exercise in 1995, after publicity of the legend in the local press, did allegedly yield parts of a motor vehicle that just might once have been a small country bus.

Jackman's bus garage at 1 School Lane was dismantled, sold and re-erected at Sonning Common, subsequently being destroyed by fire. Bill Jackman himself later worked for the Woodcote Water Co, digging trenches and may also have worked in the woods. After the war and perhaps during it, he was a storeman at RAF Woodcote.

Research is ongoing. If any reader is able to shed new light on our knowledge as presented in this book, such as surviving family memories, documentation or photographs, corrections, etc, they are most seriously encouraged to share it by writing to us c/o the publisher.

Below we illustrate some puzzles that we have been unable to answer. Inevitably research for a book like this does throw up all kinds of queries.

We know that in Reading, The Forbury, alongside Forbury Gardens, was used by carriers and the early bus operators from south Oxfordshire for 'lay-over' during the 1920s-30s. In this view the bus is not of a make we recognise and appears to be registered DP 7846, which dates from c1928 – and which is a number for which we have no record either! Might it be a Jackman or a Hall vehicle for which we have been unable to so far establish identity? *(Commercial post card)*

This view, taken only a few years later (c1933), shows two buses parked on the forecourt outside the Sutton's Seeds establishment. That nearest the road has a partially visible rear registration plate, which appears to be EY x332 (or something very similar) and might just be the Commer 20-seater 'not first registered in Oxfordshire' to which we refer in the text regarding S Hall & Sons, of Checkendon. *(Commercial post card)*

PART 2
1929-1955
KEMP'S MOTOR SERVICES
A Southward Migration

This part of our story does not begin in Oxfordshire, but in Essex, in the area around Chelmsford, which is where Harry Kemp was born in 1886, or thereabouts. In 1901, Harry was living at 19 Roman Road, Chelmsford, with his father Samuel, mother Louisa and two older brothers. It has been recorded that in 1899 Harry was apprenticed to be an electrical engineer with Crompton & Co at their Writtle Road, Chelmsford works and eventually left Crompton's Test Department to work for Birmingham Corporation as an Electrical Shift Engineer. In 1909 he married Winifred Passey (born at Fakenham, Norfolk) and by the start of 1911 was living at Nechells Park Road in Aston parish in Birmingham, where his son Hiram Charles was born on 7 January that year. It has been suggested that Harry Kemp had visited a brother who lived in America and may have heard the name 'Hiram' there! The census of 1911 records that there were also three lodgers in the Kemp residence at the time – Winifred's widowed father John Passey, her younger brother Wilfred and younger sister Hilda. In due course, Harry Kemp secured employment with Leicester Corporation as Superintendent Engineer.

By 1921 the Kemp's were living at 209 Loughborough Road in Leicester and Harry's career was to change direction for an unknown reason, probably in 1922 when he went into partnership with Thomas Shaw as Kemp's Motor Garage Company.

In October that year a licence was granted for one bus which was used on a service linking Leicester with Loughborough via Birstall, Rothley, Mountsorrel and Quorn. The bus service was then expanded under the title of Kemp & Shaw Motor Services and additional vehicles were acquired. Young Hiram Kemp worked as a boy conductor. However, the partnership between Kemp and Shaw ended in 1927. Shaw continued alone, subsequently developing the business with a new associate – Charles Allen of Mountsorrel, already a bus proprietor in his own right. Notwithstanding Harry Kemp's departure, the business was incorporated as Kemp & Shaw Ltd on 7 April 1928, prior to which the Shaw family moved into Harry Kemp's former house at 209 Loughborough Road. A fuller account of the inception of Kemp & Shaw Motor Services and subsequent life of that company is another story, well told in a booklet published in 2005 by the Leicester Transport Study Group and written by Peter Smith, Tom Shaw and Mike Greenwood.

Kemp & Shaw's second bus was this Daimler Y with 32-seat rear entrance bus body of unknown make, which was registered NR 163. It was new to Coalville Bus & Garage Company in April 1921 and acquired in May 1925. The driver is thought to be Wilfred James 'Bill' Passey, who was Harry Kemp's brother-in-law, and the boy conductor is Hiram Kemp, about 14 years old in this photograph. (Jack Passey Colln)

Meanwhile, the Kemp's left Leicester and moved south to Woodcote in 1927, accompanied by not only Wilfred (Bill) Passey, his wife, Rosa and their infant son Jack, born February that year, but also Winifred Kemp's sister Ethel, who was by then Mrs Green, together with her husband. It has been said that Harry Kemp 'arrived in Woodcote with only £100 in his pocket', but the fact is that he acquired a house called 'Greenmore' at the top of Long Toll at Greenmore Hill in Woodcote, where there was an established market garden smallholding including greenhouses, for growing soft fruit and salad vegetables. Although the area was high up in the Chilterns and it could be quite cold, the site was sheltered to a degree by trees. The produce was supplied to various customers; Hiram Kemp initially cycled to Reading, to deliver it to Vindens greengrocery shop in Friar Street. Later, he and Bill Passey drove vans and sold produce around the villages. Apparently 'Greenmore' started life as a Georgian toll-keeper's house and was extended in Victorian times to become gardeners' cottages as part of the Mapledurham estate. However, horticultural activities were not to last for long, for within a couple of years the family were once again to enter the field of road passenger transport and would soon have a virtual monopoly on bus services in the area surrounding Woodcote, with the various Kemp's, Passeys and Greens being involved to varying degrees.

Nobody seems to know for certain why Kemp chose to come to Woodcote, of all places, or why a business transition was made from market gardening to buses and coaches. From 1929, after the Wall Street Crash – the collapse of the stock market in the United States – it was a time of worldwide depression. People had less money to spend and job losses resulted in lifestyle changes. It may have been a reduced demand for his produce that made Harry Kemp change course. In view of his past experience in running buses and perhaps having noted the rather basic efforts of contemporary

Close-up of Hiram Kemp, probably taken at the same time as the photograph on page 25, with NR 163. *(Jack Passey Colln)*

local proprietors and for that matter, the rather lacklustre offering of a major concern such as Thames Valley, he may have decided that there could be better reward if he was to offer an improved level of bus service to the local community. Whatever, he made the decision.

The first recorded reference to Kemp as a bus operator in Oxfordshire was on 23 July 1929, when licences for two buses to operate a service from Reading to Didcot were granted by Reading Council's Hackney

Bill Passey, on the entrance step of one of the five Chevrolets to enter the Kemp & Shaw fleet between November 1925 and August 1926 (all RY-registered). The trees are in leaf, so it is probably spring 1926. The 'passengers' (left to right) are unknown (wearing hat), Ethel Maude 'Tet' Green (one of Bill Passey's three sisters), and her husband. *(Jack Passey Colln)*

Ethel Green, on the entrance step of one of the new Chevrolets, probably in spring 1926. *(Jack Passey Colln)*

Carriage Licensing Sub-Committee. In that month, two Daimler CB single-deck buses were acquired, possibly through London SW9 dealer, GJ Dawson. These were previously operated by United Automobile Services Ltd, which was a major concern with extensive services in north east England and East Anglia. Registered XB 8347 and PW 1935, the chassis had been acquired from the War Department after decommissioning as lorries and fitted by United with front entrance bodies built in their own workshop. PW 1935, at least, had 26 seats. They had originally entered service in 1920 and 1923/4 respectively and were then finished as a charabus. In saloon form they could be used on bus services by United, but the roof, side and rear window sections to waist level were removable in one piece. With a canvas roll-over hood fitted at the rear, they could then be used for charabanc pleasure trip duties in fine weather.

Kemp's bus service commenced on an unrecorded date in August 1929, but only between Woodcote (War Memorial) and Reading (Blagrave Street) via Goring Heath, Trench Green, Chazey Heath and Caversham. Entry to Reading was along Caversham Road, Tudor Road, Station Hill and Station Approach, returning along The Forbury, Vastern Road and Caversham Road. Under the title of 'Kemp's Bus Services', it is thought to have run every day from the outset, but an original timetable has not been traced. Reading County Borough Council granted a licence on 8 October 1929 for a third bus – another former United Automobile Daimler CB registered PW 3324.

The intention to operate from Woodcote to Didcot seems to have been delayed – perhaps whilst awaiting the third Daimler or the grant of a Reading licence for it – but the route extension was introduced from late September or early October, running from Woodcote via Crays Pond, Goring & Streatley Station, Cleeve, South Stoke, North Stoke, Mongewell and Crowmarsh Gifford to Wallingford (Market Place) and then onward to Didcot through Brightwell and North Moreton, to terminate at The White Hart. Between Wallingford and Didcot, the service was in competition with those of The City of Oxford Motor Services Ltd (COMS). On the Woodcote to Reading section, there was also some competition with the services already described of Thames Valley, Ernie Cox and Ted Page. However, Kemp's service was somewhat different as rather than running from Village to Town, it ran Town to Village to Town. Perhaps reflecting Kemp's experience in running from Leicester to Loughborough, this was a potentially more remunerative option. As well as linking centres of population, village folk could choose which town to visit. With several trips each day, there was added convenience for customers and with terminus standing time reduced, more could be achieved, leading to

Evidently taken during the Kemp & Shaw era, before the move to Woodcote, Bill Passey is riding his motorcycle-combination, with young Hiram Kemp riding pillion and Ethel Green (Bill's sister) in the sidecar. *(Jack Passey Colln)*

lower fares than those charged by other operators – a recipe for success over the competition.

However, as others had doubtless found, running bus services in the rural south west Chilterns was not a sinecure. Although the Daimlers were built with solid tyres, they had been fitted with pneumatics before acquisition by Kemp and may have had longitudinal wooden-slatted seats. On the pot-holed and unsealed road surfaces in the area at that time, the ride is recalled as being decidedly rough; the description of bone shaker has been mentioned. Tyres lasted only a fraction of the time usually expected and it was not until the roads were tarred that more normal life-expectancy was achieved. Kemp's buses are said to have carried a yellow livery, which is quite possible as United Automobile's livery in the 1920s was yellow and brown. To supplement the Daimlers, Kemp acquired a Karrier JH 26-seat bus registered WT 9156. Purchased through a dealer, it had been used by Harrogate & District Road Car Co but was new in March 1925 to Premier Transport of Keighley.

Noting the sudden appearance of this efficient new operation, Thames Valley decided they must take some action. It is thought they extended more journeys through to Woodcote on their service 7A and instead of reaching that village via Deadman's Lane and Long Toll as hitherto, they diverted via Goring Heath, Whitchurch Hill and Crays Pond, largely duplicating the services of Ernie Cox and Ted Page. Kemp retaliated by obtaining a licence from Reading Council on 17 December 1929, to use one of his buses on a new daily service which followed the original one from Reading to Goring Heath and then branched off to terminate at Whitchurch Gate. As a result of this, Ernie Cox capitulated as already recounted, whilst the appearance of Kemp caused Ted Page to reduce his Reading service and abandon that to Wallingford.

Kemp introduced a revised timetable in April 1930, wherein the Reading to Whitchurch Gate service was extended to Crays Pond and Woodcote. By September 1930, two further former United Daimler CBs are thought to have been acquired, possibly in August – PW 121 and PW 127 of 1923 vintage. Around the same time, a 14-seat REO Speedwagon FB coach was purchased, described as a charabanc and registered WT 5891. This had been new in July 1924 to Mrs Harriet Wilson of Harrogate and had also seen service with Harrogate Carriage Co and West Yorkshire Road Car. This enabled Kemp to undertake private hire or the occasional excursion.

As Reading Council had refused to licence the two extra Daimlers, it is possible that a new network of services based on Wallingford which Kemp introduced in autumn 1930, had been designed to keep them employed, through an area where local licensing procedures did not apply. Also, the approaching introduction of the measures in the Road Traffic Act 1930 encouraged Kemp to start as many services as possible, so as to be established by the time Road Service Licences would have to be applied for. Those

commenced were partially competitive with those of City of Oxford MS and were:

Wallingford-Crowmarsh-Benson-Ewelme-Britwell Salome-Watlington
Wallingford-South Moreton-Aston Upthorpe-Aston Tirrold-Blewbury then East Hagbourne or Upton and West Hagbourne to Didcot
Wallingford-direct via A4130-Didcot
Wallingford-Brightwell-Little Wittenham-Long Wittenham-Didcot
Wallingford-Shillingford-Dorchester on Thames-Burcot-Clifton Hampden-Culham-Abingdon
Wallingford-Shillingford-Warborough-Newington-Stadhampton-Chalgrove

Certain journeys were operated across Wallingford, notably from Watlington and Chalgrove to give through travel opportunities to Didcot.

The next development followed the granting of two licences (possibly for the last two Daimlers) by Reading Council for a daily service into town from Checkendon, believed to have started around mid-November 1930. This ran via Woodcote, Goring Heath, Cane End, Gallowstree Common, Kidmore End, Chalkhouse Green, Emmer Green and Caversham. This aggressively duplicated the services of Jackman and Halls between Checkendon and Woodcote and between Cane End and Reading, but also competed with Thames Valley service 7A which ran through Checkendon to Stoke Row, but only until the end of 1930. The Checkendon service completed Kemp's portfolio in advance of the application for licences from the new Traffic Commissioners, who replaced the authority of the County Borough of Reading in respect of local omnibus regulation from 1 April 1931.

Harry Kemp, on a day out, with Passey sisters Ethel and Winnie (his wife), with Rosa Passey (Bill Passey's wife) and their two children, Jack and Mary. The photograph was taken c1930 and therefore after the move to Woodcote. (Gillian Stokes Colln)

This one was not actually later owned and operated by Harry Kemp but PW 104 is presumably in approximately the condition in which these Daimler CBs were used by Kemp.
(Philip Battersby Colln)

An interesting study of the rear of a United Daimler CB, seen here in High Street, Blyth, Northumberland, shown off by PW 3310, again not one that was actually later used by Kemp.
(Commercial post card)

We have been unable to trace any photographs of the early buses that Harry Kemp put into service from Woodcote, so have resorted to illustrating them in use with a previous owner. Even so, we are unable to illustrate everything!

Harry Kemp's original vehicles were Daimler CBs, which had started life as solid-tyred military lorries before being bought by United Automobile Services who built their own single-deck bus bodies on them. They were later fitted with pneumatic tyres, well before Harry Kemp owned them. United were an extremely large pioneer bus operator serving mainly Northumberland and Durham but later North Yorkshire, Lincolnshire and also East Anglia – and even further afield! When sold by United, the vehicles which passed to Harry Kemp quite possibly did so via a London dealer and in a livery of either primrose and black, biscuit brown and yellow-ochre, or chrome yellow picked out in red, which is very likely why yellow was adopted as the original standard Kemp's livery. Kemp's' buses are known to have been referred to originally by the local populace as 'mustard pots'!

PW 127, which was one which came to Harry Kemp, is seen squeezing through a narrow gap between buildings in Heighington, County Durham, which is mid-way between Bishop Auckland and Darlington – an ideal vehicle for negotiating narrow 'un-made' lanes in the southern Chilterns.
(Denise Johnson Colln)

Kemp Ascendant

After a plan had been approved by Goring Rural District Council, a forecourt was laid out along the Long Toll frontage on the site of the market garden, south of 'Greenmore' and adjacent to the remaining greenhouses. By 1930 a depot building with a pit had been constructed, behind which was a workshop, equipped with a lathe, a valve-grinding machine and various other tools. These facilities were to aid maintenance of the buses, which in future would be more strictly monitored by Ministry of Transport Vehicle Inspectors, under the Road Traffic Act 1930.

Within the provisions of the new Act, there was an ability for a local authority which had previously required that a licence be held for a bus service, to make recommendations to the Traffic Commissioners in respect of which services they would like to see licensed, as well as presumably advising whether any restrictions had previously been attached. Reading's Town Clerk was instructed in March 1931 to request that Road Service Licences be granted for Kemp's services from Reading to Didcot, Whitchurch Hill and Checkendon. A few days beforehand, the first issue of a document known as *Notices & Proceedings for the Southern Traffic Area* was published, containing details of Kemp's applications for Road Service Licences against reference numbers J23 to J30, which were probably amongst the first to be received and listed for hearing. Most were applied for 'without modification', but three services (Wallingford to Abingdon, Wallingford to Chalgrove and from Wallingford to Didcot via Long Wittenham) were to run only from May to September, presumably as traffic in the other months was deemed insufficient. Objections were raised by COMS in respect of the applications for the Watlington/Abingdon-Wallingford-Didcot corridors and also by the Great Western Railway for Reading-Didcot, whilst S Hall & Son and Thames Valley objected to the Reading-Checkendon application.

A Traffic Court Hearing was held in Reading on 20 April 1931, whereat the Wallingford to Abingdon and the direct Wallingford to Didcot service application which supplemented the Reading-Didcot service, were refused and presumably withdrawn almost immediately. The objections from COMS were seemingly successful and Kemp 'came to an arrangement' with them at this time, or maybe later, whereby timings on other sections of shared road would be spaced to avoid conflicts. The other Kemp applications were granted, with the exception that the Watlington-Didcot service should follow the route of the main Reading service from Wallingford to Didcot, rather than looping southwards through South Moreton, Aston Tirrold and Blewbury. On the Reading services, there was a protection clause in favour of Reading Corporation Transport, prohibiting the carriage of passengers by Kemp wholly within the County Borough of Reading, except on payment of a fare in excess of that charged by the Corporation.

Apart from COMS, other small firms were still active north of the Henley to Wallingford road. JR House had a network of market day services radiating from Watlington and Henley, whilst carrier AW Higgs ran from Chalgrove to Thame on Tuesday, via Stadhampton and to Wallingford via Benson on Friday.

A decision on the applications by Kemp, Jackman and Hall for services linking Reading and Checkendon, was deferred until 3 July 1931. Kemp was obliged to curtail his service at Woodcote and not run on to Checkendon, to balance the obligation on Hall who could not deviate to serve Woodcote. As previously mentioned, Jackman's application was granted as applied for.

This concluded Kemp's bus service licensing for the time being, allowing all his services to appear in a timetable folder dated July 1931. This contained text stating that

'Kemp's Bus Services are the cheapest and most reliable in the district. They take you through the most picturesque parts of the country, right over the Chilterns, through lovely wooded country and along the Thames Valley, where some magnificent views are obtained, making travel by these routes a pleasure'.

It is reasonable to assume that Hall, Jackman and Kemp had introduced some form of ticketing, as required by the Act. Kemp used a system employed almost universally for bus and tram services at that time, whereby packs of tickets of different types and values were held in a wooden rack by spring-loaded clips and then inserted into a punch machine, which produced a ring of a bell inside it. A principal supplier of tickets and punches was, appropriately, the Bell Punch Co Ltd.

Kemp's Bus Services also applied to licence their excursion and tours activities which ran between May and September, starting from Woodcote (Red Lion). These were for the popular Hayling Island, Southsea and Bournemouth day tours and evening trips to the annual summer Aldershot Military Tattoo.

The ubiquitous Chevrolet vehicles produced in the UK by the American company General Motors, began to be marketed in 1930 as Bedford Chevrolet models. In July 1931, General Motors introduced a new range of passenger chassis – the Bedford W series. With Kemp's business now more established and seemingly doing well, the time had come to modernise the fleet and perhaps to obtain vehicles that better complied with the Construction & Use regulations required under the Road Traffic Act 1930. A major commitment was made in September 1931 when three Bedford WLB models were acquired, with 20-seat bus bodies built by Strachan or Reall. They were fitted with a 3.18 litre petrol-engine and four-speed gearbox, being registered UD 4652, UD 4656 and UD 4678. These were followed in February 1932, or maybe slightly earlier, by UD 4863, a Commer Centaur with similar Strachan bodywork. Also thought to have been acquired in 1931 were pre-owned examples of a 14-seat Chevrolet and MY 5191, a 20-seat Ford AA bus. This intake permitted the withdrawal of at least three of the Daimlers and also the Karrier JH.

MY 5191 was one of the first of the non-former United vehicles to be purchased. A Ford AA with 20-seat body of unknown make, new in 1930, it was acquired second hand in 1931 but was only retained until 1933. It seems to have kept its original livery and is seen here with Ted Fisher, a very early employee, who lived at Hill Bottom, which is between Goring Heath and Whitchurch Hill. *(John Whitehead Colln)*

UD 4652 was the first of three Bedford WLBs to be bought new in September 1931. This one and UD 4678 had 20-seat bodies by Strachan and when new are understood to have been in a 'yellowish-brown' livery with red waistband and a Kemp's fleetname on the side panels.
(Omnibus Society – original photographer CF Klapper)

UD 4656 had a 20-seat Reall body but was otherwise in the same livery. Sometime later, these three Bedfords were repainted in a simplified yellowish-brown but without a red waistband and Kemp's fleetname, but given a yellow-ochre 'flash' down each side. *(Omnibus Society – JF Parke Colln)*

UD 4863 was a Strachan 20-seater based on a Commer Centaur B40 chassis, new to Kemp by February 1932. It was delivered in an identical livery to the 1931 Bedfords. The roof-mounted route boards reminiscent of both Kemp & Shaw and United Automobiles are not thought to have lasted very long. *(Omnibus Society – Roy Marshall Colln)*

As previously noted, Ted Page had decided that continuing his Saturday service to Reading from South Stoke was no longer worthwhile. Discussions between Page and Kemp concluded in March 1932 whereby Kemp would take over the licence, doubtless for a modest unrecorded financial consideration. The following month, Kemp applied for some timetable modifications to his existing services, including the withdrawal of the section of route between Stadhampton and Chalgrove, as well as the amalgamation of the Stadhampton-Wallingford service with that from Wallingford to Didcot via Long Wittenham, which would operate all year round. He also applied to continue Page's service. Objections came from COMS and the applications from both the latter and from Kemp were not fully-resolved and granted as appropriate until 24 June 1932. In all probability, Kemp started operating the former Page service to Reading on Saturday 3 July 1932, but it was curtailed to start at Whitchurch Hill Bottom. However, the return journeys continued beyond Whitchurch Hill to Hatch Gate and Crays Pond.

During the first half of 1932, Kemp added two more vehicles to his fleet. Both had 20 seats and had originated with JB Fraser of Redcar, passing with his business to United Automobile Services on 1 August 1931. They were disposed of by United in January 1932, probably to dealer GJ Dawson. One was a rare BAT Cruiser (XG 267), the other a REO, registered PY 9131. Soon afterwards, Daimlers PW 121 and 3324 were withdrawn, with the latter being retained for some months before sale, minus engine, to the owner of Little Stoke Manor Farm, for use as an egg-sorting shed. As early as September 1932, the BAT together with REO coach WT 5891, were traded in against two former Nottingham Corporation Transport Maudslay buses with 26-seat bodywork by Vickers. These had left Nottingham in favour of the manufacturer AEC, which accepted them in part-exchange for new AEC Regent double-deckers.

The livery chosen by Kemp for his vehicles before the war, was ochre (a yellowish-brown colour), with a yellow flash on the body sides and on some, the name Kemp was sign-written in red on the rear emergency exit door.

Kemp's application to take over the Stoke Row to Reading service of WR Jackman & Son, running Monday, Tuesday, Thursday and Saturday, was granted on 9 December 1932, operating to the same route as previously. Two weeks later, Kemp applied to run the journeys at 8am from Stoke Row and returning from Reading at 12.10pm also on Wednesday and Friday, which was granted from 20 January 1933. In terms of his excursion and tours licence, Kemp was authorised in time for the 1933 season, after objections from Halls, to pick up additionally from various villages surrounding Woodcote, including Ipsden, which was not yet served by one of his bus services.

A proposal guaranteed to invoke an objection was put to the Traffic Commissioners in January 1933. This was to operate a daily service between Nettlebed and Reading via Highmoor, Stoke Row and then along the route of Thames Valley service 7. Unsurprisingly, this application was refused, so any ambition by Kemp to purge the south Chilterns entirely of the Thames Valley Traction Co remained unfulfilled.

The abolition of the relatively small Southern Traffic Area from 1 January 1934 resulted in Berkshire and the County Borough of Reading (which included most of Caversham) being transferred to an enlarged South Eastern Traffic Area, whilst Oxfordshire was added to the East Midlands Traffic Area, the offices of which were in London and Nottingham respectively. From that point onwards, this meant that the Primary Licences held by Kemp in the East Midland area, had to be supported by Backing Licences in the South Eastern Area if there was any mileage principally on the south side of the River Thames, requiring two sets of paperwork and potentially two Traffic Court Hearings.

As the 1930s progressed, some of Kemp's less well-patronised bus services were subject to adjustment in terms of their level of service, including the days of the week on which they operated, in order to match provision

XG 267, a fairly uncommon 1930-vintage BAT Cruiser with 20-seat coach body ex-United Automobile Services, was only in the Kemp's fleet for a few months, being withdrawn in September 1932. Just a hint of it, seen here in Frazer of Redcar days shows it being used as a service bus before being absorbed into the United fleet, albeit extremely briefly, for the last four months of 1931. *(Philip Battersby Colln)*

Ted Fisher, who was a Kemp's employee for most of the 1930s, sets off to work with his bike from his home at Hill Bottom. Note the white-topped cap with a 'K' badge above the brim and his early oval enamelled Ministry of Transport Public Service Vehicle driver's badge. *(John Whitehead Colln)*

Harry Kemp bought two 1928 Vickers-bodied 26-seat Maudslay ML4Bs (TO 7230 and TO 7231), which Nottingham City Transport had part-exchanged for new AEC Regent double-deckers in September 1932. Although seemingly in Kemp's fleet for five or six years, no photographs have been traced. *('Motor Transport' advertisement)*

with actual demand more closely which seemed to fluctuate in some cases. When a new timetable booklet was published in September 1933, it confirmed that the former Jackman service from Stoke Row to Reading had been reduced to run only on Saturday. However, it was increased again from around April 1934, running daily from Reading to Checkendon and on to Stoke Row on Saturday. In a consolidation exercise, this incorporated the journeys of S Hall & Son as already described and spelt the end of Kemp's separate Reading-Kidmore End-Goring Heath-Woodcote service. By October 1934, there were one or two Saturday journeys on the Reading-Whitchurch Hill-Woodcote service that were projected to run from and to Ipsden.

Again by September 1933, the service from Stadhampton to Didcot via Wallingford and Long Wittenham was reduced to run only on Friday, Saturday and Sunday. By October 1935, the Wallingford-Didcot section had been suspended, while by June 1936, the Stadhampton to Wallingford section had been withdrawn on Sunday. Subsequently, a Sunday evening cinema-goers round trip Wallingford-Long Wittenham-Didcot was provided but this had seemingly ceased by August 1937. By October 1934, the Watlington to Didcot service had largely been reduced to run only on Friday, Saturday and Sunday west of Wallingford, with the remainder of the service treated in the same way by June 1936.

In the six years from 1933, further vehicles were acquired by Kemp to replace some of those taken into stock earlier. In March 1933, Reading motor taxation records indicate that H Kemp was the owner of a new

Ford, registered RD 4378. However, whether this was actually a bus is open to question. It was licensed as Hackney but could quite possibly have been a car used as a taxi, although it is not known that Kemp's indulged in such activities. It is stated in various editions of *The Motor Transport Year Book* that a Ford was in the Kemp fleet until the late 1930s. RD 4378 may have replaced the earlier Ford MY 5191 in 1933, as the latter seems to have ended its days in 1935 as a goods vehicle owned by JH Adderley of Abingdon. By March 1935, a 26-seat Gilford 168SD, registered JC 1288 had been acquired after little use by Crosville Motor Services, which inherited it with the business of Tudor Evans of Llithfaen. Two other Gilfords were earlier purchased (UP 2082 and UP 2189), with 24-seat Duple coach bodies. They were obtained through dealer GJ Dawson, who had them in stock in November 1933, so they may have actually been purchased by Kemp as soon as early 1934. They were new to R &

C Armstrong, trading as Majestic Saloon Coaches of Ebchester, Co Durham and had passed with the Majestic business to the control of United Automobile Services in 1932, which retained Majestic as a separate subsidiary company. The ex-Majestic Gilfords were followed in May 1937 by two 1929-vintage Leyland Lioness PLC1s of a similar capacity, previously in the fleet of Birch Bros of London NW5 and with bodies built by that firm in their own workshops.

Having built up his business, it seems that Harry Kemp thought about capitalising on his success. In November 1936 he wrote to the Birmingham & Midland Motor Omnibus Co (Midland Red), suggesting that if they were to consider extending their activities in the direction of south Oxfordshire, he would be pleased to hear from them, stating that he operated eleven vehicles. A few days later, a reply came from Midland Red's Traffic Manager, Orlando Cecil Power, informing

The vehicles that helped put British intercity coach services 'on the map', so-to-speak, were Gilford 166SDs, like this one with Duple 24-seat dual-door body, new to Majestic Luxury Saloon Coaches, of Ebchester, County Durham, who put coaches, including UP 2082, on their London – Newcastle upon Tyne – Edinburgh service before being absorbed into United Automobile. This one, and UP 2189 from the same source, joined the Kemp fleet circa early 1934 and stayed for three years, helping to develop private hire business and the excursion network. *('Commercial Motor')*

After one (or possibly two) further Gilfords had been added to stock for the 1935 summer season, the next fleet additions were two 1929 Leyland Lioness PLC1 coaches (UL 4418 and UL 4419) from the famous Birch Bros, of London NW5, which, seemingly, replaced the two ex-Majestic Gilfords, circa May 1937. *(Paul Lacey Colln)*

Kemp that Midland Red had no interest but suggested in as many words that the more local Thames Valley Traction Co might have. Perhaps Kemp chose to write to the Birmingham-based operator in view of previous knowledge from the days of the Kemp & Shaw business in an area where Midland Red was dominant.

As Frank Thatcher was driving his Kemp's bus from Reading to Woodcote with a full load of passengers, on 7 August 1937, a car driven by a lady from London collided with his vehicle and spun it around at Goring Heath Crossroads. Frank had sounded his horn several times when approaching the crossroads, but witnesses stated that the car was being driven at about 40 mph. Having struck the bus, the car went up the bank and overturned, with one person seriously injured. The car driver's version of events and an estimate of the speed she was driving at were somewhat different. She was found guilty of driving without due care and attention and fined £2 and £1.6s.1d (£1.30p) costs.

Harry Kemp put a flagship vehicle into service in March 1938, which was the first in the fleet with an oil (diesel) engine, rather than being petrol-powered. It was also the first (and only pre-war) forward control vehicle, whereby the driver sat alongside the engine in a separate cab, rather than behind it within the saloon area, as in normal control vehicles. UD 9431 was a Dennis Lancet Mk II with a body also by Dennis seating as many as 39, although only licensed for 38. As these

seats were fitted within a space where there would normally be 33, it was somewhat cramped inside. Unlike normal control vehicles, the Dennis required a conductor to be employed when it was used on bus services. It had been purchased at the Commercial Motor Show at Olympia in London and was originally driven principally by Hiram Kemp, who, incidentally, was normally called John by the family, friends and the staff. Family legend has it that Hiram/John started driving (off-road) at the age of 11 in Leicester. The Dennis had a few little extras, such as a two-tone horn and a simple gradient indicator. When working on this vehicle, conductors were warned not to stand on the step and lean outwards as the sliding door had a habit of suddenly slamming shut when the coach was braking. During the Second World War, it was not unknown for up to 80 people to be squeezed into UD 9431 on busy journeys.

The four vehicles recorded as acquired in 1938/9 were more 20-seat pre-owned vehicles. None of them were exactly in their first flush of youth. There were two Commer Invader 6TKs (VX 9906 and PL 603) and two Morris Commercials, at least one recently withdrawn by the East Kent Road Car Co and as had often been the case, acquired by Kemp through GJ Dawson. This was JG 2835, an RP model, with a body constructed by East Kent themselves. These vehicles, which were new in 1932/3 had been sold by East Kent as early as 1938 as they had excessive fuel consumption. To offer

UD 9431 became the pride of Harry Kemp's fleet. It was a Dennis Lancet II, with a Dennis 39-seat coach body, which was an exhibit at the 1937 Commercial Motor Show at which Harry Kemp bought it. He had an extra two pairs of seats crammed into it by reducing the seating pitch to the minimum permissible and personalising the vehicle by having other items, like a pair of fog-lamps and a two-tone horn fitted. More to the point, this coach was the first diesel-engined and forward control vehicle in the fleet, so if it was working as a service bus it needed a crew of two. It is seen here pre-war in Caversham Road, Reading, on layover, while the crew visit a café.
(Museum of English Rural Life, University of Reading)

When it was new in March 1931, VX 9906, a Commer Invader 6K, with 20-seat body, was operated by East Bergholt & District of Colchester, passing to the Eastern National Omnibus Co in 1933, then to Fox & Hart 'Hounslow Star' before arriving with Harry Kemp in 1938. (Paul Lacey Colln)

some improvement, Kemp's example had already been fitted with a Leyland 101-type engine. The other Morris is something of a mystery. All that is remembered by one source is part of its registration number, which was recalled as JG 1xxx. East Kent had two batches of Morris Commercial Viceroy models, new in 1931, registered JG 1456-89. They had coach seating in bodies by Harrington or Beadle. Records state that the whole batch was requisitioned by the War Department in July 1940, direct from East Kent service. However, if the Kemp vehicle was one of those, perhaps there is a possibility that at least one of the batch was disposed of separately by East Kent beforehand, but no further evidence is so far available, being just one of a number of mysteries regarding the Kemp fleet.

In November 1938 complaints were received about the low level of bus service in the Kidmore End area. The Traffic Commissioners facilitated the reinstatement of some withdrawn journeys to run on a trial basis during December 1938 and January/February 1939, with the proviso that if they were not used enough, these journeys could be withdrawn again – which they were from 1 March 1939. Prior to the Traffic Commissioners' review, Harry Kemp was quoted in the *Reading Evening Gazette* as saying, "I say definitely that the extra service is not wanted. The figures during the experimental period are proof that it is not required, although the public said they wanted it."

Another war was a strong possibility and various military installations began to appear in Oxfordshire, including several airfields. One of these was at Benson, where construction began in 1937 to convert the fields into a base for military aircraft, with 5,981 feet of runways.

Unfortunately, this meant that the relatively recently-built Benson bypass and connecting road to Wallingford via the London Road Inn had to be severed. It also required demolition of the Keep Countryside Beautiful Roadhouse and filling station on the London Road, which had a rustic thatched roof over the petrol pumps. The airfield was situated in a well-known frost hollow, often recording the coldest temperatures in the UK – such as minus 17.1 degrees centigrade in January 2010. RAF Benson was officially opened on 1 April 1939 and in time was to provide additional patronage for Kemp's bus services as well as some contract work. For some while, there had been various applications for licence variations, as well as objections and counter-objections, between Kemp and City of Oxford MS regarding their respective services in the Benson and Ewelme area, which had culminated in a Traffic Commissioners' Sitting at Northampton on 15 March 1939, when agreement was reached in advance of the opening of the aerodrome. However, Kemp then applied to amend his route via Clay Lane, through the aerodrome area, rather than via the B4009 road, thus by-passing 50 houses. City of Oxford's service 39 operated daily, whereas Kemp was running just on Friday, Saturday and Sunday. The larger operator pointed out in their objection that Kemp's proposed service would not be of much value for aerodrome personnel who required daily transport. A meeting had been held between COMS and the Commanding Officer after some personnel had arrived on 1 February. He expressed satisfaction with COMS' own proposals for serving the aerodrome. Notwithstanding, Kemp's application to divert some journeys was granted.

Wartime Kemp's

When Prime Minister Neville Chamberlain announced on the wireless on the morning of Sunday 3 September 1939 that Britain was about to go to war with Germany again, so soon after the last one, the fleet of Kemp's Bus Services is thought to have consisted of eight operational vehicles: Bedford WLBs UD 4652/6/78, Commer Centaur UD 4863, Commer Invader VX 9906, Morris Commercials JG 1xxx/2835 and Dennis Lancet UD 9431. Apart from the Dennis, all were somewhat past their prime and had been worked hard during their lives.

To conserve fuel, quite stringent petrol rationing was introduced from 23 September 1939, followed by a request from Traffic Commissioners asking bus operators to reduce their mileage, especially in respect of journeys that were somewhat poorly-patronised. Kemp's introduced reductions on several of their services, including the removal of most late evening journeys and the withdrawal at some time in September 1939 of the former Page Saturday service from Whitchurch Hill Bottom to Reading and the Saturday route section beyond Checkendon to Stoke Row. Subsequently, around 1942, all Sunday morning services had to be withdrawn to save fuel, by Government Order.

Wartime conditions brought many difficulties for all bus operators. Some drivers and other staff began to be called-up for military service, resulting in labour shortages. Tyres and spare parts became in short supply and until 1942, virtually no new buses or coaches were produced, as the manufacturing plants were turned over to essential wartime production, such as military vehicles, aircraft or munitions. In order to hinder enemy aircraft, a night-time blackout was imposed, with vehicle headlights being severely masked so as to only allow a downward-directed thin strip of light to be cast and this was made more difficult for driving by having no street lighting. In Kemp's operating area, where the roads were often narrow, with no white carriageway markings down the centre or at the sides, driving a bus at night was particularly hazardous. The lack of markings was noted as putting a particular strain on Kemp's drivers, as many sections of road had high banks either side, making it difficult to distinguish where the road ended and the bank began.

Coach trips for pleasure purposes were then out of the question and traditional excursions to seaside resorts were largely pointless as most beaches along the south coast were out-of-bounds and protected by barbed wire entanglements in order to frustrate any invasion attempts.

As well as the challenge of keeping the buses running, there was also sadness for the Kemp family, for Harry's first wife – Winnie – passed away in the winter of 1939/40.

In 1940, an article was published in *Modern Transport* about Kemp's Bus Services, part of which may well have been drafted by Harry Kemp himself. As well as summarising bus service development and the then current wartime problems, it also indicated how the firm altered its operations to deal with shifting patterns of demand. Since the mid-1930s, Kemp's had not operated regular interval services throughout the week; journeys were concentrated at times or on days when they were most needed and when there was most demand, supported by duplicate journeys if loadings were heavy.

JG 2835, a Morris-Commercial RP, with a 20-seater body, had been new to the East Kent Road Car Co in 1933 and came to Kemp's in 1939, where it spent the war years. On the Reading – Kidmore End – Checkendon service, buses served Gallowstree Common by double-running, and turning as seen here, by reversing into a narrow lane. Not an easy manoeuvre if it was at night in the blackout! *(Omnibus Society – JF Parke Colln)*

UD 9431, the diesel-engined 'Pride of the Fleet' Dennis Lancet II, is seen here at Woodcote working the bus service to Reading on 15 June 1941. Note the twin horns! *(JC Gillham)*

The peak passenger demand into Reading was on Thursday and Saturday and to Wallingford and Didcot on Friday and Saturday. Thus, on other days of the week, there were noticeably fewer journeys provided.

In terms of the fleet, Kemp's were fortunate that none of their vehicles or their garage were subject to attack from hostile aircraft, although Reading did have a number of air raids. It was also fortunate that none of the buses or coaches were compulsorily requisitioned for military use, as became prevalent in 1940, as those owned were undertaking essential services and none were surplus to requirements. However, some replacement was needed for the more elderly vehicles, so a mixed bag of substitutes was acquired in 1940 and 1941, before the buying and selling of buses and coaches was forbidden, without the requisite Permit, the issue of which was strictly-controlled. Thanks to the memory of John Davies, who closely followed Kemp bus activity during the war and afterwards, we know some of characteristics of these wartime purchases.

In October 1940, two vehicles were acquired after use by White Heather Transport of Southsea. EXK 599 was a 1938 Bedford WTB with 25-seat coachwork by Duple, which had been new to United Services Transport Ltd for their Universal Sightseeing fleet in London. It had curved glass panels along the roof line, whilst the roof itself was partly of a canvas folding-back type, which Kemp's replaced with sheet metal. It ran in Universal's blue and white livery until later painted brown and blue. AYA 170 was a Dennis Ace 20-seat bus with a snout-like bonnet and radiator, which earned the type the nickname of 'Flying Pig'. New in 1934 to the well-known Somerset independent operator Hutchings & Cornelius Services Ltd of South Petherton, it remained in a red and cream livery whilst at Kemp's. It soon received a gash down the near side due to accident damage and ran for most of its time at Woodcote with a plank of wood nailed over the offending area, whilst a missing

window was covered with a sheet of plywood, such was the wartime need for 'make do and mend'. Its body was eventually removed and the chassis was still in the field next to the depot in 1950.

The following year, 1941, UD 5469 arrived, a Bedford WLB/Duple coach that had been new to W Smith (Smith Bros/Miltonian Bus Service) of Great Milton, which was in quite good condition and was not repainted either, from its red and cream livery. DKP 410 was a Dennis Arrow Minor coach, originally much-used on bus services, before spending its time on contract duties after the war, including to Huntley & Palmer's works in Reading, being regularly driven by Ernie Brant. Until at least 1950, it was used on private hire work, but did nothing for the company's image. The wood-framed body needed a lot of strengthening work. Kemp's seemed to have a penchant for Commers and another 1941 arrival, in July, was a PLNF5 model with Heaver 26-seat coach body. Registered EUO 187, it came from CT Burfitt (Grey Cars) of Ilfracombe. Its Commer engine was replaced with a Bedford one, after which there was a problem with gear ratios and it had to be driven in third gear on a flat road. These arrivals were quite welcome, as Kemp's had recently had to hire, thought to be in 1941, two AEC Regal vehicles: one was a bus from the City of Oxford MS fleet with a wire roof luggage rack, which was used for some weeks and also a coach for one week from Surrey Motors of Sutton, in their brown and yellow livery.

The vehicles now in stock allowed the withdrawal and disposal of Bedfords UD 4656 and 4678, Commer VX 9906 and Morris Commercial 'JG 1xxx'. The Morris was seen in Reading one day in 1941, towing one of the Bedfords, on the way to pastures new. The next day, the Commer was similarly observed, leaving Kemp's under its own power.

Great changes were made to the wooded landscape around Woodcote when construction started in 1941

DKP 410, a 1937 Dennis Arrow Minor, with Dennis 25-seat coach body, had quite a long career with Kemp's, being acquired in 1941, yet still being in service at the Kemp's demise in 1955. It had been new to C Bourne, Tenterden, Kent but passed to Crown Coaches, Tongham, Surrey before reaching Harry Kemp at a time of desperate shortage of suitable second hand vehicles. It is seen here on 10 May 1952 on layover in The Forbury, Reading down the hill from the usual Blagrave Street stand. When new it had a 'sun saloon' body with roll-back canvas centre roof, which Harry Kemp panelled over and also fitted an extra seat next to the driver, making it a 26-seater. (WJ Haynes)

of RAF Woodcote, which was not an airfield but a huge storage and distribution depot, both open-air and in large sheds. Designated 70MU (Maintenance Unit), it covered 176 acres of land and was bordered by three roads leading to Goring Heath, from Crays Pond, Woodcote and Exlade Street. The sides of the roads were to witness stockpiles of equipment and this, the buildings and everything else was suitably camouflaged, aided by the woodland setting. The area used extended right up through College Woods, nearly to the Methodist chapel in Long Toll, just below Kemp's premises. Construction work provided employment for a large number of local tradesmen, whilst the blasting and earthmoving is thought to have been undertaken by British Estate Services (Plant Hire) Ltd, controlled by a man called Etienne Barrett, who will feature in large measure later in this story. When it opened, civilians from the surrounding area were employed at RAF Woodcote. Although the RAF ran some of its own buses for transporting staff, some travel requirements would no doubt have provided additional custom for Kemp's bus services. Added to the evacuees from London, including some from schools in Hanwell and North Kensington, who arrived in Woodcote in three coaches as early as 3 September 1939, Kemp's few elderly vehicles would have been hard-pressed to cope with the demand. Other local wartime influxes included the pupils and staff of the Oratory School which moved in 1942 from Caversham Park to Woodcote House, near Exlade Street. This was because it was proposed that Caversham Park would be used as a hospital, but instead, the BBC took it over as a monitoring station. Residential accommodation for the BBC staff transferred from other locations was provided at Great Oaks on the road from Whitchurch Hill to Crays Pond. Shuttles to and from Caversham Park were provided by the BBC using some buses from its own motor transport department.

The war resulted in a significant change in civilian working patterns, or commuting. Every adult, male and female, not otherwise in the Armed Forces, was expected to 'do their bit' for the War Effort. For example, although engaged in a reserved occupation, Hiram Kemp became a Special Constable. Some people, especially women, worked in factories and for country dwellers, this could mean travelling considerable distances into the towns, such as Reading, Wallingford and Didcot. In the past, country bus operators such as Kemp's had mainly provided journeys orientated towards housewives' shopping requirements or evening cinema trips, but now more early morning journeys for workers and early evening returns were provided.

It is recalled that Kemp's were awarded a contract to transport soldiers from Reading to Southampton, possibly in June 1942, to form burial parties after a particularly heavy bombing raid on the city. Ernie Brant drove the Dennis Arrow Minor DKP 410, his usual bus at the time. There were also contracts for taking Prisoners of War from various camps, to work on farms.

Apparently, they used to ply Kemp's drivers with hooch, which they made from potatoes they used to scrounge from the farmers.

In those days, many radios, especially in rural areas, were powered by accumulators, which had to be recharged by a radio engineer or at a garage. A notice displayed in Dennis Lancet UD 9431 (and probably other vehicles) requested passengers not to place accumulators on luggage racks as any stray dilute sulphuric acid from within them was liable to cause extensive damage.

In time, somebody in the Ministry of War Transport realised that the lack of supply of new buses was not conducive to the maintenance of reliable, essential public transport, which could well jeopardise the War Effort. For single-deck vehicles, discussions were held with Bedford and Duple (although some other body-building contractors were to be employed), the result being a utility version of the lightweight pre-war Bedford OB chassis, which had been produced in limited numbers before production had ceased. The new model was labelled OWB and was to be fitted with a 32-seat utility 'no frills' body, with single-skin roof and wooden slatted seats. The buses, which cost around £600, were delivered with matt brown paintwork and could only be ordered against the requisite Permit, with operators having to demonstrate that they were essential for maintaining vital transport services. Certainly Kemp's were in desperate need of replacement vehicles to ease the burden on their eclectic fleet. Deliveries got underway in July 1942 and Kemp's received their first – BBW 274 with Mulliner body – three months later. Five more followed with Duple bodies (BBW 268/331/701/2 and 950) in the two year period from November 1942 and they became the backbone of the fleet. Locally, both the BBC and the RAF also used Bedford OWBs for transport of civilian staff. The Kemp intake enabled several vehicles to be stood down, including the last of the original Bedford WLBs (UD 4652) which in 1943 had its seats removed and was then used for a year or so to bring petrol supplies to Woodcote from a garage at Goring-on-Thames in drums. Bus and truck operators were not allowed to use their own fuel tanks during the war and the number of commercial sources was heavily-restricted. With little thought of Health & Safety, the bus full of 40 gallon drums of petrol must have potentially constituted a mobile fire bomb, which the Luftwaffe would have been hard-pressed to emulate. Morris Commercial JG 2835 was seemingly relegated to spare vehicle status for some time, although it made a surprise brief reappearance in Reading about 1945, after which it disappeared, the last of the pre-war 20-seat vehicles.

Having left school, Bill Passey's son Jack began to undertake conducting duties on the Dennis Lancet coach having previously done so under-age. After a short post-war compulsory period in the forces, he was to work for Kemp's and Chiltern Queens as a driver,

BBW 274 was the first of three Bedford OWBs supplied new at the end of 1942, which Harry Kemp was able to obtain having made successful applications for permits. This was the only one with a Mulliner body. The others (BBW 268 and BBW 331) were by Duple. All were supplied new with wooden slat seating for 32 passengers. Kemp's withdrew and sold these three at a time when beginning to expand the post-war contract and private hire market as they were then able to obtain new and larger capacity vehicles. BBW 274 is seen here when sold to S Huntley, East Oakley, Basingstoke in June 1949. *(WJ Haynes)*

Perhaps the best-remembered of the Kemp's' Bedford OWBs are BBW 701, BBW 702 and BBW 950, new in 1943/44 and surviving into the start of the Chiltern Queens era. Photographs of BBW 702 and BBW 950 have proved very elusive – and those of BBW 701 are fairly limited. This one, of BBW 701, showing it fitted with ex-Thames Valley upholstered seats, instead of the original wooden slatted type, therefore dates from 1950 or later, when the livery would have been red with maroon wings (and, it seems, also the front roof dome and destination box). The bus, bound for Checkendon, is on the Blagrave Street stand in Reading where the two Kemp's bus stop flags were provided here. *(John Whitehead Colln)*

in the garage and in the workshop, until the end of his working life, being multi-skilled in various trades. His sister Mary was one of the office staff and some years later married Cyril Baldwin. Towards the end of the war, Kemp's had their first lady bus drivers – Esme Swain, who was once a Parlour Maid at 'Querns', followed by a lady known as 'The Duchess' – but her real name is not yet to hand.

During the war, Traffic Commissioners were replaced by Regional Transport Commissioners and the publication of *Notices & Proceedings* was suspended. New bus services were granted under a system known as Defence Permits, but seemingly no records of these survive.

It is thought that passenger demand required the introduction of an additional bus service by Kemp's, perhaps in 1943 but certainly by May 1944. This ran on Saturday and Sunday afternoons between Reading and Wallingford, but on a more direct route than the Didcot service, running the same way as the Didcot service to Woodcote, then via Ipsden Turn, White House (Lark Stoke), Mongewell and Crowmarsh Gifford. Bedford EXK 599 was initially the usual performer. The new service ran northwards from Woodcote along Red Lane, which was part of the B479 road from Caversham to Crowmarsh Gifford. It was not to be until nearly 30 years later that a Woodcote Bypass was built, to avoid the village and to complement a significant upgrading and straightening of what was the B479, now renumbered A4074.

Normal Road Service licensing procedures were not restored until 1946, so what was probably a belated facility to replace Jackman's former service to Henley-on-Thames for the weekly Market, which was then on Thursday, may well have been started by Kemp under a Defence Permit, but whether during the war, after mileage and fuel restrictions had been eased or just after it has not yet been determined. The route meandered between Checkendon and Henley via Woodcote, Crays Pond, Whitchurch Hill, Goring Heath, Cane End, Gallowstree Common, Peppard and Rotherfield Greys, with two journeys each way.

Recovery, Growth and Austerity

On 28 August 1945, thirteen days after Japan surrendered, signifying the end of the war in south-east Asia, the Kemp business was formally incorporated as Kemp's Motor Services Ltd. It had a nominal capital of £7,500 and the directors and sole shareholders were, of course, Harry Kemp (Governing Director) of Greenmore Hill, Woodcote and Hiram Charles Kemp (Managing Director) of 'Four Winds', Crays Pond. Ethel Green was appointed Company Secretary. Subsequently, Harry Kemp semi-retired and later moved to Woodham Walter in Essex, leaving Hiram (John) Kemp in charge at Woodcote. However, Kemp senior would visit Woodcote regularly. Harry Kemp was a keen amateur radio enthusiast and had a whole room at his Essex home filled with the appropriate equipment, as well as a tall transmitter mast in the garden.

City of Oxford MS soon moved to strengthen their services in the Wallingford area. In January 1946 they applied to increase their service 38 between Didcot, Blewbury, Aston Tirrold and Wallingford and to restore a service between Ewelme and Wallingford that had been suspended some six years previously. Kemp wrote to COMS, expressing his surprise that they had gone ahead with submitting applications before it had been discussed and agreed between the parties, which as far as he could recall was the previous understanding.

Although the war was over and men were gradually returning from the forces, life for most had become much-changed. Many continued to travel to work in factories in towns and a strong local military presence was maintained. Fuel and many foodstuffs remained on ration, whilst some other goods were hard to obtain, or perhaps only in 'austerity' versions. At least people could gain some amusement by undertaking travel for pleasure again, such as outings to the coast or other attractions. With a continuing shortage of both new and pre-owned vehicles, bus and coach operators became hard-pressed to cope with these demands. The population of south Oxfordshire had increased and would continue to do so, partly through an influx of displaced persons from overseas, domiciled at various 'camps'.

In the winter of 1940, construction had started of a large camp at Scots Common, about a mile north of Checkendon, which became occupied by American troops from 1942 until D-Day in June 1944. About a month later, a German V1 rocket dropped in the vicinity and John Bennett recalls that his father was blown off the top of a lorry by the blast, where he had been watching the rocket's progress. Subsequently, the camp was used to house Italian and German Prisoners-of-War, including some who were wounded and required medical treatment. In 1948 it was acquired from the Ministry of Defence by the National Assistance Board and became a hostel for displaced Polish nationals arriving from various parts of the world, who had already spent eight years in exile. The corrugated iron Nissen huts were converted to provide very basic living accommodation, as well as a chapel, school and meeting hall, for an entire community. The residents were expected to support themselves; some gained employment on farms but quite a few worked in Reading for Huntley & Palmer, the biscuit makers, and others at the associated firm of Huntley, Boorne and Stevens, who made the biscuit tins and other metal boxes. They were transported morning and afternoon, Monday to Friday, to these firms and to H & G Simonds brewery, also in Reading, by Kemp's vehicles on a contract basis, for which an Express Road Service Licence was applied for and subsequently granted in November 1948. Transport was also provided to the Oxford factory of Pressed Steel. At the same time, Express licences were obtained to transport foreign workers to the Reading factories from Howberry Park Camp at Crowmarsh and from South Camp at Nettlebed.

John Bennett also recalls that in some respects, the rural bus services, even in the 1940s, were still somewhat similar to the old carriers, with variations to licensed routes sometimes performed informally on request or as a favour to regular customers. On the Checkendon service, the drivers would take the Bennett family beyond the terminus at Whitehall, so as to drop them at their house at Lovegrove's Corner. When going to Reading, if one wanted the bus to stop, it would do so whilst one waited indoors, if a shopping bag was hung on the garden gate.

A Kemp's timetable folder dated February 1947 reveals a number of changes. On the Reading-Wallingford-Didcot service there were more journeys, especially between the latter two points. The Reading-Wallingford service via Red Lane and Ipsden Turn ran daily with additional journeys, with an extension from/to Benson Aerodrome to facilitate an evening out in Reading for RAF personnel. On the Wallingford-Watlington route, a daily service was restored as far as Ewelme. After some years, a daily Wallingford-Didcot service via The Wittenhams was reinstated in about January 1948.

Service numbers began to appear on printed timetables (but not on vehicles) from the autumn of 1948, which in general corresponded to the final digit of the Road Service Licence reference number. These were:

1: Wallingford-Watlington
2: Reading-Wallingford-Didcot
3: Reading-Checkendon
6: Reading-Whitchurch Hill-Woodcote-Ipsden
12: Reading-Woodcote-Red Lane-Wallingford-Benson
13: Checkendon-Henley
14: Didcot-Wittenhams-Wallingford-Stadhampton

A timetable dated 27 September 1948 indicates that service 3 had been extended from Checkendon to Scots Common Polish Settlement (to give the residents a daily regular service to the jobs, shops and bright lights of Reading) and on through the narrow lanes to Nuffield. The 10pm journey from Reading on Sunday was extended beyond Nuffield to Benson Aerodrome. This was the golden era of maximum patronage for bus services, at a time of continuing petrol rationing and relatively low car ownership.

Both service 2 and service 12 gained a major timetable enhancement on 4 October 1948 when each was increased to operate every two hours on weekdays and on Sunday afternoon, with all journeys on service 12 running through to/from Benson Aerodrome. The timetables were arranged so that an even-interval hourly service resulted between Reading and Woodcote (there was also service 6 via Whitchurch Hill) and there was one bus per hour between Reading and Wallingford. After these revisions, buses were worked more intensively and to tight timings. Up until then, there had been leisurely and lengthy layovers at termini, including in Reading, where Kemp buses parked for long periods in Kings Meadow Road, near to the swimming baths.

The expanding business needed additional depot infrastructure. In 1948 some of the old greenhouses were demolished and a second garage constructed, complete with a pit for working under vehicles and an area for Bennie Warner to undertake bodywork repairs. A small building near the road became a mess room and a glasshouse was converted to a cashier's office and store. A wing of 'Greenmore' was converted into a general office. A double-deck bus could not enter either of the garages for maintenance, so a pit built into a concrete ramp was constructed parallel to the road at the top of the field, offering a vision for motorists ascending Long Toll, of a bus seemingly floating in the air and towering over the hedge.

Conscription to military service ceased in 1948, three years after the war ended, but not before Jack Passey had served his term in the RAF from 1947. In replacement came National Service from 1 January 1949. Males between seventeen and 21 years of age were required to serve for eighteen months, later extended to two years.

In time, many coach operators in the vicinity of barracks, airfields and naval bases would profit from running express services to major cities for servicemen taking weekend leave and seeking transport that was

These two views are of WN 6224, the ex-South Wales Transport 1934 Dennis Lancet, which came from Clarke, Rubery, Hereford in August 1946 and lasted in service until September 1952. Having been refurbished by Markhams, of Reading, it was out-shopped in a smart new livery of red with maroon wings and flashes, which subsequently became standard. 'Winnie', as she subsequently became known, was another forward control vehicle, with driver in a separate cab and therefore requiring a conductor. It was the first acquisition after the formation of Kemp's Motor Services Ltd The nearside view (Copyright: RHG Simpson) appears to have been taken when parked in Long Toll, Woodcote while the offside view (John Whitehead Collection – by the late LG Head) is at the Blagrave Street, Reading stand, with driver Fred Smith about to take command.

cheaper and sometimes quicker than cross-country rail services, especially as many military establishments were remote from railway stations. Kemp's were granted a licence for their first Forces Leave express service in July 1948, between Benson Aerodrome and London. For many years the terminus was Baylis Road Coach Park, near Waterloo. The six month period between the application in January 1948 and the granting of the licence was typical of time taken for objections to be considered (those from British Railways being particularly prevalent) and for a Hearing to take place. Kemp's licence was co-ordinated with one held by South Midland Motor Services Ltd and each company worked the service in alternate months, which may have been a compromise in order to deal with an objection from the Oxford-based operator.

February 1947 saw the delivery of new Duple-bodied Bedford OB service bus CBW 522, which survived into Chiltern Queens days, although this view would seem to have been taken in 1954/55, quite late in its Kemp's career, as it is in red livery with maroon wings and bonnet top and with a mushroom grey band edged in maroon. It is shown on the Blagrave Street stand in Reading bound for Wallingford. *(Omnibus Society – Roy Marshall Colln)*

Between 1946 and 1949, seventeen buses and coaches were acquired by Kemp's, three of which never entered service, being used as a source of spare parts. Some of these were expensive to buy and maintain. Thanks to John Davies, we have some additional information.

The first vehicle to arrive after the war ended was WN 6224, a Dennis Lancet bus of 1934 vintage, originally owned by South Wales Transport. It was nicknamed 'Winnie'. Before entering service, it received attention from Markham's Garage in Reading and was deemed one of the more useful and successful pre-owned specimens taken into stock in the latter part of the 1940s. Apart from contract work, it was used on the Benson to London Forces Leave service as well as a fair amount on bus services, firstly on the Reading-Whitchurch Hill-Woodcote route and later on the Reading to Wallingford section of the main Didcot service.

Despite the lengthy wait at that time between ordering a new vehicle and it being delivered, due to shortages of materials and a large backlog of orders at the popular chassis and body manufacturers, Kemp's managed to introduce three new vehicles in 1947. CBW 522 was a Bedford OB with a superior style of Duple bus body than those on the wartime utility models. It was worked hard, including almost daily on a contract from Reading to the RAF Maintenance Unit at Milton. It would work the first bus from Woodcote to Reading, go to Milton, then run the Wallingford-Reading via Red Lane service during the day, after which it would take the workers back from Milton to Reading via Streatley, ending its day on the 6.15pm departure from Reading to Checkendon. Its engine was not switched off for twelve hours.

In April 1947 came CBW 864, a new Dennis Lancet J3 with 35-seat Whitson coach body, which meant that Kemp's had something decent to use when required on private hire and excursions, as well as for more mundane work such as bus services, contracts and Forces Leave

Something to be proud of was Dennis Lancet J3 CBW 864, with 35-seat body by Whitson, Kemp's first post-war luxury coach, new in April 1947. Delivered in the recently adopted red and maroon livery, this broadside view at The Peggy Bedford (where the Great West Road and the Great South-West Road split), was probably taken after the coach was collected from the bodybuilders, Whitson of West Drayton, on Good Friday that year by Hiram Kemp and John Highe. *(Kemp family collection – by Late Hiram Kemp)*

services. Next to arrive, in June 1947, was CUD 286, a Commer Commando with a Perkins diesel engine and a 32-seat coach body. Its braking system did not match the power of the engine and Perkins diesel units were noted for causing damaging vibrations in lightweight Commer and Bedford vehicles. It spent much time on the Checkendon service but only lasted at Kemp's for around three years until it was sold to an operator in rural Norfolk. John Gutteridge delivered it there one weekend, taking his motorbike inside it so he could ride home.

OU 5721, known as 'The Buggy', was a Commer Invader which started life with Chisnell's King Alfred Motor Services in Winchester but came to Kemp's from Gregory of Hook, along with another Commer which was dismantled for spares, donating its engine to 'The Buggy'. The latter was too small for most of the contracts, apart from the Mapledurham school run and the Howberry Park Camp to Reading workers' service.

From about 1941, those vehicles due for repaint in Kemp's livery had been given a blue flash on the side, rather than yellow as hitherto. From 1947, it was decided to change the livery to red and maroon, with a K motif, featuring ribbons and laurel leaves, designed by Ken Clarke and apparently based on an RAF cap badge. Within the laurel leaves was written the Latin *Semper Eadem*, which translates as "always the same", which interestingly is also the motto on the Coat-of-Arms of the city of Leicester. Also in 1947, the

traditional Bell Punch ticket system was replaced with TIM ticket machines of the Major model, which held a blank paper roll on which was printed the relevant fare, Boarding Stage etc. Unfortunately, the Waybill for these was as tedious to complete as for the punch tickets, as each fare value had to be recorded separately. Setright were just introducing their Speed roll ticket machines and Kemp's were an early customer in 1949 when they bought them to replace the TIM machines after only two years. However, that was not before an alleged incident in Reading when an irate member of staff is supposed to have thrown a TIM ticket machine for some unknown reason at Hiram Kemp.

Three diverse vehicles dating from the 1930s appeared in spring and early summer 1948, in order to meet the increased needs of the growing bus service network. Probably one of the best-known both in the Kemp's fleet and in the early days of Chiltern Queens was BRD 922. This was an AEC Regal, once numbered T594 in London Transport's 10T10 class of vehicles for Green Line coach duties and registered EYK 229. It had been made available to the United States Army along with nine others, in September 1942. At the end of the war, most were returned to London for further use. T594, however, seems to have developed faults and was seemingly used to provide parts to keep others running. Eventually, in a somewhat derelict state, it passed to Arlington Motors, a dealer in Enfield. They

Perhaps Kemp's most famous vehicle was BRD 922, a much modified former London Transport Green Line coach of the 10T10 type – T594 (EYK 229), which had been lent to the US Army during the war but failed to be returned. It had arrived with Smith's Coaches, Reading as an empty body on a rolling chassis and Smiths gathered some suitable parts from all over the country, re-registered it in the absence of a log-book, and put it into service in their blue and orange colours. Sold to Kemp's in May 1948, Smiths painted out their orange relief with brown and it ran thus with Kemp's before repaint to Kemp's new red and maroon, as seen here on the Blagrave Street stand, in Reading on 7 May 1949. (VC Jones)

The only known photograph with Kemp's of 'Wivvy' (WV 1545) is this one taken in August 1949 in The Forbury, Reading. It is a 1933 Dennis Lancet with Heaver 32-seat body, new to Card of Devizes but which came to Kemp's from King & Donovan of Yattendon, in a grey and blue livery in July 1948. It was put into Kemp's' red and maroon but only lasted in the fleet until February 1951. (John Davies)

A 1934 Leyland Lion LT5A with 4-cylinder oil engine, VD 3424 'Vee-Dee', new to the Lanarkshire Traction Co, carried a Leyland 32-seat body with rear platform like a double-decker. It joined Kemp's fleet in June 1948. Finished in red and maroon livery, it lasted only until September 1950. Seen here in The Forbury in August 1949, the Mulliner-bodied Bedford OB behind is DBW 67, new in September 1948 but only in service until October 1951. DBW 67 seemingly had a serious traffic accident which may have caused recertification problems, so its seats were exchanged with those in an ex-City of Oxford AEC Regal (EFC 291) bought at that time and DBW 67 was sold, eventually becoming a baker's van in Worcester. (John Davies)

A sister to this rare 1934 normal control Dennis Lancet, VV 1164, was originally obtained in January 1949 with a view to preparing it for use but it was eventually cannibalised for engine spares only, for WN 6224 and WV 1545. The vehicle was new to Northampton Corporation Transport and carried a locally-built Grose 26-seat body. (Hestair-Dennis Archive)

New ground was broken with the acquisition of two 1933-vintage ex-City of Oxford Motor Services petrol-engined AEC Regent double-deckers, one for spares (JO 7875) and one for service (JO 7876) in August/ September 1948, being required mainly for increased contract work. No photographs seem to exist of them in Kemp's ownership, this wartime view showing JO 7876 in City of Oxford service. It came to an untimely end on 16 December 1950, when it collided with the low bridge in Vastern Road, Reading (which required all Reading Corporation Transport double-deck motorbuses to be of lowbridge construction) – being driven by a Kemp's coach driver at the time!! (John Whitehead Colln)

sold it to Smith's Coaches of Reading, minus engine, gearbox, radiator and seats, amongst other things. Over time, Smiths had rebuilt it with an AEC 8.8 litre diesel engine, an AEC lorry radiator and a crash gearbox, rather than the correct preselector type. When almost ready for service in 1946, a man employed by London Transport to track down sundry missing vehicles arrived in Reading and noted how non-standard the bus had become. He decided that as Smiths had bought it in good faith and done much work on it, it could stay with Smiths, as far too much modification would be needed to make it acceptable for London Transport use again. On purchase from Smiths in May 1948, it had a set of bus seats, so Kemp's had them replaced by Vincents of Reading with coach seats. It was used on a variety of work including on bus services with a conductor.

VD 3424 (usually described as 'Vee-Dee') was a 1934 Leyland Lion LT5A bus, with cut-away entrance platform at the rear corner. New to Lanarkshire Traction

Co Ltd, Kemp's acquired it, apparently for £950, after use by the successor Central Scottish Motor Traction Co. Despite the high price, it was in bad condition and continually plagued by mechanical failures. However, at that time, vehicles of any type were much sought after and these shortages led to inflated prices.

A Dennis Lancet, registered WV 1545 and known as 'Wivvy', was not in a much better state. Its wooden body was very poor and the coach disgraced itself in 1948 while on hire to Tappins Coaches, when a seat parted company with the rotten floor. It has been said that it cost an outrageous £1,100. These were followed, fortunately, by three new vehicles: DBW 66, a TSM (previously known as Tilling-Stevens) K6LA7 with Gardner engine and coach body by Vincent, a Bedford OB (DBW 67) with 28 coach seats in a bus body by Mulliner which was used mostly on service 6 and DBW 382, a Dennis Lancet J3 coach, also with a Vincent body.

DBW 67's regular driver was Tommy Coles who,

A second Tilling-Stevens luxury coach, DUD 401, this time a K6LM7 because it had a Meadows engine, and carrying a Dutfield 33-seat body, was new in May 1949. Note the 'K' emblem and motto on the side panel, the front spring-steel 'bumper' and the front and rear wheel embellishers that it had for a while. *(Kemp family collection – by Late Hiram Kemp)*

The girls' names given to the luxury coaches – and a couple of other vehicles (apart from 'Winnie' (WN 6224), 'Wivvy' (WV 1545) and 'Vee-Dee' (VD 3424)) are as follows:- UD 9431 = Rita-Ann BRD 922 = Rosemary CBW 864 = Patricia DBW 66 = Mary-Ann DBW 382 = Daphne (later Wendy) DUD 401 = Greta (later Valerie)

An unusual second hand purchase in August 1949 , especially since Kemp's had already withdrawn and sold only a year earlier the first three Bedford OWBs that they had obtained new during the war, was of EOT 48. It came from Gregory of Hook, Hants, in their green livery and had worked on hire to Kemp's before actually being purchased. It continued to run in green for a while, presumably before some extensive mechanical and bodywork repairs and fitting interior side and roof panels. It had come fitted with 32 leather upholstered seats but was re-seated to 28 using ex-Thames Valley upholstered seats in February 1950 and repainted into Kemp's red and maroon livery. It seems that the bus was obtained for and regularly employed on a school contract to Henley, which was later augmented by working the two new Henley town bus services for two years before they were taken over by AG & KM Spiers of Henley. *(MJC Dare)*

unlike the other drivers, performed the same duty every day he worked. This bus had a short life with Kemp's, during which it is thought to have been involved in an accident, as it was sold in early 1951, after its seats had been transferred to another vehicle.

To deal with increased loadings at certain times, it was decided to purchase two double-deck buses – 1933 AEC Regents with Park Royal bodies, recently removed from the fleet of City of Oxford MS. One was never put in to service by Kemp's, but the other, JO 7876, was used during the week on the workers' run from Scots Common Polish Settlement to Huntley & Palmer's in Reading and on service 12 (Reading-Benson Aerodrome) on Saturdays. With a petrol engine, it was extremely uneconomical to run, unless demand would have otherwise required two single-deck buses. It had to use Friar Street and Caversham Road in Reading (the route as traditionally taken by the Checkendon service) as it was too high to fit under Vastern Road railway bridge. This bridge proved to be its downfall when, one Saturday night in December 1950, a driver not normally on service 12, forgot and drove it that way, resulting in it becoming wedged and decapitated, needing retrieval by Thames Valley's breakdown truck. It was damaged beyond repair, so it was necessary to hire a double-decker from City of Oxford MS for two weeks over the busy Christmas and New Year period.

In 1948, Reading Corporation Transport was disposing of six, two-year-old Bedford OB buses with Duple bodies, registered CDP 231-6. These would have been in good condition, ideal for many of Kemp's' operations and would have possibly negated the need to buy some of the more dubious vehicles, but such youthful buses were of premium interest to many firms at that time. Kemp put in a tender with an offer to trump any higher bid if his was not successful. However, the Corporation obtained more money for them by selling them back to the dealer which originally supplied them – the local Great Western Motors. Thus, Kemp was thwarted.

1949 saw the arrival of three more vehicles. A rare normal control Dennis Lancet bus from the municipal Northampton fleet (although it had previously been on loan for about two years to St Helens Corporation Transport) was acquired with the intention of putting it into service, but this never happened as it was used to provide spare parts, being dumped in the field next to the garage. DUD 401 was another new TSM coach, this time with Meadows engine and a Dutfield body. EOT 48 was a 1945 Bedford OWB bus, acquired from Gregory's of Hook. Kemp's reconditioned it and put in replacement seats acquired from Thames Valley Leyland Lion buses, which were being withdrawn at the time, in place of the leather upholstered seats that were fitted when acquired.

In order that staff could receive Sickness Benefit, it was agreed that a Kemp's Motor Services Staff Benevolent Fund should be set up. At the inaugural meeting on 24 October 1949, it was decided that members would make contributions from their weekly pay and after three days of sickness, being unable to work, they should receive 3s per day, or one guinea (£1.1s or £1.05) per week.

Interlude – John Davies Remembers

Information available for this book has been much-enriched by extensive notes made by John Davies about the period 1940-50. As well as being an interested observer of the Kemp business, he was an employee between autumn 1949 and spring 1950. There follows a miscellany of some of the events and practices that he remembers.

The vehicles used on the bus services, where the driver sat behind the engine in the saloon area, were principally 'one man operated'. However, passengers did not normally pay and receive a ticket on entering. The driver would instead stop the bus at a convenient point, to walk around and collect the fares. Such places included Woodcote War Memorial, Goring Heath Post Office and the Telephone Box in Upper Woodcote Road, Caversham. Kemp's had to charge fares that were protective to Reading Corporation Transport from that stop by Sunny Brow, to and from Reading Stations via Caversham. The same applied on the Checkendon service once the Caversham & South Oxon Golf Course was passed. The Corporation would sometimes engage one of their staff in plain clothes to ride on the Kemp's bus to check if they were charged the higher protective fare rate. These Fare Conditions were to remain in force through the later Chiltern Queens era, until abolished under 1980s legislation.

The winter of 1946/7 brought many problems due to the adverse weather. Heavy snow and a prolonged period of sub-zero temperatures resulted in extensive snow accumulations and many blocked roads. Service 12 between Woodcote and Crowmarsh ran through some very exposed countryside, which encouraged the strong winds to blow the snow into deep drifts. On one occasion, a bus had to be abandoned near Ewelme and it was subsequently discovered that it was in an adjacent field, rather than on the road, such was the depth of the snow masking the extent of the highway. When the snow finally melted, extensive flooding followed. The River Thames burst its banks and Caversham was almost severed from Reading by the depth of water under the Caversham Road and Vastern Road railway bridges. Reading Corporation Transport managed to get their buses through by adding metal extension tubes to the exhaust pipes, to prevent water ingress into the engines. There was also flooding in the Didcot area. Some of Kemp's vehicles were uncomfortable to drive in flood conditions, especially 'Vee-Dee', where the water came up through the cab floor and up the driver's trouser leg.

Before the use of anti-freeze solution in winter, the buses had to be drained of water each night and re-filled in the morning. On one occasion somebody did this on the slope to the new garage and in the morning there was extensive icing, making it difficult to get the vehicles up the slope out of the depot.

One Monday morning there was a 'silver thaw'. The school contracts were being driven by the garage staff, such as Ernie Brant, Bill Passey and even Hiram Kemp, as the usual drivers had arrived back very late the previous evening from their Forces Leave long distance services. Soon it was learned that Bill Passey was off the road with WN 6224, so the last spare driver went off to help him. Only George Vaughan and John Davies remained in the garage. Eventually, they heard WV 1545 coming up Long Toll, by the chapel. Ten minutes later it seemed no nearer, so they each took a shovel and went to investigate. The road was so slippery that it was hard to stand upright; behind the Dennis Lancet were a further eight buses unable to move, with Lady Rose from Hardwicke House, in her car, in the middle of them.

Thick fog caused navigational problems, especially in the late 1940s and early 1950s – the era of the urban yellow 'pea soupers' or 'smogs', when the prevalent smoke from many domestic fires as well as industrial emissions, were mixed together with natural fog. Conductors sometimes had to walk in front of buses to guide the drivers and it is said that Alfie Smith once started to walk up Vastern Road when leading a bus into Reading, realised his mistake and returned to Caversham Road, by doing a U-turn around a Keep Left bollard with the bus following behind him.

The Bedford OWB utility buses were in due course fitted with front wings made of rubber, to reduce rattles and the need for repair due to the damage they had been receiving. However, the earliest three were sold in 1947/8 for further service, being replaced by larger vehicles but of an inferior condition. Those OWBs that remained had their seating capacity reduced to 30 in 1949 on the instruction of the Traffic Commissioners and the following year the wooden slatted seats were finally replaced with 28 upholstered seats taken from withdrawn Thames Valley buses. Bedford WTB EXK 599 went to Elliott's coach works in Caversham in 1948 to be completely rebuilt and almost as an afterthought had its seats reupholstered to prevent them looking jaded against the coach's rejuvenated appearance. It returned to service in June 1949, re-registered DUD 784, being smart enough for use on private hire, as well as on more mundane daily contract work taking Tersons' construction workers from Reading to the Slough area.

The timetable enhancements in October 1948 resulted in the drivers finding it difficult to keep to time on service 2 between Reading and Didcot. The service was split at Wallingford, so that passengers making through journeys were required to change buses. This may have been in anticipation of the use of double-deck vehicles, which would not have passed under the low bridges in Didcot. One bus, usually a Bedford but sometimes Dennis WN 6224, worked from Reading to Wallingford with a conductor, normally Alfie Smith. Another bus would run from Wallingford to Didcot and also perform journeys from Wallingford to Ewelme on the Watlington route.

After the enactment of the 1944 Education Act, there was an obligation on local authorities to make provision for free home-to-school transport for children who lived further from their nearest school than two or three miles, depending on their age. Previously, children were expected to walk considerable distances and with the closure of some of the smaller local schools and the raising of the school leaving age, this had become more of an issue, especially in the winter. Secondary education became focussed on fewer, but larger, sites serving a wider area. Where insufficient opportunity or capacity existed for the use of stage carriage services, bespoke school transport for those pupils statutorily entitled, was secured by competitive tender by the education authorities. In their portfolio of contract work, Kemp's provided school transport serving Woodcote School from Goring and South Stoke and to schools at Mapledurham, Henley, Wallingford and Sonning Common. These trips were integrated in some cases into the scheduling of vehicles and drivers for the bus services. A particularly un-remunerative job was connected with the bus service 1 journeys to Ewelme School from Benson Aerodrome. As there were too many children for the usual Bedford, a coach had to be sent to act as a duplicate. After there had nearly been an accident involving a child, the Headmaster of the school insisted that as the coach driver was in a separate cab, a conductor must be provided. The person supplied was John Davies, the Yard Boy, who at the time was under-age and not able to be licensed as a conductor. He would travel on the coach in the afternoon and when they met the Bedford at Wallingford Market Place, John would pour two Jerry cans of petrol into its fuel tank, regardless of the danger of doing so with passengers on board. They then went to Ewelme and if they were lucky they might be given bunches of watercress on the way by men they knew who worked at the watercress beds. John Davies then conducted the coach with the children on board back to Benson Aerodrome, collecting only about 4/8d in fares on the short journey and then changed to the service 12 bus back to Reading and home; not a particularly productive exercise.

The only school contract that permitted the use of double-deck JO 7876, if a single-deck vehicle was not available, was from Cleeve Crossroads and Goring-on-Thames to Woodcote School via Crays Pond. One day with John Highe driving and Peter Pearce conducting, an overhanging branch of a tree in Goring struck the bus, breaking every window on the near side of the top-deck. Unfortunately, one boy needed a stitch for a cut lip. In preparation for the introduction of JO 7876, a gang led by Bob Birch, who had some tree felling experience, apparently went out at quiet times to undertake tree lopping. However, the Traffic Commissioners had some concerns over the use of double-deck vehicles. Reading Council considered that St Peter's Hill in Caversham was unsuitable, due to its steepness, narrowness and overhanging trees. They wished for a condition to be attached to Kemp's Road Service licences, preventing the use of double-deckers. In October 1949, after inspecting the route and an alternative by way of St Anne's Hill, Albert Road and Highmoor Road, the Commissioners did not impose the condition but required that low gear be used with a fifteen miles per hour speed limit. Double-deck buses would be required to come to

a stand before ascending or descending St Peter's Hill. These measures did not satisfy a gentleman who lived on the hill, who wrote with his objection to the *Berkshire Chronicle*, stating that there had been four accidents in the past few weeks and criticising the decision of the Traffic Commissioners, "whose representatives have no knowledge of the local conditions".

Following the war, the private hire work had re-started, including for club trips, village organisation outings and taking sports teams to away matches. Some work was obtained from Reading, although Smith's Coaches secured most of it. However, Kemp's did provide the transport for Rabson Rovers, a local amateur football team. One of the furthest private hire trips was to the Grand National at Aintree in 1950, when two drivers were required with stamina for the long journey there and back – no Motorways in those days! It seems that there were few licensed excursions or tours operated at this time, but some of the drivers arranged trips at their own initiative.

Whilst involved on some overhaul work on Commer CUD 286, John Davies was attempting to lift the gearbox onto a sack barrow. In doing so he crushed a finger and was sent to Hiram Kemp's wife, who had received proper First Aid training, for a bandage. He recalls nearly fainting into her arms on the kitchen doorstep of 'Greenmore'. Hiram Kemp had married Jessie Turner in 1943; she lived locally and her father, George Turner, was at one time the chauffeur at 'Abbotsfield', the same place of employment as Ernie Cox, who we met earlier. Jessie's father and mother both came from Norfolk, where her cousin Stanley was a partner in the family-run bus firm of Turner & Butcher Ltd of Kenninghall – the same operator who acquired from Kemp's CUD 286 around April 1950 (repainted green and cream before sale) and before that, also Commer EUO 187.

Another memory of John's is of painting the interiors of the Bedford OWBs bright blue, when they were refurbished internally in 1950. Some of the paint splashed onto the toe cap of his heavy shoes, which he retained for many years for use in snowy conditions underfoot; the paint was still there in the mid-1980s.

Apparently Hiram Kemp developed a liking for American vehicles and impressive cars. Attending War Surplus Sales, he would acquire various redundant items once with or intended for the US Army. Amongst his purchases were two Willys Jeeps (registered CBW 7 and CBW 523), one of which was used by Bill Passey as a run-around. Hiram's daughter Gillian remembers being taken to school in one of these vehicles, which was retained in the family long after the Kemp's left Woodcote. Hiram Kemp also acquired vehicles manufactured by Chevrolet and Packard, including two trucks (one with a Shooting Brake body and one that was used for attending bus or coach breakdowns) and also at least one vehicle with an amphibious capability, perhaps in case of a repeat of the 1947 floods. Other war surplus goods that found their way to 'Greenmore' were a couple of Nissen Huts and boxes containing aircraft parts!

In spite of being in the Kemp's fleet for nearly five years, it is surprising how this 1937 Park Royal-bodied 20-seater Leyland Cub registered EFC 300, new to City of Oxford and bought through a dealer, was so successful at evading the enthusiasts' cameras, apart from this one of it undergoing overhaul in the depot.
(RHG Simpson)

CFC 784 was one of an initial four ex-City of Oxford 1936-vintage AEC Regents with Weyman 52-seat lowbridge bodies (two for service, two for spares) bought in March 1951. A muddy CFC 784, on a damp day, waits time in Station Square, Reading before proceeding 'round the corner' to the Kemp's Blagrave Street stand. CFC 784 was finished in a variation of standard livery, being red below upper-deck floor level and maroon above, and finished with maroon wings and lower-deck waistband. (Omnibus Society – Roy Marshall Colln)

Waiting time at Reading's Blagrave Street, stand CFC 785, the other one of the two initial 1936 AEC Regents seems to have had much more maroon than CFC 784 and it additionally carried the Kemp's name in the centre of the front fairing. The tread on the front tyres appears to be non-existent!
(Michael Rooum)

A Change in Fortunes

Although the 1950s were to prove to be the final decade for the Kemp business, it started with a little more expansion of the bus service network. In order to make the vehicle that operated a school contract to Henley more cost efficient and to save some dead mileage to and from Woodcote, some work was found for it for six days a week, fitting around its school transport commitments. It was decided to commence two short local services within Henley, starting from the Market Place: service 21 to Harpsden via Henley Station and Western Avenue and service 22 via Gainsborough Hill Estate and Wootton Estate to a terminus point interestingly described as Rotherfield Greys Road (30 mph Limit Sign). Refurbished Bedford OWB EOT 48 was in due course allocated to these services.

Seemingly to celebrate their introduction on 1 June 1950 and to accompany some revisions to the timetables of other services, an impressive A5 format timetable booklet was published at that time – comparable to the style of such publications produced by some major operators. On the front cover there was a map of the routes and on the rear cover, a diagram depicting principal services 2 and 12 between Reading and Wallingford. Within were timetables set in a clear style complete with service numbers, a list of booking agents, some paid-for advertising for local businesses and various slogans, such as:

> Road safety – take care – we do – the whole of our driving staff are entrants in the National Society for the Prevention of Accidents Safe Driving Competition
>
> We have a Lost Property Office **but** we prefer that you do not have to use it
>
> Up-to-the-minute Air-Conditioned and heated Luxury Radio Coaches for Private Hire: Your entire satisfaction is our ambition

By June 1950, various other service adjustments had taken place. On service 6, Ipsden villagers were only served by one morning journey to Reading on Monday to Friday (presumably when returning home passengers had to walk about a mile from service 12 on the main road!); service 1 was operating daily between Wallingford and Watlington either via Benson village or Benson Aerodrome and service 3 had been extended from Nuffield to Turners Court Colony. The latter establishment had been founded in 1911 in order to provide training in agricultural matters for unemployed and unemployable young men, later becoming a corrective institution or borstal. Latterly it became the Wallingford Farm Training School. Closing in April 1991, it had changed its emphasis from being a place of rehabilitation for offenders, to offering training for a wider group of young people.

The influx of vehicles into the Kemp fleet slowed somewhat in 1950 with only two acquisitions – a new Commer Avenger with 37-seat coach body by Dutfield (EBW 838), the chassis of which had been delivered to Kemp's in 1948 and then stored, and a fairly elderly 20-seat Leyland Cub bus of 1937 vintage from the City of Oxford MS fleet, registered EFC 300.

City of Oxford MS met with Wallingford Town and Parish Councils on 24 April 1950 when a proposed new service from Reading to Abingdon was mentioned and next day this was reported in *The Oxford Mail*. Having advised British Railways the previous year of his intention to run to Abingdon, it was more than coincidental that on 27 April, Hiram Kemp made an application to operate a new daily bus service numbered 19 from Reading, all the way to Abingdon, via Caversham, Chazey Heath, Cane End, Exlade Street, Woodcote, Red Lane (B479), Crowmarsh, Wallingford, Brightwell, Long Wittenham Turn, Appleford, Sutton Courtenay and Drayton. This prompted Thames Valley and COMS to object on the basis of abstraction of traffic between the two terminals and to apply on 11 May to jointly operate a service between Reading and Abingdon via Tilehurst, Purley, Pangbourne, Streatley, Wallingford, Benson, Shillingford, Dorchester-on-Thames and Clifton Hampden. Both applications were subsequently granted, with Kemp's starting on 1 September 1950 and Thames Valley (using service number 50) in partnership with City of Oxford (using service number 40) on 23 September. For Kemp's, their new service 19 was perhaps something of a speculative swansong before troubles set in, but their Reading to Abingdon through service was not to prove particularly lucrative.

Kemp's Motor Services was not to operate the Henley town services 21 and 22 for long. Applications for licences to continue the services without modification were made in September 1952 by AG & KM Spiers of Henley (then trading as Butlers Coaches, having recently acquired that firm), which were granted in November that year. However, the August 1952 issue of Kemp's timetable booklet made no reference to them, so Spiers may have actually assumed operation by then. It has been said, although not proven, that the licences were passed to Spiers, as settlement of some kind of outstanding debt. Spiers were to run Henley town services until late 1985, when they were taken over by Horseman Mini Coach Service Ltd of Reading.

Hiram Kemp made a confidential approach to Thames Valley in December 1951, offering them the opportunity to purchase the Stage Carriage licences together with twelve vehicles, involving the transfer of a limited number of drivers and conductors and one foreman. The receipts from the bus services (but not including season tickets) were £22,431 for the year ending August 1951, an increase over the previous year which had produced £16,000. Thames Valley considered the matter and consulted with City of Oxford MS, but nothing transpired. The latter felt that they could increase their own Didcot to Wallingford service 38, to replace Kemp's and that a bus could be stationed at Watlington to cover Kemp's services from there and Stadhampton to Wallingford and from Wallingford as far as Little Wittenham. Their own services between Wallingford and Abingdon were deemed adequate. Whilst only the Didcot to Wallingford service was thought to be of any real interest, it was noted that, "should no service whatsoever be provided on the other services [should Kemp's not continue], it would be an inducement to some other operator to take them over and eventually become an even greater nuisance than Kemp is at the moment."

In March and May 1951, Deacon, the Dorchester-on-Thames dealer supplied to Kemp no fewer than six rather antiquated but previously well-maintained double-deck buses in the form of 1936-vintage diesel-engined AEC Regents with Weymann 52-seat lowbridge bodies. However, two of these never entered service and were used as a source of spare parts. Emanating from the fleet of City of Oxford MS, they were acquired cheaply at a time when capital was limited and perhaps it was their condition that caused some of them not to serve Kemp's for long. They were also, no doubt, expensive to maintain, but they may have helped save money by reducing the requirement to operate relief buses on busy journeys and were needed to replace some of the more unreliable vehicles acquired after the war. After the experience with JO 7876, the low height bodies were safer for avoiding conflict with overhanging trees and low railway bridges. Three-year-old Bedford OB DBW 67 was traded in to Deacon, as part of the deal. The AECs were followed in October 1951 by two more former Oxford vehicles – another double-deck AEC Regent but with Park Royal body (CWL 654) and EFC 291, an AEC Regal single-decker with Weymann body. Indicative of mounting financial problems, no more vehicles were purchased for nearly three years thereafter. Unfortunately, CWL 654 was in service for only three weeks before being withdrawn with a twisted chassis as a result of an accident at Burghfield whilst on a contract duty.

In June 1951, some journeys on service 2 (Reading-Didcot) were diverted between Goring Heath and Woodcote via Whitchurch Hill and Crays Pond, before back-tracking to Crays Pond and on to Goring-on-Thames and Wallingford. Over time, the proportion of journeys diverting thus, was to increase. Service 14 (Didcot-Stadhampton) was renumbered 5 and reduced again to operate on Friday and Saturday between Stadhampton and Wallingford and on Friday, Saturday and Sunday between Wallingford and Didcot. Also by June 1951, some Saturday journeys on service 19 (Reading-Abingdon) and some in the evening on Thursday and Sunday were extended from Abingdon (Town Hall) to RAF Abingdon. Perhaps around September 1951, but certainly by August 1952, the Ewelme to Watlington section of service 1 (Wallingford-Watlington) was reduced again to run only on Friday, Saturday and Sunday, whilst as a further economy measure, some journeys on the Reading-Wallingford section of service 19 were withdrawn in favour of a need to make a connection at Wallingford from/to service 12. It was thought to have been some time in 1953 that service 5 was withdrawn between Long Wittenham and Didcot and the Stadhampton-Wallingford section was reduced to Friday only. Service 3 was withdrawn between Nuffield and Turners Court, after a gradual reduction in the number of journeys that ran to the 'Colony'.

The Dennis Lancet coach UD 9431, pride of the pre-war fleet, was damaged in a serious accident with a lorry at the Whitchurch Hill Turn in Goring Heath, on 4 December 1953. The following April, the coach was sent to Ardler Coachworks in Reading for repairs, but for reasons soon apparent, it was never to return.

Meanwhile, demand generated by young men on National Service resulted in development of the weekend Forces Leave Express services. In December 1951 a licence was granted for a service on Saturday

A Commer Avenger chassis delivered to and stored for two years by Kemp's, was sent to Dutfield for bodying and entered service in May 1950 as a 37-seater registered EBW 838. Finished in standard red and maroon with the 'K' emblem and motto on the side panels, this coach had an impressive chromium plated front bumper and also front and rear wheel trims like DUD 401 when new, and seems to have been yet another coach for which Hiram Kemp was extremely proud. *(Kemp family collection – by Late Hiram Kemp)*

CFC 786 was one of a pair of sister vehicles to the 1936 AEC Regents acquired in May 1951. It is seen here inbound climbing Station Hill, Reading. The livery this time is red with two maroon bands and maroon wings. *(VC Jones)*

CFC 787 was the other ex-City of Oxford lowbridge AEC Regent acquired by Kemp's in May 1951 and is seen here in very smart condition on layover at Gloucester Green Bus Station in Oxford, possibly on a private hire or on a contract to carry Polish workers to work at Pressed Steel from Scots Common or Howberry Park Settlement Camps. If a school private hire required a double-decker, CFC 787 was used, for which purpose a conscious attempt was made to keep it in 'tip-top' condition. *(RHG Simpson)*

Yet another ex-City of Oxford 1936 AEC Regent, this time with Park Royal 52-seat lowbridge bodywork, acquired in October 1951, was CWL 654. It had a lamentably short service life with Kemp's as it overturned at Burghfield working on a contract duty only three weeks after entering service and no photograph of it in service with Kemp's has been traced. However, ex-City of Oxford 1937 AEC Regal EFC 291 had also been acquired in October 1951 and carried a Weymann 32-seat 'camel hump' body. Seen here on layover in The Forbury, Reading it is nicely turned out in red with maroon wings, bonnet and waistrail, complete with 'K' motif and 'Semper Eadem' motto. Before entering service it had exchanged seats with Bedford DBW 67 before the latter was sold, receiving 26 of the 28 seats, with a new 5-seater bench being made across the rear together with two new single-seats. *(DJ Pennels)*

Pre-war Dennis Lancet II UD 9431 is parked up at Gloucester Green, Oxford, either on private hire or possibly between trips from either Scots Common or Howberry Park on the Pressed Steel contract for Polish workers in the early 1950s. *(RHG Simpson)*

Rather typical of latter-day Kemp's service buses is this rather muddy Bedford OWB, BBW 701, after it had been fitted with upholstered seats, which has just off-loaded passengers outside Reading General Station. It is in red with maroon waistband, bonnet top and wings, and carries the 'K' motif and motto. Of interest is the signwritten roof cant advertisement, which first appeared on service buses c1951/52. This one is for Field & Hawkins, outfitters, Wallingford. *(Omnibus Society)*

from RAF Benson to Oxford (Gloucester Green) and then one in 1952 for a service as required from RAF Benson to Reading Stations, to supplement the stage carriage services. An application in 1954 for an Express licence for a weekend service to Leicester, Derby and Leeds from RAF Benson, was withdrawn before determination, but a run from RAF Abingdon to London was granted in March 1954, being operated in alternate months with South Midland Motor Services, similar to the arrangement for the Benson-London service. Later in 1954 came the granting of Kemp's' final licence application for a new service at weekends – from RAF Benson to Portsmouth.

Erstwhile Checkendon carrier's daughter Lizzy Wells would travel by Kemp's bus twice a week from there to Reading, to earn a little money by selling eggs and flowers. On Saturdays and in school holidays, her Great Grandson Pat Walsh would go with her. They would stand at the crossroads at Bradley Street waiting for the bus to appear up Lovegrove's Lane. Lizzy had good hearing and would say, "I can hear the bus down Payables Farm hill, it'll be here in five minutes", so she could probably

hear the whine of the Bedford's transmission as it overran down the hill over a mile away. On arrival, the bus proceeded to the Polish Camp, before retracing its route through Checkendon and on to Reading. They would alight halfway along Caversham Road, where Lizzy would deliver the eggs and flowers to regular customers to earn a few extra shillings to spend in Reading. When older, in the mid-1950s, Pat Walsh travelled by bus from his home in Goring to secondary school in Caversham. Occasionally, one of Kemp's double-deckers would appear and one day, it met a tall lorry coming the other way between Goring Heath and the Mapledurham Turn. Both vehicles pulled tight to each side of the road, the drivers not realising that their vehicles were angled inwards causing their roofs to lock together. The boys on the top-deck saw this about to happen and ran down the stairs shouting. It took some time to get the vehicles apart and arrival at school was very late, but the boys had a good story to tell!

By August 1954, only two of the AEC Regent double-deck buses purchased in 1951, were still active, so replacements were needed. The answer came in the

Private Hire and Duplicates For Royal Blue

Nicely posed Commer Avenger **EBW 838** on layover in a quiet London street – there were such things in those days! *(Omnibus Society – Roy Marshall Colln)*

Tilling-Stevens **DUD 401** sets off from Victoria Coach Station on hire to Royal Blue, bound for Bournemouth, with **CBW 864** behind. *(Omnibus Society – Roy Marshall Colln)*

A nice study of **CBW 864** in the London suburbs on another occasion, taking a coach-load of holiday-makers off to the sea on a bright summer's day. *(Omnibus Society – Roy Marshall Colln)*

Dennis Lancet DBW 382 parked up for the weekend at Baylis Road Coach Park, near Waterloo, on a Forces Leave contract from RAF Benson. Just above the Union Jack badge on the dash panel below the driver's windscreen can be seen 'Wendy'. *(Omnibus Society – Roy Marshall Collection)*

Tilling-Stevens DUD 401, with radiator muffed against a cruel winter wind, is parked for the weekend at Baylis Road Coach Park, near Waterloo on the Forces Leave contract in the final Kemp's Motor Services Ltd livery introduced in spring 1954 – maroon with red flashes and a mushroom grey roof, window surrounds and wings. *(Omnibus Society – Roy Marshall Colln)*

form of two AEC Regents with lowbridge bodywork constructed in the Chiswick Works of the London Passenger Transport Board. DLU 157 and DYL 860 dated from 1937 and were members of London Transport's STL class. They had been sold by W North, a Leeds-based dealer, in March 1953 along with four others to Basil Williams of Emsworth Hants, for his Hants & Sussex Motor Services Ltd fleet. Williams' Hants & Sussex group of companies was also suffering severe and terminal financial problems and in 1954 was disposing of surplus vehicles, thus the two STLs passed to Kemp's. Again, these were bargain-priced purchases, indicative of the poor financial state also of Kemp's Motor Services Ltd at that time. DYL 860 was acquired without an engine. Eric Tappern went to Emsworth with Hiram Kemp to collect DLU 157 and during the journey Kemp allegedly told him that two businessmen were going to put money into the company, so perhaps an approach had already been made by people about who much more will follow.

The two buses were later joined at Woodcote by DGX 346, another STL but with a conventional highbridge body. It was intended just to be a source of spare parts and remained in London Transport country

area green and cream livery. In February 1955, Jack Passey travelled to W North's premises near Leeds on the back of Hiram Kemp's motorbike, so he could drive the STL back. This he did as far as Crowmarsh, where they arrived at 2am. The engine and pre-selector gearbox from this bus was later transferred to AEC Regal BRD 922, along with the bonnet cover.

The financial problems already alluded to had begun to make themselves visible through 1953 and 1954. It was apparent that little money was being spent on the vehicles which caused unreliability of the bus services, leading to passenger dissatisfaction. This culminated in a Licensing Authority Inquiry, which concluded on 5 November 1954 at a Sitting at the County Court in Oxford. This had been informed by evidence from Ministry of Transport Certifying Officers who reported in relation to poor timekeeping, fare collection irregularities and the poor state of the vehicles and the maintenance regime.

There was also the question of the financial position of the company. Hiram Kemp briefed the Inquiry on what had been done to improve matters. Tony Sears had been promoted from driver to Traffic Manager and Engineer, replacing a Mr Jefferies who had been

DLU 157 was a 1937 vintage AEC Regent former London Transport STL-class lowbridge double-decker. It was one of two bought from the failing Hants & Sussex operation of Basil Williams at Emsworth, Hants and is seen here on the Blagrave Street stand on 12th April 1955, before Kemp's themselves went into liquidation in May 1955. CFC 784 is behind. *(Southdown Omnibus Trust – photographer Michael Plunkett)*

DGX 346 was a standard ex-London Transport STL-class double-decker from the Country Area, one of the very last two dozen pre-war examples to be withdrawn by London Transport in August 1954. It was bought by Kemp's purely for cannibalisation for spares in February 1955 and was fetched and driven back south from W North, the Leeds dealer. *(AG Low)*

We make no excuse for illustrating BBW 701 again, this one of it about to turn from Church Road into Bridge Street, in Caversham on 5 December 1954. This rather blurred image, taken from the flat above Lloyds Bank, where John Davies resided, is included simply because it is the only one we have located which shows the final Kemp's service bus livery as introduced in 1954, comprising red with maroon wings and bonnet top and with the waistband painted mushroom grey. BBW 701 was out-shopped thus in November 1954. *(Michael Plunkett)*

Garage Foreman for a short period after Ernie Brant left. John Holder, who had previously worked for Thames Valley, had been engaged as an Inspector. New methods of fleet inspection and maintenance had been introduced and the Inspector had brought improvements in timekeeping and fare collection. Since the previous Sitting of the Inquiry, only two letters of complaint had been received, whilst a written statement was handed to the Licensing Authority which apparently indicated that arrangements had been made with a person or persons for financial backing. Applications had been made for timetable adjustments and an application to increase fares would shortly be submitted.

After some deliberation, the Licensing Authority decided not to revoke the licences of Kemp's Motor Services, but expressed concern that there had been a failure to provide services regularly and efficiently owing to lack of supervision and a poor standard of maintenance. The judgement continued: "We are, however, prepared to take the risk to enable you to put matters right, as we have in mind the very long service rendered by the Kemp family in the area, also in the light of what you have said this morning and the steps you are taking. If in the future you are unable or unwilling to raise to a high level the standard of your fleet, we shall have to make way for some other operator who can and will."

Cash flow problems meant that some account payments were delayed and suppliers demanded settlement before further deliveries of fuel, tyres, spare parts etc could be made. It is said that Hiram Kemp would meet buses in Reading mid-shift and collect takings from the drivers and on Saturday, the drivers would extract their wages in small change from their cash bag and then bank the money in their Post Office Savings Accounts.

Despite the leniency shown by the Licensing Authority, the financial issues were seemingly insurmountable

A second former London Transport lowbridge STL-class bus acquired from Hants & Sussex as a non-runner was DYL 860 but it was fully overhauled, entering service in May 1955, after Kemp's had gone into liquidation and just as Chiltern Queens was taking over. *(John Whitehead Colln)*

and sadly, Barclays Bank appointed a Receiver and Manager on 14 January 1955, under powers contained in a debenture in favour of them. The Receiver was Mr G Talfourd-Cook, of Cook, Sutton & Co, Chartered Accountants of Reading. He made some approaches in an attempt to sell the business as a going concern. On 18 February, he visited the Reading offices of Thames Valley, where he was advised that there was no interest in buying the complete Kemp business. Talfourd-Cook then asked whether Thames Valley might be interested in the licences for the Abingdon and Benson to London Forces Express services, or that for service 2 from Reading to Didcot, but he did not have much at his disposal with which to tempt a potential buyer. Some examples of revenue on the daily services, obtained for a week in May 1954, showed that service 12 took the most money at £135, followed by service 2 at £95 and service 3 at £86. Service 19 brought in only just over £20! School and other contracts yielded around £175 per week. Only service 2 was in profit, the premises were no longer owned by the business, the eighteen vehicles were in a poor state and were all due for recertification within the year, not to mention substantial debts. Apparently, an officer of Reading Corporation Transport had been to see Talfourd-Cook on the instructions of the Transport Committee, but this was thought to be just curiosity. Valliant Direct Coaches of Ealing apparently also expressed a non-committal interest.

Matters came to a head when the Regent Oil Co Ltd, which presumably was owed money for petrol and diesel, preferred a petition on 23 February 1955 for winding up and an Order to effect this compulsorily was made on 14 March in the High Court of Justice Chancery Division. Within a few days, there had been further developments which would set the course of events for the next 47 years, leading into the third and final part of our story. However, it was not to be *Semper Eadem* for the company Kemp's Motor Services Ltd, which was liquidated on 31 January 1957 and eventually dissolved

by notice in the *London Gazette* on 25 August 1959.

In retrospect, one can attempt to suggest the circumstances as to why the business failed, some of them by no means unique in terms of bus and coach concerns which had recently expanded in rural areas to cope with post-war opportunities. The Kemp business probably grew too quickly in the period 1947-52 and overtraded at a time when the bus industry in general was at its peak and one could not risk falling behind, giving others the opportunity to capitalise. The inability to buy satisfactory vehicles at a reasonable price to cope with demand has already been mentioned and borrowing money was not easy in the ten years after the end of the war. During the early 1950s, petrol rationing was eased and then lifted; wages had begun to increase and more disposable income meant that more people could afford to buy cars. Inflation was relatively low but operating costs had increased considerably, whilst from 1950 there were large increases of tax on motor fuel which by 1952 had reached two hundred per cent! Despite that, it was difficult to get sanction from the Licensing Authority to increase fares to a more remunerative level, especially if other operators with more buoyant revenue streams did not want to 'come into line' over common sections of route or between common points. Many of Kemp's fares had not significantly altered since before the war. In terms of coach work, Kemp's undertook much for Valliant Direct Coaches of Ealing at weekends, while vehicles would otherwise be parked in London between Forces Express journeys, which contributed to a neglect of the needs of the more local private hire market. When the work with Valliant came to an end, local private hire customers had taken their business elsewhere, whilst unreliability may have led to cancellation of some contracts by the education authorities for the home-to-school services.

All these factors, along with others, probably conspired to unbalance the Kemp business and to place it on an unredeemable path.

One of only two 1936 ex-City of Oxford AEC Regents remaining in service, CFC 787 was withdrawn (notwithstanding having been given a mushroom-grey 'tween-decks band in August 1954), presumably prompted by its failure to inspire the Ministry Inspector to grant a further Certificate of Fitness – hence the swift acquisition of the two ex-London Transport lowbridge STLs from Hants & Sussex. It is seen here being stripped prior to being sold for scrap. (MJC Dare)

Still dumped on site until August 1954 was CWL 654, the bus which had seen only three weeks' service before overturning and having to be withdrawn due to a twisted chassis, and one of the two ex-City of Oxford buses bought only for spares (CWL 793 and CWL 794). Sale for scrap would help the ailing Kemp business just a bit by putting a few shillings into the coffers. (AG Low)

With space at a premium after losing the facility to park vehicles on the derelict brickworks site opposite the depot, vehicles had to be parked on verges when Kemp's own premises was filled, some of it with buses that had been withdrawn. A sad-looking DKP 410, now withdrawn, is in roadside mud after serving Kemp's since 1941. It passed to Chiltern Queens but was not operated and very quickly sold. An Essex operator managed to get two years of further use from her! (Omnibus Society – DS Giles Colln)

A Final Tribute to the Kemp Family

. . . and what it did to help open up south Oxfordshire

Harry Kemp, with his second wife, Ethel 'Tet', who he had married c1947, and Valerie (grand-daughter), around the time of Harry's retirement and move to Woodham Walter, Essex

A reunion on a visit to Woodham Walter, Essex, c1956, by the Passey family, with Bill Passey at the back of the car. The two children in the car are Richard and Andrew Baldwin with their mother, Mary Baldwin (nee Passey) looking to the rear and Rosa Passey (Bill's wife) sitting on the running board. Harry and Ethel Kemp are next to the house.

Hiram Kemp, is seen here outside his shop in Caversham, in the 1960s.

Didcot had grown from a village to a small town, mainly thanks to the Great Western Railway and its huge provender stores building for the feed for all the horses it owned. The bus in this 1930s view of The Broadway is owned by City of Oxford Motor Services.

White Hall, Checkendon c1911 (but which would not have changed very much over the next two decades), with water-bound crushed stone road surfacing. The location is still recognisable today, with Whitehall Lane to the right and Lovegrove's Lane in the distance to the left, which leads to Bradley Street and Scots Common, whilst straight on is Uxmore Road, leading to Kit Lane, Stoke Row.

(Left) Reading Road, Goring Heath, c1911, with water-bound macadam road surfacing which would have been still like it 15 years later when pioneer bus services had commenced operation.

(Right) Looking down Long Toll, some way below the bus depot, towards Goring Heath, probably in the early 1930s. Note the unsealed road surface. During the war, the woods on the left became part of RAF Woodcote, which lasted until the late 1950s.
(Pangbourne and Goring)

More pre-war post card views of the environment within which Harry Kemp's bus services developed.

The Street, Crowmarsh, on the way out of Wallingford c1920, the turning for Benson Lane (for Benson and Oxford) being round the bend, on the left, and for Woodcote and Reading beyond that, on the right, Nettlebed and Henley being straight ahead. The road layout now is quite different.

The Cross Roads, Woodcote.

Woodcote War Memorial (erected 1919) and the cross roads c1958, well before Woodcote By-Pass was constructed, looking from South Stoke Road across to Reading Road, with Red Lane to the left (to Crowmarsh, Wallingford and Oxford) and Goring Road to the right (to Crays Pond, Whitchurch).

...and perhaps the fondest memory of a Kemp's bus.

This superb view of **BRD 922**, the former London Transport Green Line coach that evaded a return to London after the war, is one vehicle for which both Kemp's and Chiltern Queens are particularly famous! It is seen here over the inspection pit that Kemp's had constructed right next to the public highway – upon which buses, particularly double-deckers, are recalled as somewhat daunting as one approached the top of the hill! In this view the coach seating with which it had been fitted as clearly evident. *(Ken Swallow)*

PART 3
1955-2002
CHILTERN QUEENS Ltd

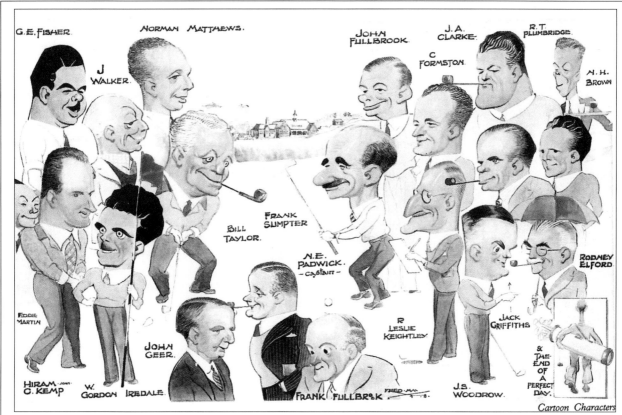

G.E. FISHER.
NORMAN MATTHEWS.
J WALKER.
JOHN FULLBROOK.
J.A. CLARKE.
C FORMSTON.
R.T. PLUMBRIDGE.
N.H. BROWN.
BILL TAYLOR.
FRANK SUMPTER
N.E. PADWICK. — Captain —
EDDIE MARTIN
HIRAM C. KEMP
W. GORDON IREDALE.
JOHN GEER.
FRANK FULLBROOK.
FRED.M.
R LESLIE KEIGHTLEY
JACK GRIFFITHS
J.S. WOODROW.
RODNEY ELFORD
& THE END OF A PERFECT DAY.
Cartoon Characters

Caricatures of Hiram Kemp to the bottom left and of JS Woodrow to the bottom right.
(Cartoon from 'Goring & Streatley Golf Club: The First Hundred Years 1895 – 1995')

Renaissance

Contrary to some expectations, the year 1955 did not see the cessation of bus and coach activities at Long Toll in Woodcote. Although economic circumstances in the mid-1950s were not especially favourable to the passenger transport industry and the heady patronage levels for bus services of the late 1940s were not to return, two businessmen of some means and standing felt that with investment and a fresh approach it could be worthwhile to salvage the moribund Kemp's Motor Services concern, at an attractive purchase price in view of the circumstances. Thus, Etienne CE Barrett and John S Woodrow arrived on the scene. About to be enacted was a Renaissance, a word appropriately used by the late Mike Dare as the title of his article in *Buses Illustrated* published in January 1963.

At the time of the 1911 Census, the Barrett family were living at 213 Shakespeare Road, Herne Hill in south London. Etienne Cyril Ernest Barrett was then about eleven years old (born c1899) and had two

younger brothers and a baby sister. He later won a three year scholarship at the Beaufoy School of Engineering and served in the latter part of the First World War in the Royal Naval Air Service. He then worked for an engineering firm in London until 1929 when he moved to Reading to take up an appointment as depot manager for CH Pugh Ltd. In 1938 he was appointed a director of British Estates Services Ltd, which had been incorporated in January 1934. Subsequently, he was to become involved in a number of businesses in the Reading area, notably in the field of property ownership and development, concrete, brick and tile making and construction activities. Further British Estate companies were incorporated in the early nineteen forties – British Estate Services (Plant Hire) Ltd and British Estate Services (Transport) Ltd and then British Estate Services (Properties) Ltd in 1947, of which Barrett was governing director at the time of his death.

Barrett became acquainted with John Stanley Woodrow. In the 1911 census, Woodrow was nine years of age and living with his parents, a brother and two sisters, at Swadlincote in Derbyshire, near Burton-upon-Trent. His father Henry had been born at Wisbech in Cambridgeshire and was described as a 'Colliery Deputy, Above Ground'. His mother, Margaret Woodrow was born at Church Gresley, which is near Swadlincote. John Woodrow was to become a Chartered Accountant by profession and both he and Barrett sought ways of diversifying their interests, sometimes individually, sometimes in partnership with each other. They acquired businesses that were for sale and also took control of those that were failing or had failed.

Stanley Woodrow had achieved success in various business ventures, such as his directorship in the Pulsometer Engineering Co Ltd, a pump manufacturer, of Nine Elms Works, Oxford Road, Reading. A much re-constituted business known as Sigmund Pulsometer Pumps still exists, although no longer in Reading.

Barrett lived on the Bath Road, near Calcot and Woodrow in Clevedon Road, Tilehurst. Their political interests led them to be selected as candidates who were then elected to the County Borough of Reading as Conservative Councillors, later becoming Aldermen and subsequently spending a year each as Mayor of Reading. It has been suggested that they wielded considerable power in the town. Barrett was first elected to the Council in 1947, was Mayor in 1963 and served as a councillor with one short break until local government reorganisation in 1974. Woodrow was made an Alderman and elected Mayor of Reading in 1961, having been conferred an OBE in the 1959 New Year's Honours for his work as Chairman of the Reading & District National Savings Movement.

Stanley Woodrow had joined Goring & Streatley Golf Club in 1936, was Club Captain in 1954 and was subsequently made Chairman of the Club and later President, being described in the book on the club's history as, "a prime mover in many events and was a powerful if somewhat autocratic figure in the club". Interestingly, Hiram Kemp was also a member, having joined in 1942 and it is stated in the afore-mentioned book that during wartime fuel rationing he would arrive at the club by pony and trap or on horseback. It was noted that at one time he used a bus or coach to provide transport to the golf club for members in the area and also sponsored a competition trophy, known appropriately as the Kemp Cup. No doubt it was during the war that Hiram Kemp's wife Jessie is recorded as having donated eggs as prizes for the card-playing circle at the golf club. The Kemps kept hens as well as a pig at one time – until it bit Hiram Kemp and was sent to be converted into bacon. The golf club had various members from the local business community and it is tempting to speculate that it may well have been networking with Hiram Kemp that alerted Woodrow to the fact that the Kemp's Motor Services Ltd business might be suitable for some investment, but instead, ultimately became available in terms of the acquisition of certain assets.

It is said that one Sunday morning, Etienne Barrett and his son Colin visited the Kemp premises and looked at the vehicles, the condition of which did not look too promising and they apparently wondered how bus services could actually be run with them. However, Barrett and Woodrow decided to make an offer to the Receiver and the Bank for the premises, licences, vehicles and any remaining goodwill of Kemp's Motor Services Ltd, but formed a new company to do so. The name Fair Mile Motor Services was considered, as was Barwood Passenger Transport (a play on the names Barrett and Woodrow), but it was Barrett's son Colin's idea that won the day as he suggested the inspired, memorable and slightly mysterious name of Chiltern Queens. He remembers that the idea came to him whilst working at the British Estate Services filling station, where the vehicles of Sodbury Queen Coaches of Chipping Sodbury in Gloucestershire, would call in to be re-fuelled en-route to and from London. Of the various suggestions, Mrs Florence Woodrow, who apparently was tasked with making the final choice, favoured Colin's. However, the 'Queens' part of the name was to be unpopular with some of the staff. Chiltern Queens Ltd was incorporated on 11 May 1955, with a nominal capital of £6,000, with Barrett and Woodrow both holding 3,000 £1 shares. A deposit on the purchase price agreed with the Receiver had been paid on 30 April. Road Service Licences to continue Kemp's operations were authorised from 19 June 1955.

News of developments at Woodcote inevitably reached other parties. On 19 March 1955, Thames Valley's Traffic Manager, John Dally, having heard a rumour that the Kemp's business had been purchased by Barrett and Woodrow, stated in a memo that, "I cannot vouch for this rumour, although there is usually no smoke without fire". City of Oxford MS was corresponding with Hiram Kemp on the subject of fares anomalies as early as April 1955, with the Chiltern Queens name being used on the letters and also on timetable sheets issued at that time. The transfer arrangements for the business were assisted by Hiram Kemp staying on initially as General Manager, but in March 1956 he was replaced by a promoted Tony Sears.

As already mentioned, Tony had worked for Kemp's, was later appointed Traffic Manager and Engineer and was therefore one of several people staying on into the Chiltern Queens era. He was to successfully steer that company for over 40 years. He was born in Bexhill, Sussex, moving to Reading from Hastings in 1939. After an apprenticeship with Abbey Motors in Reading, he saw wartime employment as a machine tool fitter for aircraft production. At the end of the war he got a job as a bus engine fitter with Thames Valley in Reading, after which he was obliged to spend two years with the Royal Air Force as conscription was still in effect. On leaving military service, he joined his brothers Len and Jack at the Marine Division of Thornycroft, at Caversham. With a liking for the countryside and for meeting people, he

John Stanley Woodrow, Chartered Accountant, one time Member of the Grand Council of the Federation of British Industry, Director of Pulsometer Engineering Ltd, Chairman of Thames Valley Water Board, and President of the Reading Chamber of Trade, Reading Borough Councillor (later Alderman), conferred an OBE in the 1959 New Year's Honours for work as Chairman of the Reading & District National Savings Movement, was Mayor of Reading 1961/62, was subsequently Deputy Lieutenant of Berkshire, received a CBE in 1970 and was made a Freeman of Reading in 1971. *(Reading Central Library – Local History Archive)*

Etienne Cyril Ernest Barrett, Company Director of British Estate Services Ltd, Reading Borough Councillor from 1947 (later Alderman), was Mayor of Reading 1962/63 and subsequently served as a Reading Councillor with one short break until local government re-organisation in 1974 (including serving at one time as Chairman of the Transport Committee). *(Reading Borough Council – Mayoral Archive)*

decided he would like to be a bus driver and thus joined Kemp's as such in 1950. He did enjoy being a country bus driver/conductor and remembers bringing home bunches of watercress, which was grown at Ewelme. When he transferred to coach duties, he was allocated Dennis Lancet CBW 864, also undertaking workshop tasks during quiet periods. When operating Forces Leave express journeys to London or Birmingham, the servicemen apparently preferred to travel on Tony's coach rather than any others on the same departure, as CBW 864 had an excellent turn of speed and they arrived home for the weekend quicker.

Other members of the Kemp's management who transferred in 1955 were John Holder, the Inspector, who was made Assistant Manager until replaced by a Mr Cramp in March 1956 and Cyril Minchin who stayed until about 1971. Tony Sears' brother Len later arrived to take charge of the workshop but stayed for only a relatively short time.

When Hiram Kemp left Woodcote, he moved to Marlow and ran a public house called The Railway Hotel, also apparently driving part-time on school contracts for Spiers Coaches. Subsequently, having run The New

Inn at Curridge, near Newbury, he moved in December 1960 to Caversham where he ran a greengrocer's and general store for some years.

The acquisition of the Kemp's business by Chiltern Queens included the stage carriage services then operating, excursions and tours licences from Woodcote and villages such as Ipsden, Stoke Row, Goring and Checkendon, Forces Leave services from RAF Benson to London, Oxford and Reading Station, the Works services to Reading from Nettlebed (South Camp) and Scots Common (Polish Hostel) and some school transport contracts. Twenty vehicles entered Chiltern Queens ownership, in addition to which Dennis Lancet UD 9431 was still at Ardler Coachworks in Reading, under lien, waiting for somebody to pay the bill for repair work. In service at the time were AEC Regent double-deckers CFC 784, DLU 157 and DYL 860; AEC Regal BRD 922; Bedford WTB DUD 784; Bedford OWBs BBW 701/2, 950 and EOT 48; Bedford OB CBW 522; Dennis Lancets CBW 864 and DBW 382; TSM K6s DBW 66 and DUD 401 and Commer Avenger EBW 838. Already withdrawn by Kemp's and not operated under Chiltern Queens auspices were AEC double-deckers

This rear view of **BRD 922** in the workshop on 31 October 1955 is a record that the bus had lost its destination box in the rear dome, having seemingly done so even before it arrived with Kemp's. The Bedford **OWB** outside the building is **EOT 48**, withdrawn June 1955, identified from its advert. *(Norman Rayfield)*

CFC 786 and DGX 346, AEC Regal EFC 291, Leyland Cub EFC 300 and Dennis Arrow Minor DKP 410.

The operational vehicles carried varying paint schemes, with nine of them having been repainted by Kemp's the previous year, coinciding with a change to a predominantly maroon and grey livery:

Red with maroon wings, flashes and/or bands: BBW 702/950, EOT 48, BRD 922, CBW 864, DBW 382

Maroon with red flashes, grey roofs, window surrounds and wings: DUD 784, DBW 66, DUD 401 and EBW 838

Red with maroon wings and bonnet and grey bands: BBW 701 and CBW 522

Maroon lower panels, red upper panels, grey wings and window surrounds, silver roof: DLU 157 and DYL 860 and maybe CFC 784.

From the outset, the directors stated that they intended to overhaul and rebuild the best of the Kemp's vehicles in order to prolong their useful life, but for others they realised that replacements were required in order to present a better image and attract new business. Standardisation was sought but that was beyond the means of the new company. Within a short time of the takeover, two five-year-old Leyland Comet coaches with Strachan bodywork were sourced. The previous operator of HRK 901 and 906 was Homeland Tours of Croydon. The former was 27 feet long and had 33 seats; the latter was 30 feet long and had 37 seats. For some time, these coaches ran in their original maroon, red and ivory livery. In June 1955, Bedford OWB bus BBW 701 was repainted all-red; this was considered unsatisfactory so a grey band was added the following month and similar BBW 950 repainted to match. For coaches, it was decided that in future they should be deep Brunswick green with a grey roof, wings and flashes; the first to be so painted was TSM coach DUD 401.

In July 1955, three Maudslay Marathon coaches with half-cab 33-seat bodywork were acquired from Majestic

Coaches of London E10 and gained the new coach livery. Two (LPF 250 and LPH 429) had bodies by Whitson and one (LPK 200) by West Nor. In the same month, the first operational former Kemp's vehicle was withdrawn – Bedford OWB bus BBW 702 – which remained dumped on the premises for some months as was often the custom, before being stripped for useful parts and then sold for scrap. In the following years, several redundant vehicles would be sold to local scrap dealers, including Deacon of Dorchester on Thames, Main of Benson and Smith of Woodcote. Some were actually dismantled on site adjacent to the depot.

Somewhat coincidentally, the original Kemp family public transport enterprise in Leicester, Kemp & Shaw Ltd, had its share capital acquired by the Birmingham & Midland Motor Omnibus Co Ltd (Midland Red) on 30 July 1955. It was retained as a separate subsidiary company until 1 January 1959.

An investment by Chiltern Queens, thanks to a bank loan, followed in October 1955, in an attempt to portray a modern outlook and to emulate the underfloor-engined buses being operated by neighbours Thames Valley and City of Oxford MS. Three brand new AEC Reliance chassis with somewhat basic 44-seat bus bodies by Duple (Midland) were obtained, bearing registrations LMO 743-5. These acquitted themselves so well that their worth was soon proven and it was decided that all future new deliveries would be of the AEC Reliance marque. The three buses were to enjoy substantial longevity, being active until 1975/6. A new standard bus livery of red with cream window surround was carried. All future vehicle purchases were to be funded solely from profits on earnings.

There was a need to rationalise the stage carriage services, to improve cost-effectiveness and travel opportunity for the public, as well as to remove some 'dead wood'. Applications for revisions were made to the Licensing Authority in the summer of 1955. In a letter to John Dally of Thames Valley, Hiram Kemp stated that, "we shall be tidying up a number of illogical and somewhat useless odds and ends, such as our services out to the Wittenhams, Stadhampton and Watlington. By crossing back and forth between Abingdon and Stadhampton, we shall make connections in Wallingford with other services on each arrival. Also, by the extension of our Reading to Benson Aerodrome service to embrace Ewelme and Watlington we shall render the need for a separate licence to Watlington unnecessary".

The only service to emerge unaltered (and still delineated by the number 13) was the Thursday run to Henley-on-Thames from Checkendon and Woodcote.

The very first second hand Chiltern Queens acquisitions, bought in June 1955 to augment the ex-Kemp's fleet, were two Leyland Comets, formerly with Homeland Tours, of Croydon, which had Strachan bodies and were new in 1950. HRK 901 was a 33-seater (and 27ft long), which ran much of its time in Chiltern Queens' service in its Homeland Tours livery of maroon, red and cream but did latterly receive green and grey, as seen here on a private hire to Margate, outside the famous Dreamland Amusement Park. *(Surfleet Transport Photographs)*

The other ex-Homeland Tours Leyland Comet bought in June 1955 was HRK 906, similar to HRK 901 but 30ft long and with 37 seats. It is seen here at Upper Heyford, in deepest Oxfordshire, on 28 July 1957 on an Omnibus Society study tour of independent bus undertakings in Buckinghamshire and Oxfordshire, still in its Homeland Tours livery. *(Les Simpson)*

Kemp's rolling stock under new ownership – I

This selection shows the condition of some of Kemp's vehicles as taken over by Chiltern Queens in May 1955. *(All photographs Copyright: Omnibus Society – DS Giles Colln)*

At the right we see **BRD 922**, parked on the roadside, with **DKP 410** behind.

DUD 784 was the second hand Bedford **WLB** which was refurbished by **J Samuel Elliot Ltd** of Caversham (who had converted many of the 40 London Transport Green Line 10T10s into 'Clubmobiles' for the US Air Force during the war) and re-registered from **EXK 599** in June 1949, still looking quite presentable. Leyland Cub **EFC 300** is in the depot and AEC Regal **EFC 291** is behind, while the double-decker is **DGX 346**, the London Transport Country Area STL-type bought for spares.

Just about off the highway and not quite into the hedge (as Long Toll starts its long decent through the woods) and next to **EFC 291** is **CFC 784**, whilst behind, on the pit is, presumably, **DYL 860**, the lowbridge ex-Hants & Sussex former London STL not yet in service but with work in hand.

Kemp's rolling stock under new ownership – 2

The surviving ex-City of Oxford 1936-vintage **AEC Regent** double-decker taken into Chiltern Queens' stock was **CFC 784**, seen here on 31 October 1955 outside the depot. Note the American car outside 'Greenmore' – most likely Hiram Kemp's Packard saloon **DAL 474**. Since the May 1955 takeover, the bus has had ex-London Transport seats fitted out of **DGX 346** and a partial repaint of maroon to the lower-deck panels, mushroom grey to lower-deck window surrounds and areas at the front, and a silver roof – all to help achieve Ministry of Transport re-certification. In spite of all, it suffered a major engine failure in March 1956 and never ran again. *(Norman Rayfield)*

The livery of **DLU 157** was also modified after the May 1955 Chiltern Queens' takeover, the bus being seen here on the Blagrave Street stand, in Reading on 31 October 1955 with lower-deck window surrounds now mushroom grey, the cream between-decks band and areas at the front repainted similarly, and the roof repainted in another coat of silver. *(Norman Rayfield)*

DYL 860, on layover in Wallingford Market Place soon after entering service in May 1955, was finished in the same livery into which **DLU 157** was subsequently repainted. *(MJC Dare)*

One of three 1947 Maudslay Marathon III half-cab coaches which also joined the fleet in July 1955, which came from Majestic Coaches, of London E10, LPF 250 carried a Whitson 33-seat body and was soon in service repainted into Chiltern Queens green and grey. It is here on a private hire at Leighton Park School, in Reading, probably having brought a football team from The Oratory School, Woodcote. *(AG Low)*

An identical 1947 Maudslay Marathon III with Whitson 33-seat body to LPF 250 was LPH 429, seen here in 1956 in London's Baylis Road Coach Park. Note that the roof of the coach was painted green rather than grey! *(AB Cross)*

The third 1947 example of a Maudslay Marathon III, LPK 200, carried a West Nor 33-seat body and is seen here at Chiltern Queens' depot on 28 July 1957 during the Omnibus Society study tour of Buckinghamshire and Oxfordshire independent bus operators. It was the first of the three to be withdrawn, in autumn 1960. *(Omnibus Society – Roy Marshall Colln)*

The other seven services were cleverly re-organised into four, with licences being eventually granted by the Licensing Authority, after correspondence, meetings and agreement with COMS over fares details, to enable the new arrangements to be operative by 22 December 1955. Full details are given in Appendix 2 but the revised services were unusually given letter designations rather than numbers:

A: Reading-Goring Heath-Woodcote-Ipsden-Wallingford-Didcot

B: Reading-Goring Heath-Goring-North Stoke-Wallingford-Benson-Ewelme-Watlington (with some journeys via Woodcote)

C: Stadhampton-Wallingford-Long Wittenham-Sutton Courtenay-Abingdon

D: Nuffield-Scots Common-Checkendon-Cane End-Chalkhouse Green-Emmer Green-Reading. (Nuffield was only served by one journey each way on Thursday)

Curiously, one Saturday journey and one Sunday journey over former service 19 remained for a short time, linking Reading with Abingdon via Woodcote and Wallingford. This was shown as such in the December 1955 timetable booklet, but not the one dated February 1956. Further alterations had occurred by the latter date. Service A gained a completely different timetable which included the deletion of some Thursday-only journeys which two months earlier had oddly retained (on paper) the number 12. Service C had a reduction in the number of journeys, whilst the new timetable on service D only extended to Nuffield on the last daily journey from Reading.

In contrast to the previous six months, 1956 seems to have been mainly a period of consolidation, although school contract and private hire work began to increase, having seen a drop in the latter Kemp years, when things had become difficult. Additional Road Service Licenses were applied for in February and March 1956 for 'assisted travel scheme' services for civilian workers at RAF Woodcote, from Woodcote village, Checkendon, Stoke Row and Sonning Common: from South Stoke and Goring: from Reading (Oxford Road) and from Caversham (George Street). These ran Mondays to Saturdays at times required for the start and end of shifts.

Frustratingly, after much work was carried out in order to get it re-certified, AEC Regent double-decker CFC 784 had to be withdrawn in March 1956 after engine failure. Some of

the repair and repainting work on other vehicles was sent to outside firms. Bedford OB bus CBW 522 went to Andover for repaint and returned in green and grey coach livery in error, rather than red and cream bus livery. Bedford OWB BBW 701 was given a body rebuild in July 1956, its seats replaced with some originally in the London STL-type double-decker (DGX 346) which Kemp's had acquired for spare parts. The remains of the latter were then dumped in the woods behind the garage.

An additional weekend Express Leave Service from RAF Benson to Nottingham was licensed from 1 July. The first quarter of 1957 witnessed the arrival of two former City of Oxford MS Guy Arab utility low height double-deckers of 1943 vintage – JWL 729 & 731. Probably before departure from Oxford, the duck egg blue bands in the COMS livery were repainted maroon. Acquired via Deacon, the Dorchester-on-Thames dealer, they were operated in COMS red and maroon, generally on service B. DLU 157, one of the ex-London STLs, was repainted red and cream, but still with silver roof. However, the other STL (DYL 860) was withdrawn in April 1957 and sold to Deacon, possibly in part exchange for a further COMS Guy, JWL 858, which arrived the following month.

An anecdote from 1957 has been recounted. Etienne Barrett, who was driving in his Buick car with his Secretary, came across Bedford OWB BBW 950 at Goring Heath which had steam coming from its radiator. The driver was George Goodenough and the conductor was Jack Spokes. Passing by was one of the AEC Reliances, substituting for a double-deck duty, but without a conductor. Barrett got out of the car and having asked why a small bus should have a conductor, whereas the AEC did not, when it was covering for a two-man duty, he then demanded to know why steam

As recounted in the text, soon after the Chiltern Queens takeover, Bedford OB service bus CBW 522 was sent off to an outside contractor for repaint and came back in green and grey coach livery instead of red and cream. Seen here on the usual Blagrave Street stand, in Reading, with some replacement panels fitted to the offside, very likely an accident repair, the bus has been pressed into service with the job incomplete, with the aluminium strapping still to fit before being sent for its repainting. However, the bus was withdrawn in July 1957. *(MJC Dare)*

Three brand new Identical service buses in a smart red and cream livery ordered very soon after Chiltern Queens was founded, materialised very quickly, in October 1955. Based on AEC Reliance chassis, they carried fairly plain 44-seat Duple (Midland) bodies. With a make-over (or two) they lasted in service an incredible 20-plus years. Seen here at Blagrave Street, Reading, LMO 743, photographed on 18 March 1960, depicts a somewhat basic underfloor-engined single-deck service bus of the period. (JC Gillham)

A nearside view of LMO 744, taken at Chiltern Queens' premises at Woodcote, not without one or two battle scars from the country lanes of rural south Oxfordshire, on the occasion of the Omnibus Society visit on 28 July 1957. (Omnibus Society – Roy Marshall Colln)

LMO 745 pauses with her complement of Reading-bound passengers in Long Toll, outside the Chiltern Queens depot, presumably while the driver disappears to make himself comfortable – or perhaps he is actually taking the photograph. A country bus carrying a sign-written advertisement somehow certainly does give an air of permanence. (MJC Dare)

Former Kemp's Whitson-bodied coach CBW 864 poses to show off her new green and grey Chiltern Queens livery while parked up in London's Baylis Road Coach Park, probably during the Weekend Forces Leave contract which Chiltern Queens had taken over. In July 1960, this vehicle was the second ex-Kemp's Dennis Lancet J3 to be rebodied by Plaxton and was to give a further eleven years service.
(John Whitehead Colln)

Another ex-Kemp's coach showing off its Chiltern Queens green and grey livery on its Vincent body is Gardner-engined Tilling-Stevens DBW 66 as it thunders down Goring Road, connecting Woodcote with Crays Pond on 30 April 1963 with Percy Sherwood in charge. It was to remain in service until November 1963.
(AJ Douglas)

The other Tilling-Stevens, Meadows-engined DUD 401 with Dutfield body, turned out to be the last ex-Kemp's half-cab coach in service. It received an extensive body overhaul in 1959 after a period de-licenced, was re-certified and was not finally withdrawn until November 1964. It is seen here in the muddy yard of the derelict brickworks site opposite the depot. *(AG Low)*

was coming out of the Bedford. Apparently the water pump was leaking, so a small convoy continued on to the depot at Woodcote. Barrett instructed that the radiator should be removed, but Tony Sears disagreed, as he needed the bus for service with probably no substitute available. As the heated argument continued, Jack Passey was heard to exclaim, "just what am I supposed to do for the best?" Eventually, Barrett was persuaded, reluctantly, that the radiator should not be removed.

The grey band on Bedford OWB bus BBW 950 was repainted cream in July 1957, whilst AEC Regal BRD 922 became green and grey and Bedford OB bus CBW 522 was withdrawn. Despite being repainted, BRD 922 was destined to be withdrawn from service as soon as December that year and then spent the next eighteen months or so dumped at the side of the brickworks. Whilst there, its rear number plate became detached, revealing its original registration EYK 229 on the original plate underneath. To end the year, two eight-year-old 29-seat Guy Vixen coaches (NPC 727 and NPE 61) with bodywork by Wadham, arrived in December from Whites of Camberley in Surrey, the first of three pairs of vehicles from that source that came to Woodcote in three consecutive years. The Vixens entered service the following spring, still in Whites grey and green livery.

A decision by the directors regarding future vehicle policy spelt the end of life on the road in 1958 for the two 1943 Guy Arabs, after little more than a year and the last London STL. This was hastened by an unfortunate early-morning incident in Blagrave Street, Reading, involving Guy Arab JWL 729 in February. It had arrived on service B and was left unattended. In due course, Bedford OWB BBW 701 driven by Nelson Prior, arrived from Checkendon, whereupon the Bedford's brakes failed and it ran into the back of the Guy. The latter was promptly withdrawn and later donated its engine to similar JWL 858.

By the latter part of the 1950s, patronage and revenue on many rural bus services was significantly declining as car ownership increased and as preferences for social activities changed. The television at home replaced the trip to the cinema and the telephone became more widespread, avoiding the need to travel by bus to visit friends and relatives in neighbouring towns and villages. With reduced revenues, operation of rear entrance double-deckers with conductors was no longer required for the number of people being carried, even during peak hours, nor was it economically justifiable. Cost reductions were required, thus conductors could be dispensed with and as practiced since the earliest days of Kemp's Bus Services, all vehicles that were suitable could be 'one-man operated', with the driver collecting the fares.

It became the practice to allocate two drivers in rotation to each of the single-deck buses used on the main stage carriage services. George Painter and Fred Coles were in charge of AEC Reliance LMO 743, Brian

Critchfield and Gerry Higgs on LMO 744 and Alan Tull and Des Spokes on LMO 745, whilst Cyril Lilley was the regular driver on service D to Checkendon, initially using BBW 701, the last Bedford OWB in the fleet.

Around this time, the management of Chiltern Queens stated that in future years they would look to purchase a mixture of new and decent pre-owned vehicles, whilst a few existing vehicles would be subject to extensive rebuilding or re-bodying, to make them more up to date and appealing to customers. As part of this, the old half-cab Vincent body on Dennis Lancet DBW 382 was removed and the chassis given a new body by Plaxton in June 1958. When it returned, it had the appearance of certain new coaches coming into service at that time, at much less cost than a new vehicle and giving it an extended life for private hire and excursion work. Chiltern Queens was unusual in keeping three distinct fleets – bus, coach and contract. Apart from the long distance runs for the military sites, contract vehicles did not accumulate high mileage, so the older vehicles tended to be used, some in red and cream bus livery and some in the green and grey coach colour scheme. Naturally, the best coaches undertook private hire and excursions and had their own drivers who kept them in spotless condition. That is not to suggest that the other vehicles were any less pristine, for they were regularly washed by the Cleaner.

As well as the usual school transport contracts, there was one for the Farm Training School at Turners Court Colony. However, contracts run under Road Service Licences for staff transport to Huntley & Palmer's biscuit factory and Huntley, Boorne and Stevens' engineering works, both in Reading, seem to have ceased around the mid-nineteen fifties.

Opposite the depot premises in Long Toll was a former brickworks site. Derelict since the war, Kemp's had unofficially parked vehicles there as their own premises had become inadequate for the size of their fleet. Hiram Kemp had apparently wanted to buy it but the company's financial position in the early nineteen fifties precluded it. Eventually the vehicle parking had to cease. Chiltern Queens vehicles were therefore being parked at the side of the road, which concerned the local Council. On the proviso that this would stop, the Council granted planning permission for the brickworks site to be used; in due course it would be developed by Chiltern Queens.

Comfort facilities for staff at the bus depot could be described as primitive. There was one 'privy' style toilet in a corrugated iron hut, complete with bucket. After some lobbying, involving showing photographs to demonstrate how dire the facilities were, the Council did eventually grant planning permission for a proper toilet block to be built and furnished.

Two new AEC Reliance chassis, this time with air brakes, were ordered; MUD 975 materialised in July 1958 with a Duple Britannia 43-seat centre entrance coach body, followed by NBW 407 the following month

The three Guy Arab II utility double-deckers which came from City of Oxford via a dealer in 1957 carried Roe lowbridge bodywork with 55 seats. Notwithstanding the extended bonnets of Arab Mk IIs, they were powered by 5LW Gardner engines, so were somewhat sluggish on the Chiltern hills and the writer has fond memories of one example making heavy weather of the hill out of Goring towards Crays Pond. Note the painted-out fleetname and the duck-egg blue of the Oxford livery in this view of a well-laden JWL 729 passing Reading General Station on its way to the Blagrave Street stand. The Arabs were never otherwise repainted out of City of Oxford livery.
(Surfleet Transport Photographs)

JWL 858, which joined the Chiltern Queens fleet just a little later than the other two, is in the muddy yard next to the derelict brickworks at the Woodcote depot circa winter 1957/58 with a newly signwritten nearside advertisement but also has the lower-deck in use as a temporary store for a set of bus seats! *(AG Low)*

with a 45-seat Plaxton Highway bus body, allegedly the first such vehicle in southern England. It was placed in charge of Charlie Lee and Bill Wise. The removal of conductors from the bus services was thus facilitated, although the final ex-Oxford Guy, JWL 858, was retained for service use if required until November 1959.

1958 marked a nadir in Labour Relations, as such things were then known, between London Transport, its staff and the Transport & General Workers Union. Demands for wage increases for bus operating and engineering staff were resisted, perhaps for complex political reasons, culminating in a strike from 4 May after which not a single bus, coach or trolleybus left its depot for a full seven weeks. London Transport Executive made the unprecedented decision to grant authorisation to a small number of organisations and coach firms to run a few token services as a gesture during the Strike. One such was Chiltern Queens who were granted a licence to run between Chiswick and Hyde Park Corner, with a minimum fare of 6d. Bedford OWB BBW 701 (driven by Gerry Higgs) and Commer Avenger EBW 838 (driven by Jack Passey) went to London for about two weeks. This

was a useful opportunity to boost revenue at a time when it was diminishing on the local services. This may have been the occasion when Chiltern Queens hired another Bedford OWB (BBW 291) from House of Watlington, to use on bus services for a short period that year.

Meanwhile, back in Oxfordshire and Berkshire, service C was altered in June 1958. The section of route between Stadhampton and Warborough was reduced to operate only on Fridays, whilst on reaching Long Wittenham via Wallingford, the route was diverted to run to Didcot, rather than to Abingdon; the Sunday service was withdrawn. These changes may well have been prompted by an attempt to cut losses. Although petrol rationing had been in force during the Suez crisis in 1957, it was in October 1958 that hire purchase controls were removed and sales of cars shot up by 70 per cent compared to the previous year. From then on, reductions in rural bus services nationwide became routine.

Some statistics relating to Chiltern Queens survive from an internal City of Oxford MS memo in summer 1958. Twenty drivers were employed for stage carriage services and six for private hire and contract work. Rates

By the time of the Omnibus Society visit on 28 July 1957, BRD 922 had been repainted into green and grey, possibly for use on contract work as it had coach seats. It had previously received a partial repaint whilst red, with cream window surrounds, soon after the Chiltern Queens takeover in May 1955. However, being repainted in coach livery did not preclude its use as a service bus – but its days were beginning to be counted and it was withdrawn in December 1957, although not broken up until 1959. *(JC Gillham)*

(Left & below) The first of three pairs of vehicle to be bought from **White's Coaches of Camberley, Surrey**, arrived during December 1957, as **BRD 922** was withdrawn. This intake was of 1949 vintage **Guy Vixen** 29-seaters, each with **Wadham** bodywork, registered **NPC 727** and **NPE 61**. They entered service in spring 1958, initially still in White's grey and green livery and seem to have been used on local contract work. They were eventually repainted and lasted quite a while, not being withdrawn until summer 1964. During its time with **Chiltern Queens**, NPC 727 was fitted with a Bedford engine.
(John Whitehead Colln (NPC 727); RHG Simpson (NPE 61))

of pay were 3s 11½d (20p) per hour, with small supplements for longer hours. For driver/conductors, these rates were increased by 2d per hour. Several times in a week, a drivers' duty which finished at 11pm was followed by a 6am start next morning. If a driver was more than five minutes late for duty, he would be sent home and a spare driver allocated. Takings on the Didcot-Reading service averaged £10 per day.

In September 1958, COMS objected to an application by Chiltern Queens in connection with a new journey on service A between Wallingford and Didcot, which was originally to carry a restriction permitting carriage of school children only. COMS service 38 did not arrive in Didcot in time for school assembly, and so enquiries had later been received from teachers and catering staff at the school who also wished to travel on the same bus as the children, in order to arrive before 9am. COMS lodged an objection with the Traffic Commissioners and Chiltern Queens backed down and agreed to maintain the restriction. This small matter demonstrates how difficult and frustrating it was under the restrictive licensing system to provide new facilities.

After its London adventure, Commer EBW 838 was withdrawn in October 1958, having sustained accident damage. Michael Allen recalls an amusing anecdote about this coach. When it was being tested on one occasion by Mr Clasper, a Ministry of Transport inspector, for renewal of its Certificate of Fitness, he lay across the seats and pushed out the side of the body with his feet. This demonstrated that the body was nearing the end of its usefulness.

Arrivals in 1958 were the next pair of coaches from Whites of Camberley – an Albion Victor and a TSM K6 – and an Austin CXB with rare 29-seat Mann Egerton bodywork, registered EEA 8 and costing a princely £65. These were meant for contract duties and the TSM (NPF 552) spent its short time at Woodcote in Whites grey and green livery. By the end of the year, apart from the rebodied Dennis DBW 382, only four former Kemp's vehicles remained in service.

At the start of 1959, a Dennis Falcon L6 with 30-seat bus bodywork by Gurney Nutting was purchased. Dating from 1952, this vehicle, registered SPD 207, was

DBW 382 was the first of two ex-Kemp's Dennis Lancet J3s to be sent to Plaxton for re-bodying in a modern style to help make the Chiltern Queens private hire image more appealing. Seen here in its new form with a Consort body, after its return in late summer 1958, it turns into Caversham Road from Vastern Road many years before installation of what is currently known as the TGI Friday roundabout. CBW 864 was dealt with in a similar manner – but not until summer 1960, when it was fitted with an Embassy body. *(RHG Simpson)*

originally used as a demonstration model by the chassis manufacturer and had previously been operated by Yellow Bus Services of Guildford. The services of that firm were acquired by Aldershot & District in June 1958 but the Yellow Bus vehicles had been sold separately through dealers. In due course SPD 207 replaced the last Bedford OWB (BBW 701) on the Checkendon service, becoming the regular bus on that route until 1967.

Changing military requirements caused the run-down of RAF Woodcote in the second half of 1958 and by 29 January 1959 the remaining stores and personnel were transferred to 3MU Milton, near Didcot and the Woodcote 70MU site closed down. Chiltern Queens was thereafter denied the job of transporting civilian workers to the site on contracted services, but the name persisted on their timetables for many years afterwards. By 1961 all the large buildings had been demolished, although the remains of some smaller installations can still be found in the woods today, if one knows where to look.

DUD 401, one of the former Kemp's TSMs, was extensively rebuilt by July 1959, giving it a further lease of life until autumn 1964. As it retained a half-cab layout, it continued to look dated. Further Whites of Camberley cast-offs destined for contract duties with Chiltern Queens were KGU 599, a Dennis Lancet J3, and Albion Victor NPA 462, a twin to NPA 461 already being operated.

Whilst it has been noted that 1959 was a very good year for Private Hire business for the coach fleet, bus service C's performance was still causing concern. On 8 June 1959 an application was granted to reduce the whole service from Stadhampton to Didcot to operate only on Fridays, with four journeys each way; Stadhampton and Newington were only served in the afternoon.

It was high time Chiltern Queens kept abreast of developments in coach design and added an up-to-the-minute underfloor-engined example to stock, hence **MUD 975**, an AEC Reliance with Duple Britannia 43-seat centre-entrance body, a real classic of the 1950s. She was new in July 1958 and stayed in stock for 22 years! Here she is, posed in the depot yard.
(Omnibus Society – Roy Marshall Colln)

The opportunity was also taken in summer 1958 to augment the three LMO-registered AEC Reliance service buses with another, resulting in **NBW 407**, which carried a particularly pleasing Plaxton Highway 45-seat body. This, too, had a 22-year working life and is seen here on 13th June 1959 on the stand in Blagrave Street, Reading.
(JH Aston)

A shadow of its former self when it was new to Kemp's, the green and grey coach livery as applied to Commer Avenger **EBW 838**, also carrying a Dutfield body, does not really inspire a 'please hire me' in the writer's opinion! Although seen here on the stand in Blagrave Street, Reading, possibly deputising for a service bus, it was more often used on contract work and was eventually withdrawn after an accident in October 1958, after only eight years' service and shortly after use in London during the prolonged 1958 London bus strike. *(Omnibus Society – Roy Marshall Colln)*

The first of the 1958 intake of second hand vehicles from White's Coaches of Camberley, in September that year, was NPA 461, seen in the yard after repaint into Chiltern Queens' coach livery. A 1949 Albion Victor with a Whitson 31-seat body, she was a rugged vehicle of a useful size suited to local contract work and stayed in service until May 1965. *(MJC Dare)*

The other 1958 intake from White's Coaches of Camberley was NPF 552, a 1949 Meadows-engined Tilling-Stevens K6LM7 with Dutfield 33-seat body, the same combination and age as ex-Kemp's DUD 401, although the body style differed. Seen here in the brickworks yard soon after delivery, it stayed in White's grey and green livery the whole time it was with Chiltern Queens, for it failed to impress and stayed in stock less than a year, being withdrawn in July 1959. *(John Whitehead Colln)*

An unusual addition to stock in November 1958 was EEA 8, a 29-seat Mann Egerton-bodied Austin CXB, which is reputed to have cost the princely sum of £65. In a red and cream livery, which it retained the whole of its time with Chiltern Queens until withdrawn in May 1961, it came from Taylor's Coaches of Carterton, to replace utility Bedford BBW 950, and was thus used mainly on bus services from Wallingford to the Wittenhams and Warborough. *(John Whitehead Colln)*

SPD 207 was a second hand purchase by Chiltern Queens in January 1959 which will forever be synonymous with the Checkendon-Reading service, for it was in continuous use on it until May 1967. New in May 1952 to Yellow Bus Service of Stoughton, Guildford, it was a Dennis Falcon with Gurney Nutting 30-seat body. The original cream livery was adapted by giving the bus a red roof and side panels carrying Chiltern Queens fleetname transfers, and is seen here on the Blagrave Street stand on 13th June 1959. (JH Aston)

This view of DUD 784 was taken in Long Toll outside the depot in February 1959. It had been withdrawn from passenger service in July 1958 having been repainted into green and grey and was subsequently used as the crew ferry bus and garage run-about, hence its operation on trade plates at the time. When sold for scrap in 1960, it was replaced on this latter duty for a short while by Bedford OWB BBW 701. (PM Moth)

The last utility Bedford in stock was BBW 701, which received a body rebuild and repaint with cream window surrounds in July 1956 and also included being re-seated with ex-London Transport seats salvaged from double-decker CFC 784 when finally withdrawn due to engine failure, but which had come out of green ex-London STL DGX 346. It is seen here in the brickworks yard opposite the depot having been dumped for a year or so after its own withdrawal from service before being sold for breaking c1961. (MJC Dare)

The 1959 intake of two vehicles from White's Coaches of Camberley came in July and entered service in the late autumn. Both were ten years old and the first, NPA 462, an Albion Victor with Whitson 31-seat body, was a sister to NPA 461 bought the previous year. *(J Walker)*

The other 1959 acquisition from White's Coaches was KGU 599, a Dennis Lancet J3 with Burlingham 35-seat body, evidently bought for contract work rather than private hire now that Chiltern Queens could offer much more up-to-date vehicles for private hire use. In this view the vehicle is on bald tyres and appears withdrawn, which took place in April 1962. *(Omnibus Society – Peter Yeomans Colln)*

The Swinging 'Sixties

The new decade brought many things – men walking on the Moon, the end of National Service, JF Kennedy, the Profumo Affair, a Labour government in 1964, The Beatles, Hippies, great socio-economic change, more disposable income, Dr Beeching's rail modernisation programme and more affordable cars, to name but a few, but sadly it did not offer much in the way of better prosperity for rural bus services and coaching. Public transport generally was on the decline – people wanted cars for flexible travel opportunity and better roads. Transport Minister (1959-64) Ernest Marples was happy to oblige. Of the towns served by Chiltern Queens services, Watlington lost its railway branch line to Princes Risborough in July 1957, Wallingford its short branch to the main line at Cholsey & Moulsford in June 1959 and Didcot its cross-country line to Newbury in September 1962 – all before the Beeching Plan took effect. It is unlikely that Chiltern Queens gained any extra revenue as a result of these line closures.

1960 was marked by the passing, in Essex, of Harry Kemp on 12 October, but matters at Chiltern Queens seemed relatively uneventful that year. The only vehicle to enter the fleet was a Bedford CALV minibus with a body conversion by Martin Walter of Folkestone, featuring slam doors at the rear. It seated eleven passengers with those behind the driver arranged along the sides, so it was not the most comfortable vehicle. It was probably envisaged that it would be useful for private hire jobs for small parties, such as darts teams travelling to an away match. One of the Maudslay Marathon coaches (LPK 200) was withdrawn in October and then spent the customary sojourn 'out to grass', before being scrapped on site the following year. The other former Kemp's Dennis Lancet J3 (CBW 864) was given a new Plaxton full-front body in July 1960, similar to that already on DBW 382, again disguising its true vintage to unsuspecting customers.

Not much happened in the fleet during 1960 and the only new vehicle was, surprisingly, a Bedford CALV 11-seat minibus registered SBW 562. Such vehicles were gaining popularity with coach hire operators at the time, because the supply of new small-capacity coaches was drying up. This one lasted a commendable 11 years in service and is seen here parked at Gloucester Green, Oxford, in March 1963. (RHG Simpson)

This was the result when Whitson-bodied Maudslay Marathon III coach LPH 429 was rebuilt with a 'full-front' during winter 1960/61. As such, it could be used as a one-man service bus, albeit in green and grey coach livery, as well as a school contract and local private hire vehicle. It is seen here northbound in Caversham Road, Reading passing the British Railways Western Region signal works on 14 August 1962. (FW York)

The last half-cab coach to be purchased for use by Chiltern Queens was HRU 755, another 1949 Dennis Lancet J3 with 33-seat body, this time by Plaxton. It came in April 1961 from Bluebird Coaches of Weymouth. It lasted until 1967 and is seen in The Forbury, Reading (just down the hill from the Blagrave Street stand), with the platforms of Reading (Southern) Station in the background and a rare view of the tea stall on the right of the picture. *(AG Low)*

In June 1961, another out-of-character second hand purchase was a so-called lightweight, which came from Super Coaches of Upminster, Essex. It was 704 JMB, a 1960 Thames-Trader with Burlingham Seagull 60 41-seat body – and was therefore almost new. It ran most of its 11 year life with Chiltern Queens in its original cream livery and is seen here having a wash outside the workshop in May 1962. *(MJC Dare)*

Over the winter of 1960/1, another Maudslay Marathon coach, LPH 429, was overhauled and rebuilt with a full front, to the design of Tony Sears, after which it was used partly as a spare vehicle for the bus services, although it carried coach livery. An unusual feature was that the radiator grille was of a style more normally seen on AEC Regent V double-deckers of the period.

In March 1961, the last double-decker, Guy Arab JWL 858, was finally sold to a London scrap dealer. Although it had not seen service for some time, as it ran down the hill on tow, the engine sprang into life. This temporarily resulted in the bus towing the breakdown lorry sent to retrieve it! In the same month, the surviving Bedford OWB, BBW 701, became the new crew ferry bus and garage run-around vehicle, functions previously performed by DUD 784, the Bedford WTB coach. Shortly afterwards Austin coach EEA 8 was withdrawn, soon after the arrival of the last half-cab vehicle, purchased for contract duties. This was HRU 755 – a Dennis Lancet J3 with Plaxton bodywork which had been new in 1949 to

Bluebird Coaches of Weymouth. In complete contrast, the second arrival of the year, in June, was a lightweight Ford Thames 570E coach with Burlingham body, from Super Coaches of Upminster. Little progress was being made in terms of aspirations of fleet standardisation. Apart from a ten-year-old Bedford SB coach acquired in 1967, there were to be no more lightweight vehicles (as traditionally described) acquired for service throughout the rest of the company's existence, unless one counts the Mercedes-Benz midibuses that would come in the 1990s.

Useful additional work gained by Chiltern Queens, like many other small operators in southern and western England if they had acceptable vehicles, was providing relief coaches for use on busy express services run by concerns such as Royal Blue, to coastal resorts during peak summer periods. In late August 1961, for example, the two rebodied Dennis Lancet J3s and AEC Reliance MUD 975 were so engaged, operating to the West Country from London's Victoria Coach Station.

Significant rationalisation was applied to bus service D. For some time, the only journeys operated on the section beyond Scots Common to Nuffield had been one each way mid-morning and a late evening journey each way on Saturdays. However, from 16 October 1961, the section of route beyond Checkendon via Scots Common to Nuffield was withdrawn and there were fewer journeys over the rest of the route to Reading with none on Sundays. Patronage had now diminished following the closure of the Polish settlement at Scots Common. Today, the site is Cox's wood yard. Subsequently, the timetable was further reduced to four journeys from Checkendon to Reading, with three back. There was also a mid-morning short journey from Reading out to Gallowstree Common and return, which lasted until March 1969.

Chiltern Queens were still not finished in seeking out examples of Dennis Lancet IIIs which might be for sale, for they were a much trusted type. In March 1962 they found a pair, one of which (OTD 948) was a 30ft long J10 version, which entered service, and a J3 (FUT 452), which was broken for spares. OTD 948 dated from 1952, with a Yeates 35-seat full-front body, so, like LPH 429 in its rebuilt form, it could be used as a service bus as well as a coach for contract work. It is on the stand in Blagrave Street, Reading. Both acquisitions came from Todd, of Whitchurch, Aylesbury. *(AG Low)*

The last Dennis Lancet coach to be acquired for service, in March 1962, was a 1952 J10 model, registered OTD 948. Its full-front 35-seat bodywork by Yeates made it look less dated and it came from Todd of Whitchurch in Buckinghamshire, along with an older J3 model (FUT 452) which was acquired for spare parts. The J10 effectively replaced another J3 (KGU 599), which was withdrawn the following month. It was rumoured that the latter might be given a new Plaxton body, but that did not happen.

Two quite significant vehicles entered what was already a very interesting fleet. The very latest in luxury coach design materialised in May 1962 in the form of a 51-seat AEC Reliance with the new Plaxton Panorama body. Registered VBW 581, it had heating and air-conditioning, was the first vehicle of 36 foot length purchased and was the first such vehicle in the area, although very soon followed by a similar one for Spiers of Henley-on-Thames. On 15 May, around fifteen members of the Reading Transport Society were treated to a demonstration run in the new coach, starting from the British Estate Services Garage in Reading, out to Stoke Row, after which they were entertained to tea by the company. On account of its size, the new coach was dubbed 'Queen Mary', its regular driver being Roland 'Bubbles' Sherwood. In contrast, September brought a unique bus to Woodcote in the form of the Dennis Pelican underfloor-engined single-decker with 44-seat Duple (Midland) bodywork. Although two other Pelican chassis were constructed, they were never bodied. 530 BPG was built in 1956 as a demonstrator, but no orders were received by Dennis,

which abandoned the project. It was taken off their hands in March 1957 by an operator local to them – Yellow Bus Services of Guildford, who later sold it on to Trimdon Motor Services in County Durham. It reached Chiltern Queens via Daisy Bus Service of Broughton, Lincolnshire. Former driver Michael Allen recalls that it was not very reliable and initially was mainly used on the Reading-Didcot service A.

The winter of 1962/3 was severe, with much snow and ice for weeks on end. Michael Allen was employed on workshop duties but was often called upon to go out and drive on a bus service. He recounts that, "on Boxing Day 1962 the snow started and I had to do a long duty of 11½ hours with very little break. I was driving AEC Reliance LMO 743 on service B and by the time I left Reading at 8.50pm it was snowing hard. When coming back from Ewelme, the roads were very bad approaching Whitchurch Hill and coming up from Goring to Woodcote but I got home safely. Over the next four weeks the road conditions got much worse but there was only one day that we could not run – a Sunday in February 1963. AEC Reliances LMO 743-5 were not fitted with heaters or demisters at that time." These buses and the Dennis Pelican had to have major body repair work after the bad winter, with re-styled front panels on the LMOs and also a complete re-spray for LMO 745. Painting was done by the hot spray method, expertly in-house by Ron Back, who had joined the company in the workshop in autumn 1958 from Elliots in Caversham. In summer 1963, the Dennis Falcon L6 (SPD 207) was much-improved after an extensive rebuilding, returning to service in green and grey coach livery, whilst on 11 April that year, Ron Back went to Scarborough to collect the second new

In May 1962, this vehicle was truly ground-breaking! It was one of two of the newly-permitted 36ft long AEC Reliances to enter service in the area. Both had 51-seat Plaxton Panorama bodies, this one (VBW 581) with Chiltern Queens, who were just pipped to the post by AG & KM Spiers of Henley, who had VBW 763. Quite remarkably, over 50 years later both survive in preservation. When new, Etienne Barrett was unable to resist the opportunity to give local short demonstration excursions and, quickly dubbed 'Queen Mary', VBW 581, running on Chiltern Queens' trade plates 056 BW, is here awaiting passengers at his British Estate Services filling station at World's End, Bath Road, Reading on 16 May 1962. (MJC Dare)

Just as famous a member of Chiltern Queens' stock list as the ex-London Transport Green Line coach, was 530 BPG, the Dennis Pelican former show model and demonstrator, dating from 1956. With Duple Midland 40-seat body (later up-seated to 44-seats) it had already had three owners after being a demonstrator before reaching Chiltern Queens in September 1962 – which might suggest that it had reliability problems. However, it lasted in service until 1970. It is seen here ascending Station Hill, Reading, to terminate on the Blagrave Street stand. Note the bleak surroundings opposite Reading Station, before Western Tower, the Bus Station and the Top Rank ballroom/bingo hall were built – and everything since demolished! (AG Low)

36 foot AEC Reliance/Plaxton coach. XBW 242 was predictably christened 'Queen Elizabeth'.

National Service in the Armed Forces was abolished from 31 December 1960, with the last conscripts departing in May 1963. This diminished the requirement for the weekend Forces Express Leave services, as substantial patronage came from National Servicemen. However, the express services, including that from RAF Benson to London, continued to run for some while, recalled by Tony Sears as until about 1978, although it was not until 1982 that the licence for the London service was allowed to lapse. Licences for services to Portsmouth and Newcastle-Upon-Tyne were eventually also surrendered, along with one to Nottingham which had been granted in July 1957 following an objection from Tom Tappin Ltd, which ran an RAF Benson to Birmingham Leave service.

The first foray overseas for Chiltern Queens coaches was apparently on 28 July 1963, when a large party from Bracknell departed for France, Belgium and Germany,

travelling in rebodied Dennis Lancets CBW 864 and DBW 382 and also AEC Reliance MUD 975.

Early 1964 witnessed the return to service after repaint and overhaul of DUD 401, the last former Kemp's half-cab coach remaining in use, but it did not see the year out before withdrawal. Arrivals that year included the first two of several pre-owned vacuum-braked AEC Reliance coaches to be acquired over the following four years. Dating from the period 1954-62, they carried 41-seat bodywork by Plaxton, Duple, Yeates or Burlingham, with either front or centre entrances. Some came through the well-known dealer, Lancashire Motor Traders of Oldham. There was also 850 ABK, a 1962 air-braked Reliance with 43-seat front entrance Duple Britannia body, which was purchased with accident damage, so Chiltern Queens rebuilt its front end and it entered service on 1 May 1965. Slightly more antique for 1964 was LLU 420, an AEC Regal III with full-front body by Gurney Nutting. This was acquired from a Mr Thomas, a dealer and showman from Reading, for use

Dennis Falcon SPD 207 underwent an extensive rebuilding of its Gurney Nutting body during summer 1963 and it was out-shopped with cosmetic changes to its appearance and in green and grey coach livery, although it continued to be found working usually on the Checkendon – Reading bus service. It was finally withdrawn in May 1967.
(RHG Simpson)

The obviously positive appreciation of 'Queen Mary' (VBW 581) prompted the ordering of a second example, which was collected from Plaxton, Scarborough, on 11th April 1963. Inevitably, XBW 242 became 'Queen Elizabeth' and is seen here on an excursion to Hayling Island (also known as Reading-by-the-Sea) on 6 July 1970.
(FW York)

on school contracts and it put in over two years service. AEC Reliance LMO 744 was repainted and then ran on *deisel* (sic) fuel – as the legend by the filler cap proclaimed.

Over time, the two bus stop flags at the Chiltern Queens stops in Blagrave Street, Reading, had suffered weathering to their paintwork. Nine years after Kemp's ceased operating, one of these flags read 'Kemp's Bus Stop, Routes 3 and 19', whilst the other read 'Routes 2, 6 and 12'. They had originally been erected in 1950 as part of the promotion for new Kemp's service 19 to Abingdon.

In time for Christmas shopping in 1963, a contract with a Road Service Licence was started on Saturdays at the behest of the Squire of Mapledurham estate, who apparently underwrote it, to link the Thames-side village of that name to Reading, for the benefit of estate workers and their families. A coach would be used, including Maudslay LPH 429. Mapledurham itself is some distance from the main Reading-Crowmarsh road

and although a licence is recorded as formally granted from 8 January 1964, the service did not endure.

Excavations for the foundations of a new bus garage building were started in summer 1962, in the brickworks yard. Constructed by Condor Ltd of Winchester, work proceeded slowly – by winter 1963/4 it was partially completed and could be used for vehicle parking. Previously, a large crane had been brought in to lift the roof into position. For whatever reason, it remained on site and was still there in the mid nineteen nineties, rusting amongst the brambles behind the building.

Some while afterwards, planning permission was granted for the erection of a 6,000 square feet building on the original Kemp site. Once the framework with a corrugated asbestos roof had been built, it was found that the entrance was inaccessible in general use for the type of vehicles then operated. After a considerable time, the building was finished and rented to beer and wine merchant Hawkings & Platt. A Thornycroft open-sided lorry was converted into a Brewer's dray in the

NWF 286, new in July 1954, was an **AEC** Reliance coach with Plaxton Venturer centre-entrance 41-seat body acquired in June 1964 and seen here looking very smart in the substantially complete new depot building erected the previous year on the brickworks site. *(AG Low)*

850 ABK, an AEC Reliance with Duple Britannia 43-seat body rather complimented **MUD 975** bought new – except that this second hand purchase was front entrance whereas **MUD 975** had a centre entrance. **850 ABK** was new in June 1962, so was only two years old when it came from Don's Coaches of Southsea in June 1964 – but with major front end accident damage. It entered Chiltern Queens service on 1 May 1965 having been completely rebuilt and is seen here in Dorchester-on-Thames on 21 July 1965. When eventually withdrawn in 1989 and sold into preservation, it had served Chiltern Queens for an incredible 24 years! *(AJ Douglas)*

Another fairly odd choice for Chiltern Queens to add to stock was LLU 420, a 35-seater full-fronted AEC Regal III with bodywork by Gurney Nutting. New in 1951, it joined the fleet for use mainly on school contracts, so its age and somewhat dated appearance was not particularly important – and may have had something to do with how much it cost! It is seen here well-posed outside the depot premises.
(John Whitehead Colln)

Another AEC Reliance carrying a Plaxton Venturer 41-seat centre-entrance body, to compliment NWF 286, was JCX 756, seen here emerging from the brickworks yard after a scattering of snow in 1965, soon after acquisition. New in March 1955, Chiltern Queens was its third owner, in November 1964, and was used until de-licenced in January 1969, deleted from stock in March 1970 and eventually broken up on site. (MJC Dare)

Chiltern Queens workshop, for use by the new tenant for deliveries throughout the Thames Valley. After a lengthy period, these activities had to cease as an eviction order was issued by the local authority, as they breached planning consent. Thereafter, apart from hosting the construction of a horse box for Stan Woodrow's son, a few odd paint-spraying jobs and storage, the building remained empty.

On 13 December 1963, a bus on service B was stopped at Crowmarsh by Ministry of Transport Vehicle Examiners who noted that driver Brian Critchfield had 70 passengers on board. The vehicle would have had 44 seats and space for eight standing passengers. The offence was brought to Henley Magistrates' Court in March 1964, when the company pleaded guilty. Mr Barrett, then Deputy Mayor of Reading, said that by arrangement with the Council's Education Department, the bus left Wallingford around 4pm to carry the children home to Benson. Normally there would have been enough room legally for everybody but there were extra adults travelling in the busy run-up to Christmas. He was rather bullish by saying that it was 'monstrous' that such an overloading situation should be prosecuted, when country bus services were not frequent and that otherwise, the children would have to wait an hour and a half in the cold for the next bus. The legal representative for the Traffic Commissioner asked Mr Barrett if his company was in business for profit, to which the latter replied, "yes, but we never make any!" Chiltern Queens were fined £1 and the driver 10s.

Checkendon Parish Council had conducted what would today be called a 'consultation exercise' to gain opinions on what local people thought of their bus service. Comments on the vehicles included, "dirty, cold, draughty, old and decrepit". There was also too little time allowed in Reading in the afternoon for shopping. A public meeting was called in March

1964, where Tony Sears had to explain that not only could they not run more journeys, but that fares would have to be shortly increased as well. The company had met three wage awards without increasing fares, but this need was now urgent. The Checkendon service was particularly un-remunerative and many of the roads precluded the use of more modern vehicles, which were wider. Tony thought the only way to improve matters would be for a subsidy to be funded by the Taxpayer. It was not until the Transport Act 1968 that local authorities were given the ability to do just that, but many chose not to.

Chiltern Queens' newest flagship made its public debut on 2 April 1965 when it was entered in the British Coach Rally at Blackpool, driven by Ron Back. DUD 753C was a 36 foot Leyland Leopard which, like the new AECs, had a 51-seat Plaxton Panorama body.

In August 1965, the fleet composition was given as: thirteen AEC, six Dennis and one each of Maudslay, Ford, Bedford (the minibus), Albion and Leyland. Nine other vehicles were still present at Woodcote either being dismantled or awaiting scrapping. On 11 September 1965, AEC Reliance coach LDL 696 was hired to transport a wedding party, complete with traditional white ribbons.

Often a girl, who was courting a Wallingford boy, was the only passenger on the last bus back to Ewelme on service B. In October 1965, the Traffic Commissioners granted permission to curtail this journey. At the Traffic Court Hearing, necessitated by a Representation by Ewelme Parish Council, they were advised by Tony Sears that the girl had now married and there were now no passengers at all going to Ewelme on that journey and that no more than five passengers were ever on the bus beyond Crays Pond.

After receiving an overhaul and a different engine, the Dennis Pelican was used on 24 April 1966 for a tour by local bus enthusiasts over some of Chiltern Queens' stage carriage routes. A stop was made for tea at Wallingford and the bus was driven by Michael Allen and by Mike Dare in his dual roles of part-time Chiltern Queens driver and Hon Secretary of Reading Transport Society.

In autumn 1966, Dennis Falcon SPD 207 suffered accident damage, so was substituted temporarily on the Checkendon service by AEC Regal LLU 420. In turn, this meant that the Thursday shoppers on service 13 to Henley enjoyed a one-man-operated vehicle from the coach fleet. In the late 1960s, AEC Reliance coaches

New ground was broken in January 1965 with the delivery of another 51-seat Plaxton Panorama – but this time on a Leyland Leopard chassis. As time would tell, this was certainly not an automatic abandonment of the tried-and-tested AEC Reliance, for Chiltern Queens had three new and fifteen second hand of the latter between January 1965 and April 1974, after which new vehicles were, for a while, Leyland Leopards. DUD 753C was entry 40 at the 1965 British Coach Rally, at Blackpool, on 2 April and is seen here outside the new depot building being prepared prior to departure. (MJC Dare)

Another classic coach design of the 1950s, of which Chiltern Queens had only one, was the Duple Elizabethan, which, in fact, preceded the Britannia. LNV 303 was a fairly early AEC Reliance, dating from May 1955, and was nearly ten years old when acquired from York Bros, Northampton, in March 1965. However, it put in over eight years of further service with Chiltern Queens and is seen posed here in the yard at Woodcote. (MJC Dare)

Also a fairly early AEC Reliance, new in spring 1955, was LDL 896, which arrived with Chiltern Queens in June 1965 and similarly remained in service until July 1973. It carried a Yeates Riviera 41-seat centre-entrance body and is seen here parked up inside the new depot building. It was new to Shotters, of Brighstone on the Isle of Wight and when new attended the 1955 British Coach Rally at Brighton. (RHG Simpson)

Second Hand Coach Additions – 1

More coaches with Plaxton Venturer 41-seat centre-entrance bodies on 1955 vintage AEC Reliance chassis came in 1966. UUG 39 came from George's Coaches of Kirkburton, Huddersfield, in February, having been new to Wallace Arnold, Leeds.
(RHG Simpson)

Something of a pure chance was the purchase of sister vehicle UUG 37 in July 1966. This one, which had been with Hills of Tredegar, Monmouthshire, after sale by Wallace Arnold, Leeds, is parked up in the new depot building.
(RHG Simpson)

Yet another Plaxton body design to join Chiltern Queens, needless to say on an AEC Reliance chassis, was this one. KBV 778, dating from August 1958, was the Consort II centre-entrance 41-seater. Drawn up outside the workshop, this one had been new to Ribblesdale of Blackburn, and was acquired through a dealer in January 1967, being withdrawn in May 1975. *(RHG Simpson)*

Second Hand Coach Additions – 2

After four years of buying second hand centre-entrance coaches, the intake in April 1967 was this 1962 AEC Reliance with Burlingham Seagull 60 41-seat front-entrance body. 135 KD was acquired through Lancashire Motor Traders of Salford, having had two previous owners, then survived twelve years in service with Chiltern Queens. *(Omnibus Society – Roy Marshall Colln)*

A surprise purchase amongst all the AEC Reliances was OUN 628, a 1957 Bedford SBG with Duple Super Vega 41-seat body, now fitted with a diesel engine, which also arrived from Lancashire Motor Traders in April 1967, having seen service from new based in Wrexham. It was six years in Chiltern Queens' service, until 1973, so it was 16 years old when withdrawn, quite commendable for a lightweight. *(RHG Simpson)*

Another Yeates-bodied AEC Reliance was this Europa 41-seater new in April 1960, registered 26 MTF, which joined the Chiltern Queens fleet in August 1967 and was in service until October 1975 – 15½ years of service life, over eight years of which were with Chiltern Queens. It, too, came via Lancashire Motor Traders, having had only one previous owner, but it was in a bit of a state and received a thorough rebuild before entering Chiltern Queens' service. *(Omnibus Society – Roy Marshall Colln)*

There was an intake of only two vehicles, both second hand, into the fleet in 1968, both in February, one coach and one service bus. The coach was VBD 78, a 1960 AEC Reliance with front-entrance 41-seat Duple Britannia body, seen here parked up in Weymouth. New to York Bros, Northampton, it was 18 years old by the time it was retired ten years later, in February 1978. *(John Whitehead Colln)*

The service bus that was purchased in February 1968 was JNR 298, a 1953 AEC Regal IV with Willowbrook 43-seat dual-purpose body (ie coach seats in a bus body). The Regal IV was a heavyweight forerunner to the AEC Reliance and was renowned for heavy fuel consumption. This one lasted just shy of four years with Chiltern Queens. *(Philip Smith)*

NWF 286, UUG 39 and LNV 303, despite having centre entrances, were often used on the latter service.

A fares revision on 20 June 1966 included the abolition of return fares.

Alderman Barrett became Chairman of the Transport Committee after the Conservatives regained control of Reading County Borough Council in May 1967. For some time he had been opposed to purchasing a second batch of Bristol buses for Reading Corporation Transport, preferring AECs as one might expect. At the July meeting of the Transport Committee his opinion was voted down and a decision made to order 28 further Bristol bus chassis. Barrett resigned the Chair on 2 August in protest.

Falling patronage and profitability saw inevitable further reductions on the bus services towards the end of the 1960s. The remaining Sunday journeys on services A and B were withdrawn on 16 June 1968, leaving a large area without public transport on that day. AEC Reliance LMO 744 had the dubious honour of performing the last Sunday duty. The Sunday service on the Ewelme to Watlington section of service B had disappeared some time previously. The South Eastern Area Traffic Commissioners put out a plea to other operators who might be interested in running between Reading and Didcot on Sundays, but there were no takers. More cuts were to come in 1969, when the Stadhampton to Warborough section of Friday service C was withdrawn on 21 February, to be followed by significant timetable reductions on the other services from March and April of that year, including withdrawal of early morning and late evening journeys.

A somewhat surprising February 1968 acquisition was JNR 298, a fifteen-year-old AEC Regal IV dual-purpose (ie originally intended for use as a bus or coach) vehicle, with 43-seat bodywork by Willowbrook. Probably secured at a bargain price due to its age and type, this was the regular vehicle allocated to service D until late 1971, replacing AEC Reliance coach JCX 756.

There occurred in January 1969 one of the periodical clear-outs of the yard at Woodcote, when four vehicles were sold for scrap to Passey (a coincidental name), a scrap dealer at Benson. These were Dennis Lancets KGU 599, HRU 755, OTD 948 and Dennis Falcon SPD 207. However, a new Pride of the Fleet was about to arrive. TUD 167G was the first 12m AEC Reliance to be built, with one of the first of the new bodywork examples from Plaxton – the Panorama Elite. It had 57 seats, on runners so that the number and layout could be adjusted. This was a higher capacity than the double-deckers of the 1950s. It was exhibited by Plaxton on their stand at the Commercial Motor Show in September 1968 and was then used by them as a demonstrator. It reached its intended customer in April 1969 and was dubbed 'QE2', after the new Cunard liner. The extra length of the new 12m Reliance meant that some modifications were necessary to the garage building, after the coach was backed in one day and demolished part of the rear wall. Fortunately, for economy, only lime mortar had been used in the original wall, otherwise damage to the coach might have been more extensive. The new coach was a confident end to the decade but it did not mean that the next one would be any easier in certain ways for a small bus and coach operator in a rural area.

The LMO Triplets live the gruelling life of a country bus

LMO 743 has almost reached the top of the hill, after the climb up Long Toll to the Chiltern Queens depot. With what appears to be a fresh coating of stone chippings on the road surface, it is quite easy to imagine the tar smell on a hot summer's day and the barking exhaust of the bus once more toiling along its usual route. *(Peter Trevaskis)*

There were times when service buses had to be in service in less than perfect condition! Note the scored and creased panels on LMO 744, quite apart from the more obvious missing offside headlamp, seen here on the stand in Blagrave Street, Reading. *(Arnold Richardson)*

The same bus, LMO 744, outside Didcot station a little later in its life, having acquired a cosmetic front 'bumper' (which would be of no practical use) ran in service for some weeks minus some off-side panelling resulting from the cruel operating conditions caused by the severe winter weather in early 1963, when it was fitted temporarily with three tiers of lifeguard tubing to prevent anyone from falling under the bus when it was moving – fortunately not obvious to intending passengers boarding the bus on the nearside at a bus stop! *(RHG Simpson)*

Some Memories of the Early Years

The second ex-Kemp's Dennis Lancet J3 to be re-bodied by Plaxton, this time with an Embassy body, was **CBW 864**, which was received in July 1960. Two years earlier, **DBW 382** had received a Consort body. Both were 37-seaters. *(MJC Dare)*

Gardner-engined former Kemp's Vincent-bodied Tilling-Stevens **DBW 66** was, in its time, an important and reliable component of Chiltern Queens' original coach fleet, upon which the dependability of the undertaking came to be built. *(John Whitehead)*

More Memories of the Early Years

JWL 858 was the last survivor of the trio of ex-City of Oxford lowbridge Guy Arabs put into service in 1957, although in all cases the stay was brief. Amongst the several reasons was the severe reduction in the contract services serving the Polish community at Checkendon and Howberry Park and the closure of RAF Woodcote, and the continuing reduction of stage carriage traffic, which made it uneconomic to employ conductors when services could now be operated by modern one-man-operated single-deckers. *(John Whitehead)*

The rear ends of service buses being comparatively infrequently photographed, we thought it proper to make amends! Here is NBW 407 at the Reading terminal point on Station Hill. *(Anon)*

Willowbrook-bodied JNR 298, new to Brown Bros, Sapcote in July 1953 and later with Robinson, Burbage, was an AEC Regal IV fitted with synchromesh gearbox, which joined Chiltern Queens in February 1968. It is leading the way, chased by NBW 407, outbound along Caversham Road, Reading, at the same location as the pre-war photo of UD 9431 earlier.
(John Whitehead – from Peter Whitworth Colln)

The very latest in coach styling at the 1968 Commercial Motor Show, at Earls Court, London, was this AEC Reliance with Plaxton Panorama Elite 57-seat bodywork, seen here in the demonstration park in full Chiltern Queens green and grey livery. Usually photographed at the event carrying registration plate 'PLA 69', its true identity was TUD 167G and after the Show it went on a demonstration tour before delivery to Chiltern Queens in April 1969 – where, of course, it became dubbed 'QE 2'! It led a long life with the undertaking. *(AG Low)*

LMO 744, one of the three long-serving AEC Reliance service buses, seen here at Didcot Station on the last operation by Chiltern Queens of a Sunday service, on Sunday, 30 June 1968. *(Philip Smith)*

97

The Difficult 'Seventies

The 1970s possibly marked the lowest point in the fortunes of the overall UK bus industry, in its regulated form that had existed since 1931. It was a period of general drops in patronage, need for subsidy, labour supply problems and all too frequent fare increases. In many cases, it was just a matter of managing decline for the state-owned National Bus Co subsidiaries like City of Oxford MS and the Thames Valley & Aldershot Omnibus Co (Alder Valley), as well for as the municipally-owned sector and many independent operators.

The first year of the new decade opened with the acquisition of two more of Chiltern Queens' favoured, tried and tested AEC Reliances. BMK 344A was a 1963 model with 45-seat Duple Commodore body, which arrived from Ivory Coaches of Tetbury, Gloucestershire in February. This permitted the withdrawal of older AEC/Plaxton coach JCX 756. At the other end of the year, a 1957 bus version was purchased from the fleet of Aldershot & District; RCG 618 had a 43-seat body by Weymann. Purchased on 1 December, it was in service only eight days later, smartly repainted in red and cream livery.

BMK 344A, new in June 1963, carried a 45-seat Duple Commodore body, and came from Ivory Coaches, Tetbury, entering the Chiltern Queens fleet in February 1970 and surviving until June 1984. It is seen here in the forecourt of Tilehurst Station, Reading, presumably on rail replacement. *(MJC Dare)*

This Weymann-bodied AEC Reliance was the first of several new to Aldershot & District to enter the Chiltern Queens fleet. RCG 618, new in February 1957, joined Chiltern Queens in December 1970 and was not withdrawn until June 1981. It is seen here on the original Blagrave Street stand, adjacent to Reading Station. *(John Whitehead Colln)*

JNR 298, the 1953 Willowbrook-bodied AEC Regal IV, is on layover in Vastern Road, Reading. The view is included to illustrate how Chiltern Queens' service buses had to be found somewhere for layover, in this case in a road now vastly different. *(Chris Aston Omnicolour Pix)*

During 1969 and 1970, the workshop staff had overhauled and rebuilt stalwart Reliance buses LMO 743-5, featuring re-styled fronts complete with flashing indicators and reflective number plates. In July 1970, there were owned 26 vehicles of which no fewer than eighteen were AEC Reliances. There were also the two rebodied Dennis Lancets, the AEC Regal IV, the Dennis Pelican, the Leyland Leopard, one Ford coach, one Bedford coach and the Bedford minibus. The Dennis Pelican came off the road in October that year.

On 19 September 1970, there was an Open Day at the Didcot Railway Centre as well as the regular Battle of Britain Day at RAF Benson. Large crowds attended and Chiltern Queens' bus services A and B were very busy. In addition, a fifteen minute interval shuttle service was operated to and from Wallingford by AEC Reliance coaches MUD 975, VBD 78, 850 ABK, XBW 242, LNV 303 and 135 KD during the afternoon.

During early 1971, AECs LMO 744 and RCG 618 were given Certificates of Fitness valid until 1976 – a tribute to the care and attention lavished by the workshop staff on vehicles of such age. The Bedford minibus lost its Public Service Vehicle status in March that year, but was retained as a company support vehicle for a few months longer. The influx of AEC Reliances continued with 591 STT, a 1964 coach and brand new ABW 777J, with 53-seat Plaxton Panorama Elite bodywork, both in

April. In December 1971 the bus fleet was bolstered by the arrival of WVA 453, with Willowbrook bus bodywork, from OK Motor Services of Bishop Auckland, County Durham.

Whilst the bus services were probably of dubious viability, the Directors announced a profit of £5,000 for the previous financial year, largely coming from extensive private hire work. More and more, such activity and that of school contracts were cross-subsidising stage carriage operations. Bus fares had not been increased for four years and one of fifteen per cent was applied for to coincide with the switchover day to Decimal currency in February 1971. Fortunately it was declared not to have unduly impacted on passenger numbers, which had shown slight signs of increase. The minimum fare was still no more than 1½ new pence.

AEC bus LMO 743 sustained severe accident damage on 3 September 1971, when the front end and entrance area were completely wrecked. A rebuild was soon underway, in contrast to many other concerns who would have written off a bus dating from 1955. Another example of Chiltern Queens' policy of vehicle longevity was seen when Dennis Lancet CBW 864 was re-certified until 1973, although it was to see little further use, being withdrawn from service in October 1971.

After 21 years of employment with Kemp's and Chiltern Queens, mainly on the Reading-Checkendon service, driver Cyril 'Tiger' Lilley retired on 8 April 1972.

During the late 1960s the LMO 'Triplets' were each given a makeover, all generally similar but not identical – and for different reasons, such as accident damage repair or pre-recertification work.

LMO 745, done first, in November 1966, has retained standard headlamps but in recessed panels, no 'bumpers', and standard (non-reflective) registration plates, and although a waistband has been introduced, the treatment below the windscreens is shallower than eventually on her sisters. Seen here inside the depot on completion of the rejuvenation, LMO 743 nearby has not yet been treated.
(Arnold Richardson)

LMO 744, at the Blagrave Street stand in Reading, although retaining standard headlamps but in recessed panels, has 'corner bumpers' and reflective registration plates and a waistband added which is deeper at the front compared with LMO 745. Note the former Kemp's' bus stop flag.
(Geoff Lumb)

LMO 743 has dual headlamps in recessed panels, 'corner bumpers', reflective registration plates and a waistband like LMO 744, all of which considerably enhances the appearance of these vehicles. This one is seen at a new stand location, with passenger shelter, at the foot of Station Hill, Reading, brought into use on 11th December 1972. *(RCW Smith)*

591 STT was a second Duple Commodore-bodied 45-seater AEC Reliance, this one being obtained through AG & KM Spiers in Henley, which entered Chiltern Queens service in April 1971. (MJC Dare)

ABW 777J, new in April 1971, was an AEC Reliance with Plaxton Panorama Elite II 53-seat bodywork, every inch a coach to be proud of – and all-British – seen here outside the depot on Chiltern Queens' limited trade plate 917 BW and being spruced up having been fetched from Plaxtons at Scarborough. (MJC Dare)

In December 1971, AEC Reliance WVA 453, with Willowbrook 45-seat body, came to Chiltern Queens from OK Motor Services Ltd of Bishop Auckland, although it had been new in May 1960 to Irvine, Salsburgh near Motherwell. It was in Chiltern Queens' service until July 1978 and is seen here waiting time at the Station Hill stand in Reading. (John Whitehead Colln)

Many of his regular customers turned out all along the route to bid him farewell and to thank him for loyally serving them, as he took LMO 744 (now the usual bus on service D) for his last runs.

When the Dennis Pelican was withdrawn in October 1970 there were hopes that somebody would purchase it as a preserved vehicle. As that did not occur, the body was removed, re-panelled and rebuilt with a new front. Further modifications were required to enable it to be mounted onto a 1958 AEC Reliance chassis that had been acquired in January 1970 with a Duple coach body, registered YNX 478. Work on the vehicle continued through 1972 and it was licensed from New Year's Day 1973. The Dennis Pelican chassis languished in the depot yard until it was scrapped in May 1977.

AEC Reliance models with the small, horizontally-mounted AH470 engine, were prone to cylinder head gasket failure. A burst hose, due to pressure build up in the cooling system related to the wet cylinder liner

AH470 engine on coach XBW 242, occurred whilst returning from the continent on a contract for RAF Bracknell Staff College. As usual, Ron Back was driving in case of any problem, which he dealt with. Afterwards, Barrett and Sears visited AEC at Southall and the coach was returned for investigation. Tony Sears learned from Don Allmey, a former AEC employee, that the AV470 vertically-mounted engine used in trucks had the same cylinder block, but had dry cylinder liners. Tony Sears and Ron Back toured various scrap dealers to obtain a low mileage AV470 engine on which to experiment. During spare moments, Tony worked on the acquired engine himself, before trial installation in XBW 242. The success of this resulted in the fitting of several Chiltern Queens Reliances with AV 470 engines, which were acquired from various sources, overhauled and fitted.

Further refreshment of the AEC Reliance coach fleet occurred in March 1972 with the acquisition of two 1970 models with Plaxton Panorama Elite bodywork

A 1958 AEC Reliance with Duple 41-seat coach body, YNX 478, bought for spares, was eventually used for a very different purpose. Its original body was broken up and the chassis fitted with the suitably modified Duple Midland bus body on Dennis Pelican 530 BPG. The end result is seen here at the Station Hill stand in Reading on 29 April 1975. (John Whitehead Colln)

The Pelican chassis itself was dumped out to grass and is seen here on 20 July 1974. It was eventually cut up in May 1977. (RCW Smith)

Both **FPX 701H** and **OBK 602H** were new in February 1970 and had been with Byng, Portsmouth, before being acquired by Chiltern Queens in March 1972. These AEC Reliances both carried Plaxton Panorama Elite 51-seat (FPX 701H) and 45-seat (OBK 602H) bodies and were with Chiltern Queens until the early/mid-1990s. In the early 1970s, 20 years earlier, the undertaking was developing its private hire, excursion and extended tours markets and the use of similar new and second hand more-or-less identical vehicles was perceived to be a distinct advantage. *(Both photographs PM Moth)*

from Byng's Luxury Coaches of Portsmouth, registered FPX 701H and OBK 602H. In the same month, something of a landmark vehicle entered service. To aid the bus industry, the Government of the day introduced a Bus Grant, allowing an operator to claim 50 per cent of the cost of new vehicles which were suitable for use on stage carriage services and which were required to spend a certain proportion of their time on such work. This allowed Chiltern Queens to order a new service bus fourteen years after the previous one. A 10m AEC Reliance (naturally!) chassis was bodied by Plaxton with their attractive 47-seat Derwent body. EUD 256K had interior window surrounds, lower side panels and seat backs in wood-effect Formica, red moquette for the seat cushions and bright red flooring. Modern provisions for the time, such as fluorescent lighting, air operated doors, windscreen washer, bell strips and generous

provisions of heaters, added to its appeal to passengers and drivers – a major step change from what had come before at Woodcote.

A less-momentous event was the withdrawal in July 1972 of the Ford Thames/Burlingham coach 704 JMB. Although never particularly popular, it had managed eleven years in the fleet.

Whilst a significant amount of narrow, twisting, rural roads were traversed by Chiltern Queens bus services, that between Chazey Heath and the Whitchurch Turn was especially challenging when driving a bus. Oxfordshire County Council had not been cutting the grass verges or the overhanging foliage from hedges, making visibility poor; there had been several accidents. In protest, the drivers on services A and B refused to use the route from 12 June 1972 and diverted instead via the A4074 through Cane End and then along Deadman's Lane.

EUD 256K was the first of two Bus Grant funded new service buses heralding a new era. With AEC Reliance 36ft chassis and Plaxton Derwent II 47-seat body, it entered service in March 1972 and was eventually withdrawn nearly a quarter century later, in 1996, a most important candidate for preservation at the Oxford Bus Museum, at Long Hanborough. *(Michael Allen Colln)*

Burlingham-bodied Thames Trader 704 JMB had entered the fleet in June 1961 and survived until July 1972, a remarkable time for a lightweight. For nearly all its life it ran in its original operator's cream livery and only for its final few months did it receive standard green and grey coach livery. *(DE Gillard Colln)*

This 1958 Duple-bodied AEC Reliance registered XWD 3, came from Spencer, High Wycombe in June 1973, purely for spares and is seen here dumped outside the new depot, which was built on the site of the long-derelict brickworks opposite the original Kemp's premises. *(John Whitehead Colln)*

The company management unofficially supported their boycott. Three days later, the story made the London *Evening News*, but the County Council acted slowly to trim the hedges and improve visibility. It was not until 7 August that the matter was resolved and the services returned to normal line of route. Having said that, within a week AEC Reliance LMO 745 was involved in a collision on the same piece of road. Subsequently, an application was made for a new service E, along the temporary alternative route mentioned above, but this did not reach fruition.

As mentioned earlier, the Transport Act of 1968 allowed local authorities to offer revenue support to bus services. Chiltern Queens applied to Reading County Borough Council for a grant of £679 per annum, which was approved in autumn 1972. Also in connection with Reading, the bus stand in Blagrave Street used by Kemp's and Chiltern Queens for some 40 years was abandoned after use on 9 December 1972, with a new stand with a small shelter coming into use two days later, on the north side of Station Hill, adjacent to stops used by Reading Corporation services.

More vehicular changes occurred during the spring and early summer of 1973. Various coaches were withdrawn – Bedford OUN 628 and AECs NWF 286, LNV 303 and LDL 896. As was the custom, they took up residence in the yard until scrapped or sold some time later. Joining them there was a job-lot of three coaches purchased in June 1973 from R Spencer of High Wycombe – a Bedford SB1 and two AEC Reliances. The Bedford (YBD 506) and Reliance/Harrington 2922 DK were re-sold without being used, whilst Reliance/Duple XWD 3 was used as a source of spare parts and then broken up. However, acquired for use was another Reliance/Weymann bus (SOU 440) from the erstwhile Aldershot & District fleet, still in their livery after use by Alder Valley. Its entry into service was delayed by an engine defect.

Many bus operators were experiencing difficulties in recruiting and retaining drivers, not least Chiltern Queens. A staff shortage led to several early morning journeys being withdrawn from 15 October 1973. Ongoing problems in obtaining sufficient drivers came to a head when it was found no longer possible to run service D between Reading and Checkendon. Oxfordshire County Council therefore arranged for City of Oxford MS to temporarily operate the majority of the journeys and agreed to meet their operating expenses over and above receipts by guaranteeing maximum revenue support of £500 per month. The arrangement started on 22 April 1974, with COMS obtaining their own Road Service Licence rather than running 'on hire' to Chiltern Queens. However, the latter continued to operate the 9.30am journey from Checkendon to Reading themselves. COMS numbered the service as 37. This 'temporary solution' was to last for 26 months. COMS employed various single-deck vehicle types based at Wallingford, including AEC Reliances,

AEC Swifts and Ford R-series buses with Willowbrook bodies. This was the era of National Bus Co poppy red livery and the Oxford-South Midland fleetname, as South Midland Motor Services Ltd had been absorbed by COMS on 1 January 1971.

1974 was noteworthy for the arrival of another new Bus Grant-funded single-deck bus. It appeared on 5 February, being a Leyland Leopard with Plaxton Derwent body containing 55 seats and registered OJO 835M. It was allocated to drivers Philip Smith and Mike Allen which caused some resentment from some other staff members. Shortly afterwards, the practice of allocating specific buses to named drivers ceased. Also that year, the Bedford SB coach (OUN 628) was sold for further public service – a somewhat rare occurrence for Chiltern Queens – to Brian Reed of Maidenhead.

Early in the following year, buses regularly allocated were OJO 835M and YNX 478 to service A and EUD 256K and NBW 407 to service B and there had been an increase in patronage.

A Bedford YRQ service bus was inspected in 1975, but no order was placed. Instead, the new arrivals that year were three former Aldershot & District 1963 AEC Reliances with Park Royal 49-seat dual-purpose bodywork. Initially used on their original owner's Farnham to London express service, 474 FCG, 478 FCG and 471 FCG were in the ownership of Spiers Coaches of Henley-on Thames, prior to passing to Chiltern Queens in February, August and September 1975 respectively. They had not actually been used by Spiers, having been purchased from a scrap dealer for certain spare parts. Each of these was to have a different life at Woodcote; 474 FCG needed a fair amount of work but was re-certified, equipped with 53 bus seats and put into service in spring 1975. 478 FCG was stored but then rebuilt and similarly re-seated to go on the road early in 1977. Interestingly, the latter acquired seat frames taken from Reading Corporation Sunbeam S7-type trolleybus no. 170 of 1950! When Reading abandoned this form of electric traction in 1968, the trolleybus served as a temporary classroom at Sonning Primary School until the mid-nineteen seventies, when Chiltern Queens purchased the seats when it was sold for scrap. These two impressive AEC vehicles looked very smart in the red and cream bus livery, but 471 FCG had its body removed and never entered service. When 474 and 478 were first observed in Reading, there were raised eyebrows at Alder Valley (of which Aldershot & District had become part) as they had been sold by them on the understanding that they were for scrap only(!)

The first modest fare increase for four years came on 27 January 1975, another on 26 August the same year and then one on 2 June 1976. Yet another occurred from 14 March 1977, following the loss of certain revenue support subsidies. Such increases were sadly commonplace throughout the bus industry at the time as operating costs were continually rising and local authority subsidy in some areas was difficult to obtain.

A second Aldershot & District Weymann-bodied AEC Reliance service bus, **SOU 440**, was obtained in May 1973 and entered service in January 1974. It came from Alder Valley still in Aldershot & District green livery, although the latter had become part of Alder Valley in January 1972. It is seen here on the bus stand outside Didcot Parkway station. *(Geoff Lumb)*

The second new Bus Grant funded service bus to be obtained was **OJO 835M**, again with Plaxton Derwent II body, although this time with 55 seats – and on a Leyland Leopard chassis. It arrived in February 1974 and is seen here loading at Station Hill, Reading (albeit on 23 September 1989!) This was only the second vehicle new to Chiltern Queens on a Leyland Leopard chassis. *(John Whitehead Colln)*

AG & KM Spiers of Henley had obtained three identical former Aldershot & District Park Royal-bodied 53-seater AEC Reliances dating from 1963 for spares from a scrap dealer, which they sold on to Chiltern Queens in 1975. Two were considered sufficiently complete and in good condition to be reprieved for a few years from their immediate destiny! First to enter service was 474 FCG, seen here loading at the Station Hill stand in Reading. *(John Whitehead Colln)*

It has proved difficult to find illustrations of service buses taken 'on the road' rather than at termini, so we make no excuses for including these two!

EUD 256K is seen here inbound in Woodcote Road, Caversham. *(John Whitehead Colln)*

OJO 835M, seen here on 20th July 1974 in Whitehouse Road, Woodcote. *(RCW Smith)*

Reading-bound YNX 478, climbs Whitehouse Road, Woodcote on 20 July 1974, indicating to stop to pick up the photographer opposite Bridlepath. *(RCW Smith)*

The original trio of 1955 AEC Reliance buses (LMO 743-5) were all out of use by the end of 1976, although they resided in the yard until June 1981 when sold to a scrap dealer. LMO 745 was the last in use, but just on school transport duties. After a long and eventful life, they owed the company nothing, with the bold decision to buy them by the fledgling Chiltern Queens being fully-rewarded.

One of the Chiltern Queens drivers had the thought that he could take over service D Reading-Checkendon himself, at a time that it was still being operated by COMS, if he could acquire one of Chiltern Queens' buses. Having approached his employer and started to distribute some publicity material, the directors instructed that any such plan should be abandoned forthwith. However, Chiltern Queens were finally able to re-assume the operation of service D from 1 June 1976 with a reduced timetable of two journeys each way, but with the route extended to start and finish at Woodcote on the proviso that the revenue covered the operating costs. This was fortunate as City of Oxford MS withdrew after 29 May as Oxfordshire County Council had withdrawn the subsidy arrangement. COMS Ford

R1014 single-deck bus no. 648 had performed on the last day.

April 1976 witnessed the arrival of a new Leyland Leopard coach SFC 32P, with Plaxton Supreme 57-seat body. The engine of erstwhile AEC Regal LLU 420 was acquired by the Sandtoft Trolleybus Museum near Doncaster, in which part-time driver Michael Dare was heavily involved, to act as a generator to supply power to the overhead line.

Only one vehicle was purchased in 1977 – a 41-seat AEC Reliance/Plaxton coach from 1964, registered ANL 807B. Of the two former Aldershot & District Reliance buses, RCG 618 was recertified after being out of use for around eighteen months, whilst SOU 440 was withdrawn for scrap following extensive accident damage, having inserted itself into a garden wall in Caversham Park, with attendant publicity.

Reliance coach OBK 602H was slowly altered during 1977/8 into an 'Executive' layout, with only 28 seats, but with tables, toilet, cocktail bar, coffee machine and stereo sound system. This was intended to stimulate private hire business from the upper end of that market, from corporate groups and the like, but it saw very little use.

To start off the 1976 coaching season, SFC 32P arrived new in April. Another Leyland Leopard, this one carried the latest Plaxton Supreme 57-seat body. (*Graham Geoghegan*)

On completion of the conversion, Barrett and Woodrow arranged a dinner at the Savoy Hotel in London, to which those directly involved were ferried in luxury in the coach; champagne was of course on the menu.

In May 1977 there was one of the periodic purges of redundant vehicles languishing in the yard. On this occasion, elderly AEC coaches UUG 37/39 and LNV 303 were reduced to scrap metal, along with the chassis of NWF 286, 471 FCG and that of Dennis Pelican 530 BPG.

The late nineteen-seventies saw some notable vehicle developments. A distinctly unusual purchase in May 1978 was of a Mercedes Benz 0302 coach with a 45-seat Mercedes body. Registered GMC 747J, it came from Worldwide Coaches of London SE5 and compared to the normal diet of AECs and Leylands, it could be regarded as somewhat exotic. This was followed in the first quarter of 1979 by the arrival of two new Leyland Leopard/Plaxton coaches. Once delivered, both were stored for a considerable period before use. The first was not registered until it entered service in May 1982 – over three years later, when it was given the mark PJH 582X. The second was registered UUD 623T but did not go on the road until July 1981. The latter had qualified for the 50 per cent grant offered by the Government, being suitable for use on bus services, but the delay in putting it into service meant that the grant had to be repaid. Apparently the decision to store them was Barrett's and it took intervention from Woodrow, who appeared unaware of their existence, to get them into use, after

persuasion from Tony Sears. Barrett's reason for the lengthy delay between purchase and in putting them into service is unclear – grant funding was available for one of them, or perhaps some money needed to be spent, or they came at an attractive price, or it was wished to obtain examples of the trusted Leyland Leopard, before production ceased. They had been stored in an unheated building and severe corrosion had occurred to their electrical systems, resulting in on-the-road failures and expense to rectify. At the other end of the scale, the disused ex-Kemp's Dennis Lancet DBW 382 was sold into Preservation in September 1979.

In autumn 1979, Mr Barrett inspected two 1965 AEC Reliance buses that Reading Corporation Transport had for sale, these being nos. 251 and 252 in the Reading fleet. They were registered CRD 151/2C and carried Neepsend dual-door bodywork. Although Barrett and Tony Sears were interested in acquiring them, Chief Engineer Ron Back apparently vetoed the idea as he was concerned that their 34-seat capacity would be inadequate on school services and that he would also be required to panel over the centre exit doors.

Adjustments were made to bus services A and B from 2 January 1979. Although the drivers were experienced in knowing when and where to wait on the single-track roads in expectation of a red bus roof approaching from the opposite direction, service A was diverted after Chazey Heath to operate via Cane End, Deadman's Lane and Long Toll to Woodcote, along a variant of the temporary route used during the 1972 boycott of the

The only 1977 purchase was a 1964 second hand AEC Reliance coach with 41-seat Plaxton Panorama body, which came from Lilley, Basingstoke, in May. As can be seen, parked in the yard opposite the depot, ANL 807B was a nice, tidy addition to the fleet, which remained in stock until the early 1990s. *(John Whitehead Colln)*

Something of a departure from established practice was GMC 747J, a Mercedes-Benz 0302 with Mercedes 45-seat body, new in 1971 to World Wide Travel, London SE5, which joined the Chiltern Queens fleet in May 1978 and survived ten years. *(R Gordon)*

Two more state-of-the-art Leyland Leopard coaches, fitted with 53-seat Plaxton Supreme Express IV bodies, arrived in spring 1979 – but they were put into what amounted to long-term storage. The first, UUD 623T, did not go on the road until July 1981. It is seen here in the depot yard. The second, left un-registered, eventually went into service in May 1982, when it became PJH 582X. *(John Whitehead Colln)*

B4526. Buses were then no longer required to meet on narrow sections of road and service A no longer passed through Trench Green or Goring Heath.

Back in 1963, the Reading Transport Society had been permitted to temporarily store next to the depot at Woodcote for a few months, a former South Shields Karrier trolleybus (no. 204), dating from 1936. Etienne Barrett was a Vice-President of the society during its formative years. The successor, British Trolleybus Society, purchased and then repatriated in 1979 from Santander in Spain, former London Transport Q1-type trolleybus no. 1812. On its arrival in the UK, it too took up temporary residence at Woodcote until it could be moved elsewhere.

De-Regulated 'Eighties

After nearly 50 years of protective (but stifling of much experimental innovation) road service licensing, the next decade was the one that allowed far greater freedom for bus and coach operators to control their own destiny in terms of bus services, tours and excursions offered. A phased abolition was enacted of quantity controls, fare regulation and fear of objection from competitors, through new legislation promoted by Margaret Thatcher's Conservative government. Initially, whilst coaching activities enjoyed a boost, the bus sector was still to have lean times, especially in rural areas. Demonstration of this was shown on 31 March 1980 when Chiltern Queens applied a 20 per cent fare increase.

The Transport Act 1980 removed the need for a Road Service Licence for longer-distance express services, tours and excursions. By then, Chiltern Queens' activities with the latter were much reduced as leisure travel habits changed, but licences for popular excursions, allowing picking up in most of the local villages, were held until they lapsed in the early 1980s, being no longer required. However, new day trips or holiday tours could more easily be promoted without the traditional mountain of paperwork, lawyers, solicitors and the tedious process of fighting one's objectors in the Traffic Court. For stage carriage services, the burden of proof was removed, inasmuch as applications for new, amended or cancelled services were normally granted automatically. A potential objector had to prove that the proposals were against the public interest, rather than the applicant having to prove that they were in the public interest, as had been the case since 1931.

One of the company's founders, John Woodrow, passed away on 8 December 1980, leaving control in the hands of Etienne Barrett. Woodrow is remembered as a man of few words, who in past years would arrive at the depot unannounced on a Sunday morning, in his Bentley (or contrasting Morris Minor), keenly observing and taking in everything, but saying little to any staff who happened to be there. His obituary in the *Reading Chronicle* states that he and his wife moved to Reading in 1933 and that as well as political interests, at various times he had been a member of the Grand Council of the Federation of British Industry, Chairman of Thames Valley Water Board, President of Reading Chamber of Trade and Deputy Lieutenant of Berkshire. He had received the CBE in 1970 and was made a Freeman of Reading the following year.

1980 was also the year when three more AEC Reliances were purchased to update the bus fleet. They carried a style of attractive bodywork originally designed for companies in the erstwhile British Electric Traction group. TYD 122G of 1969 had a 45-seat body by Willowbrook and although acquired from Tillingbourne Bus Co of Gomshall in Surrey, it originated with the much-lamented Hutchings & Cornelius Services Ltd of South Petherton in Somerset and arrived still in their livery. In due course it received the former trolleybus seats from 478 FCG. It was followed by a pair of 36 foot Reliances from the nearby City of Oxford MS fleet, with Marshall 49-seat dual-purpose bodywork with coach-type seating – TJO 54/5K. Later, in 1987, these two vehicles were fitted with 53 bus seats which had originally been in London Transport Daimler Fleetline DMS-class double-deckers. Leaving the fleet were the two AEC Reliances bought new in 1958 – coach MUD 975, which was sold to a steam loco preservation group as living accommodation at the Barry locomotive scrap yard of Dai Woodham (no MOT, a couple of replacement part-worn tyres and a top-up of diesel included in the stated £200 purchase price) and bus NBW 407, which was later scrapped. Between January 1981 and August 1985, no vehicles whatsoever were acquired, perhaps indicative of the need for economy, but extensive refurbishment of the existing fleet continued.

Chiltern Queens experienced in 1981 an example of service development now made easier under the relaxed national legislation. Pangbourne Coaches Ltd applied for, and introduced, a bus service to Henley-on-Thames on Mondays to Saturdays. Starting at Pangbourne, it ran via Whitchurch, Whitchurch Hill, Crays Pond, Woodcote, Cane End, Gallowstree Common, Sonning Common, Peppard and Rotherfield Greys, although originally it was intended to also serve Checkendon and Stoke Row as well. On Thursdays it only ran from Pangbourne to Woodcote, in deference to Chiltern Queens' own service to Henley. Wednesday and Saturday evening journeys did not survive long. By 1983, it had been rationalised to two round trips at shopping times on Fridays only between Pangbourne and Henley, supplementing Chiltern Queens' own service 13 on Thursdays.

The last surviving journey on service B beyond Ewelme to Watlington and back was deleted from the timetable in February 1981. Leyland Leopard OJO 835M and driver David Lee had been involved in something that would see the bus on national television on 2 April 1981. Part of an episode of 'Sorry', starring the late Ronnie Corbett was filmed in Wallingford Market Place. Ronnie was seen running after the bus, banging on the side panels, in an unsuccessful attempt to stop it. Meanwhile, back in the real world, the last Dennis owned, ex-Kemp's CBW 864, was finally sold, fortunately for preservation.

In connection with adjustments to revenue support subsidy, Oxfordshire County Council conducted a review of bus services in the south of the county, with a number of revisions (mainly involving a reduction in service) introduced from 4 January 1982. The Long Wittenham to Didcot section of service C was withdrawn, with the Friday morning bus being diagrammed to run from Long Wittenham to Wallingford, then empty to Warborough, to run back into Wallingford. To return the shoppers home, it ran first to Long Wittenham and then empty

The first of three second hand AEC Reliance service buses to be purchased in 1980 was 45-seat Willowbrook-bodied **TYD 122G** of 1969. It came from Tillingbourne Bus Co, Gomshall, Surrey, although it was new to Hutchings & Cornelius Services Ltd, South Petherton, Somerset.
(John Whitehead Colln)

The other two 1980 service bus purchases, **TJO 54K** and **TJO 55K**, came from much closer to home – City of Oxford Motor Services. These 1971 AEC Reliance sisters had Marshall (of Cambridge) dual-purpose bodies, each fitted with 49 coach seats as in **TJO 55K** seen on 9 August 1986 – but in 1987 both were fitted as 53-seaters with ex-London Transport bus seats as seen in **TJO 54K**.
(Graham Geoghegan (TJO 54K); Merchant Navy Loco Preservation Society (TJO 55K))

back to Wallingford before proceeding to Warborough – a shadow of the service run in the mid nineteen-fifties. Further reductions were made to the main Reading services, which then only sustained somewhat skeletal timetables. On service A, certain journeys between Wallingford and Didcot were diverted via South Moreton and overall, there were only two journeys each way which traversed the whole route from Reading to Didcot. On service B, only one journey each way did the full distance from Ewelme to Reading. The most frequent section was between Wallingford and Ewelme, which retained four round trips. Service D retained two journeys each way. These changes together allowed the use of one less bus and driver.

The rest of 1982 was fairly uneventful, although there was yet another fare increase on 1 March and 478 FCG, one of the former Aldershot & District AEC/Park Royal vehicles, was withdrawn in October. To give a token shopping facility to Wallingford, one Friday journey on service A was diverted from 15 July 1983 between

Didcot and South Moreton to run in a loop to the south, through East Hagbourne, Blewbury, Aston Tirrold and Aston Upthorpe. This was in replacement of COMS service 320.

In October 1983, Etienne Barrett handed the role of overseeing the business to family members and also to Stan Woodrow's son. Mr Barrett then spent a period overseas in sunnier climes.

As with Kemp's, Chiltern Queens Road Service Licence arrangements had involved two different Traffic Areas divided by the River Thames – East Midland and South Eastern. However, in April 1984, Oxfordshire was transferred to the South Eastern area, with Chiltern Queens' Operator's Licence number, which had been allocated from April 1982 under the new operator licensing system, changing from PE80 to PK 1011. Subsequently, in June 1991, the counties of Oxfordshire and Berkshire (the latter now various Unitary Authorities) were made part of the Western Traffic Area and the Operator's Licence number changed again to PH 5972.

After virtually 30 years of the Chiltern Queens' coach fleet being dark Brunswick green and grey, it was decided it was time for a change. Many coach operators thought much the same and by the mid-1970s, in Britain it had become an era of 'go faster stripes' and other experimental ways of catching the eye with style and colour. In autumn 1984, Chiltern Queens went for horizontal stripes in dark Brunswick green, a peppermint green, and white, and a new style of lettering for the fleetname, too. Here, TUD 167G is in the 'new' depot with two signwriters at work. *(Kevin Lane – Graham Wise Colln)*

The end result of the new livery as worn by TUD 167G is seen here on a private hire to the Races. Other members of the Chiltern Queens coach fleet to be repainted similarly were AEC Reliances FPX 701H and ABW 777J, together with Mercedes-Benz GMC 747J. However, the new livery did not find particular favour and, in any case, the passage of time and new ideas brought about more change. Hence, something new was adopted before the green, peppermint and white scheme spread any further. *(PM Moth)*

51-seat Leyland/Plaxton coach DUD 753C, had been out of use for around four years. Despite being nineteen years old, it was made ready for the road again in 1984, as there was a requirement for a higher capacity vehicle on a school contract. A more up-to-date coach livery, featuring a striped layout of two shades of green, with white, first appeared on AEC Reliance TUD 167G in autumn 1984; shortly afterwards, AECs FPX 701H and ABW 777J and Mercedes GMC 747J also gained the new colours. A locally-based design agency in Woodcote had been commissioned to design a new livery, which featured the Chiltern Queens name in a large classical typeface and a large golden crown emblem. The new scheme was runner-up in a national livery competition organised by trade magazine *Commercial Motor*.

Apparently due to their frustration at the lack of investment in more modern vehicles, two long-serving Chiltern Queens employees, driver David Lee and workshop manager Ron Back, decided to strike out on their own and obtained an Operator's Licence in June 1984 for their new Davron Travel venture. They bought a German MAN SR280 coach, registered 3108 RU, which was originally kept at a site in Cholsey, but they later obtained parking at Bishops Yard in Greenmore, Woodcote as their Operating Centre, a short distance from the Chiltern Queens premises. A second coach was acquired in July 1986 – WTV 965S, a Leyland Leopard with Plaxton body. A cream and brown livery was adopted.

Service 13 (Woodcote-Henley) had survived largely unaltered since 1955, but from 10 April 1984 gained a Tuesday morning service, with one round trip from Gallowstree Common into Henley. From 11 June, service D suffered a reduction when all Saturday journeys were withdrawn. The afternoon journeys on Mondays to Fridays were retained, but in the morning only a feeder journey was provided from Checkendon to Woodcote, where a connection was made with service B to and from Reading. Aligning with school transport requirements, a new service E commenced on 4 September that year from Woodcote, Crays Pond, Goring, Streatley, Moulsford and Cholsey to Wallingford, where it connected with service A to/from Didcot Girls'

School. Initially, it was restricted to use only by scholars beyond Goring & Streatley station.

The deaths of two of the principal characters in this story occurred during 1985. The first was of Hiram Kemp, erstwhile proprietor of Kemp's Motor Services, who died on 17 January. In the first week of April, Chiltern Queens were mourning the passing of Etienne Barrett, just one month before the company's thirtieth anniversary. He was 85 and was noted as having been a 'colourful' character. In a short tribute in *Bus Fare*, a journal of the British Trolleybus Society, he was remembered as having a keen sense of thrift, as evidenced by the fact that buses and coaches were rebuilt or repaired until such time as they were run into the ground and only fit for scrap, as opposed to purchasing replacements, unless convinced by somebody that it was absolutely necessary. In the nineteen seventies it is said that he wanted to have the out-of-use LMO-registered AEC Reliance buses put back into service, but this had been vetoed by Ron Back and Tony Sears as being false economy, especially as they were fitted with vacuum brakes and somewhat underpowered engines.

The company then entered Probate, which was to be the case for the best part of nine years. To some degree this prevented further development and caused much uncertainty. It was particularly unfortunate as it coincided with the approaching challenges brought by the intention to deregulate the bus industry. It also meant that the company was unable to fully develop itself to take account of the changing needs and expectations of the coach travel market. Company direction and practices were about to alter and some felt that things would never be the same again, despite the best efforts of the staff led by Tony Sears.

Pangbourne Coaches Ltd ceased trading at the end of March 1985, with their vehicles being sold. Their two bus services and the subsidies for them passed to Chiltern Queens in the week commencing 1 April. One became service F, being a Tuesday shoppers service from Woodcote to Pangbourne via Crays Pond, Whitchurch Hill and Whitchurch, whilst the other was added to service 13, which was revised to operate from

Starting in summer 1985, some of Chiltern Queens' coaches were given ageless registrations in exchange for their originals, in an attempt to disguise the age of the vehicle.

Leyland Leopard UUD 623T became 591 STT, the original coach with this registration becoming JTF 825B before being sold. The 'new' 591 STT is seen here at Didcot Parkway station in a new award-winning Chiltern Queens coach livery to replace the dark Brunswick green and grey scheme which had been used for 30 years, the Brunswick green and peppermint stripe experimental livery having not found favour.
(Arnold Richardson)

AEC Reliance VBW 581 (alias 'Queen Mary') became AJH 241A in May 1986 and Leyland Leopard SFC 32P took 'old' number VBW 581, which, being a private hire vehicle, was repainted in the new coach livery. AJH 241A, however, was a 'contract hire' vehicle, so it stayed dark Brunswick green and grey.

(Graham Geoghegan ('new' VBW 581); John Whitehead Colln (AJH 241A))

Used mostly on its bus services, Davron Travel's third coach, a Ford R1114 with Duple Dominant 53-seat body, registered **WDH 324S**, was acquired in October 1986. *(Trevor Back)*

How times have changed! Chiltern Queens' service **G** (originally 13) went back to Kemp's days – or even Bill Jackman. By 24 June 1988, when this view of 474 FCG was taken in Henley Market Place, the route was being operated under contract to Oxfordshire County Council as a socially-necessary service on Thursdays and Fridays. The Mercedes-Benz minibus in the background is owned by Bee-Line and operating the Henley Town Services. *(Chris Spencer)*

FPX 701H, parked up near Highmoor on 18 November 1989, is seen here in the only colour photograph we have been able to find, which illustrates the experimental contract livery of Brunswick green and peppermint stripe into which **TUD 167G, FPX 701H, ABW 777J** and **GMC 747J** were repainted in autumn 1984. *(Chris Spencer)*

In July 1986 another coach was acquired by Davron Travel, being WTV 965S, a Duple-bodied Leyland Leopard. It is seen here at the Station Hill stand, in Reading, on the service to Woodcote. *(Kevin Lane)*

Checkendon to Henley on Thursdays and Fridays. From the same week, the timetable on service D became just one round trip to Reading on Monday-Thursday mornings and one evening peak journey from Reading on Monday-Friday.

It was becoming fashionable for some operators to disguise the true age of vehicles from possibly unsuspecting customers, by having them re-registered with ageless or cherished marks. Therefore, in summer 1985, the Mercedes coach GMC 747J became XBW 242, so the 'old' XBW 242 became AJH 163A. Leyland Leopard UUD 623T became 591 STT, a mark taken from an AEC Reliance coach just withdrawn.

When AEC/Duple coach BMK 344A had been withdrawn in June 1984, it was sold to the 63rd Reading Scout Group, which continued to keep it at the Chiltern Queens depot. Two months later, the Scouts took it on an eight hundred mile trip to the Lake District. However, on 27 April 1985 it was stolen by vandals, collided with a railway bridge at Goring and was then driven into the River Thames at Ferry Lane in South Stoke! Only the offside rear wheel remained on dry land. It was recovered the next day, during which the engine started, enabling it to back up Ferry Lane to be attached to Reading Garage's recovery truck.

Chiltern Queens did not, from new, buy Leyland's Tiger chassis, which eventually replaced the Leopard. Since the early nineteen seventies, the UK market had been buying Volvo products from Sweden and in August 1985 Chiltern Queens acquired a 1980 model Volvo B58 with Plaxton body (LUA 244V), which started a trend in terms of main choice of chassis manufacturer, until the demise of the company. This coach was also painted in the new coach livery of white with two green stripes.

The government published a White Paper entitled *Buses* in 1984, which paved the way for the eventual enactment of the Transport Act 1985, the architect of which was Minister Nicholas Ridley, within the 'privatisation' administration of Margaret Thatcher. She believed in the 'free market' and opportunities for entrepreneurs, neither of which aligned with the restrictive road service licensing regime in place since 1931, nor with the ownership of most of the UK bus industry being in state or municipal

control. One of the Act's key provisions, along with the break-up and sale of National Bus Co subsidiaries (like City of Oxford MS) to the private sector and the need for Councils like Reading to set up arms-length companies for their bus activities, was that bus services would no longer require a Road Service Licence. Objections from other operators and Traffic Court Hearings would be consigned to history. Instead, operators had to register their intention to start, change or cancel a service at least 42 days in advance of the planned implementation date. They could therefore control their own destiny in terms of services that could be run without local authority support. The term 'Stage Carriage Service' was replaced with 'Local Bus Service'. In spring 1986, operators had to register what they wished to run commercially from 26 October that year. Local authorities could then decide whether they wished to supplement them by securing 'socially-necessary' services, mainly through a competitive tendering process.

For Chiltern Queens, there was very little in terms of bus services that could be sustained without support of some kind, so the only intentions they registered with the Traffic Commissioner were to operate two journeys on Mondays to Fridays and one on Saturdays over service A between Reading, Woodcote, Goring and Wallingford, as well as one journey each way on school days over service E from Woodcote to Didcot Girls School via Wallingford. However, Lee & Back's Davron Travel took advantage of the new competitive freedom and registered a commercial service running every 90 minutes on weekdays from Checkendon to Reading via Woodcote, Crays Pond, Whitchurch Hill, Goring Heath, Cane End, Chazey Heath and Caversham. This was through the heart of Chiltern Queens territory and was a significant improvement on what was then being offered on service B and for Checkendon in terms of service D.

Meanwhile, life had to go on at Chiltern Queens. From the week commencing 1 April 1986, bus service changes were introduced. A Friday morning facility was provided over the route of service D, by the diversion of a service B journey on that day between Whitchurch Turn and Caversham via Cane End, Gallowstree Common, Kidmore End, Chalkhouse Green and Emmer

Green. The Friday journeys on service 13 were diverted to serve Harpsden, on the outskirts of Henley, whilst an opportunity for reaching the retail attractions of Oxford had been offered since November 1985 by service G on Wednesdays, from Woodcote, Goring, Brightwell, Long Wittenham and Clifton Hampden. A new Volvo B10M/Plaxton coach (C644 SJM) was delivered in May, whilst Leyland coach SFC 32P took the registration of AEC Reliance VBW 581, which had to become AJH 241A.

During the spring and summer, local authorities invited tenders to run the contracted bus services that were felt necessary to supplement those registered as commercial operations. In rural south Oxfordshire, the latter were not particularly prolific. However, Chiltern Queens were successful in winning contracts that preserved some of what they had been running and from 27 October 1986, most of their services were being funded by Oxfordshire County Council. Details (together with subsequent changes) are given in Appendix 2, but in summary the new situation was:

A: Wallingford-Goring-Woodcote-Reading (Monday-Saturday) – replaced in part by C

B: Withdrawn – replaced in part by A, C and Davron service

C: Long Wittenham/Warborough-Wallingford (Friday) – re-designated D

D: Withdrawn – replaced in parts by Davron service and Alder Valley 136

E: Woodcote-Goring-Cholsey-Wallingford-Didcot (Monday-Saturday peak hours) – re-designated B

F: Woodcote-Whitchurch-Pangbourne (Tuesday) – re-designated E

G: Woodcote-Goring-Long Wittenham-Oxford (Wednesday) – re-designated F

13: Checkendon-Woodcote-Peppard-Henley (Thursday/Friday) – re-designated G

C: new service: Ewelme-Wallingford-Brightwell-South Moreton-Didcot (Monday-Saturday) – replacing parts of A and B

Prior to this, the last application made by Chiltern Queens for a Road Service Licence under the old system, was to introduce in September 1986 a route contracted to St Joseph's School in Reading, for carrying students from the Shiplake and Henley area. Licences for services from various points to Cranford House School in Moulsford, on a similar basis, whereby the coach was hired as a whole, had been held since the 1970s.

Initially, Davron Travel used coaches on their new bus service, acquiring a third in October 1986 in the form of a 53-seat Ford R1114 with Duple Dominant body. That previous Chiltern Queens employees were competing for business alongside their former employer meant that relations were apparently variable, although two Chiltern Queens coaches (AJH 163A and DUD 753C) were loaned to Davron during times of need in 1988. However, initially, the Chiltern Queens staff was instructed not to assist Davron if a need arose. In June 1989 Davron took delivery of a more suitable bus in the form of F986 TTF, a new Mercedes 811D with Optare Star Rider 33-seat body.

From 3 December 1986, a Wednesday facility from Woodcote to the Calcot Savacentre supermarket in the western fringes of Reading was introduced. Free travel was offered on the Reading to Calcot section of route.

Between December 1986 and the end of the decade, seven vehicles were acquired by Chiltern Queens as detailed in Appendix 4; three Volvo/Plaxton coaches, a Leyland Leopard/Alexander bus, an AEC Reliance/Plaxton bus CYA 181J (also once owned by Hutchings & Cornelius) and a rather utilitarian AEC Reliance/Marshall 54-seat bus, which returned to 'civvy street' having previously been operated by the Royal Air Force. This vehicle, now registered BMO 891T, displayed notices internally giving instructions on how to convert the seating into stretchers, as it had been capable of being used as an ambulance when in military use. There was also RFC 10T, a Leyland Leopard with 49-seat Duple Dominant coach body, acquired in May 1989.

Evidently well pleased with their original **MAN** coach, Davron Travel bought a second **MAN SR280**, registered **B915 CMR**. *(Trevor Back)*

Davron Travel also bought a new Mercedes-Benz 811D midibus with 33-seat Optare Star Rider body in June 1989, registered **F986 TTF**, a far more suitable vehicle for working their bus services, seen here vying for space at the Chiltern Queens stand on Station Hill, Reading. *(AG Low)*

BMO 891T was what turned out to be the very last **AEC Reliance** to be bought by Chiltern Queens. It was fairly unusual in that it was an ex-military vehicle (RAF registration 48 AC 82) with Marshall 54-seat body constructed with double doors at the rear and quickly convertible as an ambulance. New in 1979, it joined the Chiltern Queens fleet in October 1988, was out-shopped in 'new' coach livery, operated mainly on school contract work and was withdrawn in May 1994. It is seen here at the depot on 12th September 1991.
(John Whitehead Colln)

After five years of no new or second hand rolling stock being acquired – and with first the demise of AEC and then Leyland Motors, thoughts had to turn to European chassis manufacturers. Volvo seemed to be the best option and after a 1980 Volvo B58 with 51-seat Plaxton body, registered LUA 244V (and seen here with driver Chris Lewington in charge), was obtained in August 1985, two Volvo B10M-61s, both with 53-seat Plaxton bodies, followed. C644 SJM was brand new in May 1986 and B911 SPR was second hand, ex-Excelsior, Bournemouth, in December 1986. While C644 SJM was finished in the new coach livery, B911 SPR (seen here with the Late Bill Wheeler in charge) was in an identical scheme but in two shades of blue with white and lettered Hiscock Tours. John Hiscock, now deceased, ran a tours, excursions and theatre booking agency at Cleeve, near Goring, a business which had followed on from the EG Page business of years before.
(Graham Geoghegan)

Leyland Leopard HCS 795N, with Alexander 53-seat body, new in 1975, came from Clydeside in November 1987. It was a somewhat unusual choice but was required to meet a need at the time and put in nearly 6½ years of service with Chiltern Queens before sale for continued use. It is seen here in the depot yard on 2 April 1991. (Chris Spencer)

A further new Volvo B10M-61 with Plaxton 48-seat body – and this time one fitted with a toilet – came in December 1987, registered E533 PRU.
(Graham Geoghegan)

In December 1988, a further Plaxton 53-seat Volvo B10M-61 joined the fleet. New in 1987, D262 HFX was another to come from Excelsior, Bournemouth. (Graham Geoghegan)

Two 1978 Duple Dominant 49-seat Leyland Leopards for use as service buses joined the fleet second hand from City of Oxford. RFC 10T arrived in May 1989 and RFC 12T in October 1990. This was the start of giving white roofs to service buses instead of red, to update their appearance. The two are seen here together in the depot yard on 12th September 1991.
(John Whitehead Colln)

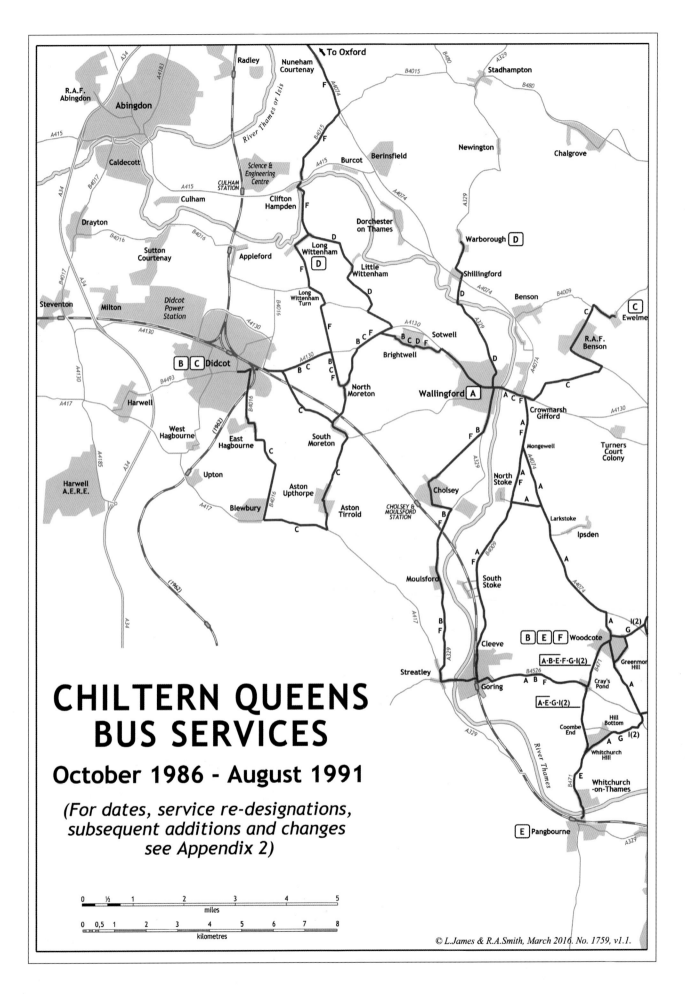

CHILTERN QUEENS
BUS SERVICES

October 1986 - August 1991

*(For dates, service re-designations,
subsequent additions and changes
see Appendix 2)*

© L.James & R.A.Smith, March 2016. No. 1759, v1.1.

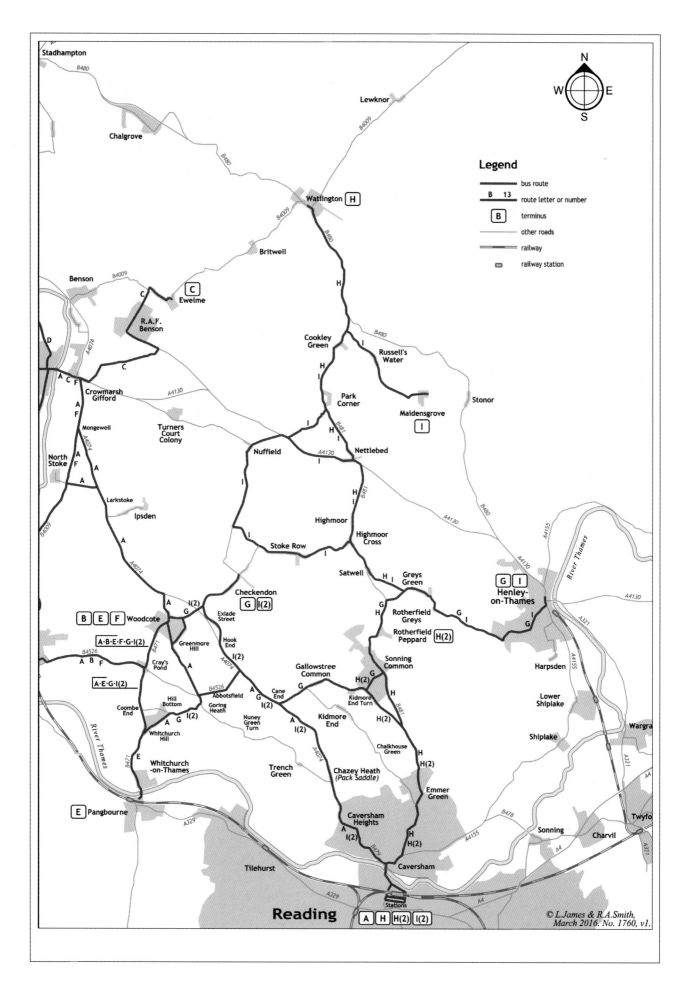

PJH 582X, the 1979 Leyland Leopard, with Plaxton 53-seat body, was stored until May 1982 before entering service in the 'old' livery. It is seen here having received the later coach livery and appears to be on the Henley College service 2225 ready to work the afternoon return trip to Stokenchurch via Marlow. *(Graham Geoghegan)*

This was suitable for use on one-man operated bus services, as its previous owner, City of Oxford MS, had done, being equipped with powered folding doors and apertures in the front roof dome for a destination blind. Six more similar coaches came from the same source at various times up to 1993. Smartly re-painted red and ivory, these attractive vehicles became a mainstay on the bus services and some school contracts. The last AEC Reliances (as mentioned above) were purchased in 1988, but their days were numbered for the type in general, as Leyland products became the new standard for Chiltern Queens vehicles on bus service work.

Volvo coach B911 SPR, purchased in December 1986, had a dual blue and white livery with appropriate lettering in connection with work for Hiscock Tours, remaining thus until late 1995. Chiltern Queens did not promote its own coach holiday programme but worked with travel firms such as Hiscock Travel, run by John Hiscock, based in Goring-on-Thames. Interestingly, the origins of that firm had been with the excursions and tours activity of Ted Page, who as recalled in Part 1, ran a bus service from South Stoke to Reading in the nineteen-twenties.

At the end of August 1987, the very old-established firm of House of Watlington ceased operations. They had run bus services thence to Reading, Wallingford, Thame and Henley. Oxfordshire County Council was faced with the task of finding replacement operators. Contracts for two services were secured by Chiltern Queens from 1 September 1987, who initially used

EUD 256K and TYD 122G. The services were Watlington to Reading via Nettlebed, Satwell, Rotherfield Peppard and Sonning Common on Mondays to Saturdays and Maidensgrove to Henley via Nettlebed or Nuffield and Stoke Row, on Tuesday, Thursday and Saturday. These were designated H and I respectively, but in July 1991 they passed in a modified form to Motts Travel of Stoke Mandeville, Buckinghamshire, numbered M1 and M36 respectively. Motts traded as Yellow Bus (confirmed by the bus livery used) and some journeys on the M1 actually ran to Reading all the way from Aylesbury, Princes Risborough, High Wycombe and Stokenchurch. Another service which had been operated by House was a Friday link between Ipsden and Wallingford which had replaced a former Chiltern Queens facility; this contract was awarded as service 214 to City of Oxford Motor Services. Although most of the House school contracts passed to Motts Travel, Chiltern Queens did gain some.

In 1988, two Chiltern Queens vehicles were entered in the AEC Society Rally at Southall – at that erstwhile manufacturer's premises. Appropriately, these were AEC Reliances 850 ABK and OBK 602H.

Davron Travel altered their service from 28 November 1988, when there was a small reduction in the number of journeys and whereby departures from Reading between 11.15am and 5.15pm followed the route to Checkendon via Goring Heath and Woodcote, but then returned to Cane End and Reading in a more direct way via Exlade Street.

More new ground was broken in October 1990 with the putting into service of this brand new Scania K93CRB coach fitted with Plaxton 55-seat body and registered H788 RWJ. It is seen here loading up with elderly ladies – with the pre-occupied driver, Pete Turner, not doing too much to help them aboard! Not thinking about the tip, then, Pete? *(Graham Geoghegan)*

New Direction 'Nineties

The final full decade of the Chiltern Queens business started with the arrival of a new coach with a chassis from another Swedish manufacturer of commercial vehicles – Scania. H788 RWJ was a Scania K93, with 55-seat Paramount bodywork by Plaxton, being delivered in October 1990.

At the start of the nineteen-nineties, the company's future ownership was still not resolved. Following the death of Etienne Barrett, there were issues over his estate; it took a considerable time to sort out matters surrounding Chiltern Queens. At one point following Barrett's passing, the firm, it has been suggested, had been offered for sale and expressions of interest were received. By the mid nineteen eighties, sons Colin and Mark Barrett had been appointed directors, along with Tony Sears, who became Managing Director; Etienne Barrett's widow, Daphne, was Company Secretary, whilst Kim Hadwell, his daughter, was appointed in October 1992, replacing Mark Barrett.

Following illness, a partner in the Davron Travel venture, David Lee, sadly passed away on 5 January 1991, leaving Ron Back to continue on his own for a short time. However, Davron coach B915 CMR, a MAN SR280 and F986 TTF, the Mercedes 811D/Optare bus, passed to Chiltern Queens on 1 July 1991, along with the bus service to Reading. The Mercedes was given

the Chiltern Queens coach livery but continued to be used on bus services. Ron Back subsequently obtained a new Operator's Licence in August 1991 and he and his son Trevor (a part-time driver for Chiltern Queens) converted a Mercedes 310 van into a 12-seat minibus (A986 ARD) and ran it for about three years under the name of R&T Travel.

The loss of the contracts for services H and I, once operated by House of Watlington, mentioned earlier, was balanced not only by the acquisition of the Davron service, which became the new service I, but by a new competitive commercial service from 29 July 1991. Thames Valley (later Alder Valley) service 7 had become service 137 in 1980, later passing to Alder Valley North Ltd when the Reading and Aldershot divisions of Alder Valley were split on 1 January 1986 ready for privatisation. When sold on 25 January 1987, Alder Valley North became The Berks Bucks Bus Co Ltd, trading as The Bee Line, but Council-owned Reading Buses acquired the Reading and Newbury-based services of The Bee Line on 16 August 1992. These included service 137 from Reading to Stoke Row via Caversham, Emmer Green, Sonning Common and Peppard, although the contracted evening and Sunday journeys were already part of Reading Buses service 54, operating across Reading from Calcot. The

With the cessation of Davron Travel's activities, their **MAN SR280** 53-seater, **B915 CMR**, joined the Chiltern Queens fleet in July 1991 and was quickly repainted into coach livery. It did not stay long as it was, evidently, not to Chiltern Queens' liking, being withdrawn in March 1993. It is seen here on 4 April 1992, by which time Chiltern Queens had been allocated a stand at stop SA immediately outside Reading Station instead of near the foot of Station Hill. *(Chris Spencer)*

Davron Travel's Optare-bodied Mercedes-Benz midibus **F986 TTF** also joined the Chiltern Queens fleet and, repainted into coach livery, it is seen on service bus duties at the new stand outside Reading Station. *(Laurie James Colln)*

When Davron Travel decided to cease operations, which it did on 30 June 1991, the foregoing two vehicles passed to Chiltern Queens. Ron Back and his son, Trevor, then converted a Mercedes-Benz 310 van into a 12-seat minibus registered **A986 ARD** and ran R & T Travel with it for around three years. *(Trevor Back)*

More Duple Dominant-bodied Leyland Leopard coaches second hand from City of Oxford, that could be used on both bus work and school contracts, were acquired during the early-to-mid 1990s. YFC 18V was a 1979 model which came in November 1991 and is seen here again posed at stop **SA** outside Reading Station. *(Graham Geoghegan)*

This smart 1988-vintage Alexander-bodied dual-purpose 29-seater Mercedes-Benz 811D midibus, registered F344 TSC, was collected from its previous owner on 5 March 1992 as a very suitable vehicle for town work almost immediately it became known that Chiltern Queens had been successful in tendering for the Henley Town Services. *(Chris Spencer)*

The next ex-City of Oxford Duple-bodied Leyland Leopard to join Chiltern Queens, again new in 1979, which came in November 1992, was **BBW 22V**. It is seen here loading in Wallingford Market Place on an afternoon journey to Ewelme, with long-term driver Michael Allen in charge. *(Graham Geoghegan)*

Another second hand Volvo B10M-61 – this time with Caetano 49-seat body (and with a toilet) and new in 1986, registered C114 PUJ, came in March 1993. (*Graham Geoghegan*)

This 1981 Leyland Leopard with Wadham Stringer Vanguard 54-seat body, registered PPJ 65W (formerly 50 AC 08) was another ex-military (RAF) coach, which joined the fleet in November 1993. Painted red and white for use on school contracts, it is seen here in the depot yard on 7 March 1998. (*RCW Smith*)

Reading-Stoke Row route was on the eastern edge of the Woodcote operators' core territory, although Kemp's had attempted to gain a foothold on it back in the nineteen-thirties. Thus, at their own initiative, Chiltern Queens introduced a new service H on weekdays between Reading and Rotherfield Peppard, with around seven journeys. An early morning journey to Reading and an evening peak period one back also served Stoke Row on Mondays to Fridays from 27 April 1992, when the service was re-designated J.

A feature of the post-deregulation UK bus industry was the extensive use of minibuses and smaller vehicles seating between sixteen and 29 passengers. Deployment ranged from high frequency town services with good overall patronage, to country routes where a small vehicle was quite sufficient for the traffic on offer. Minibuses were cheaper to buy than a large single-deck bus, were cheaper to maintain, could negotiate narrow roads such as in housing estates or in the countryside and in some cases the driver could be paid less. These factors contributed to reducing costs when commercial viability or keeping one's tender price as low as possible, were essential to survival. From 1992, smaller vehicles became a feature of Chiltern Queens bus services until the first years of the new millennium.

By this time, there was evidence locally of how much bus patronage had declined since the peak years of the late 1940s and early 1950s. The 1991 Woodcote Village Appraisal survey revealed that 95 per cent of households had access to their own motorised transport of some sort and of the commuters who responded to the survey, only 8 per cent used public bus services.

From the week commencing 27 April 1992, the contract for service G (previously 13) from Checkendon to Henley on Thursdays was lost to Horseman Coaches and numbered 57. However, Chiltern Queens decided to continue their service G on a commercial basis in competition, with a round trip to Henley on Thursday mornings from Sonning Common (Grove Road/Peppard Road), Peppard and Rotherfield Greys. Horseman also won the contract on re-tender for Chiltern Queens service E from Woodcote to Pangbourne on Tuesdays and numbered it 58. Horseman are a large coach operator based in Reading concentrating mainly on schools services, tours and private hire; they reappear later as a key player, towards the end of this story. The aforementioned service losses were balanced by Chiltern Queens taking over Henley town services H1-3/5 under contract to Oxfordshire County Council, also from 27 April, replacing operation by The Bee Line. A

TSV 804 was another second hand Volvo B10M-61, this time with Jonckheere 48-seat bodywork. It dated from 1986 (having been originally registered C28 GNK), and joined Chiltern Queens in September 1994. *(Graham Geoghegan)*

D34 ENH was yet another second hand Volvo B10M-61, which was acquired in September 1994. Dating from 1987, this one had a Duple 55-seat body.
(Graham Geoghegan)

Mercedes Benz 811D bus with 29 seats (F344 TSC) had been acquired to use on them on 5 March 1992.

In due course, Daphne Barrett was appointed a director, although she had little direct involvement in company affairs. There were also some personnel changes to record. Adam Harris was appointed as General Manager, to assist Tony Sears, who then acted in an advisory capacity although retaining his directorship. The trade press noted that Adam originally worked in engineering and advertising, before joining his father-in-law's Harries Coaches business at Stourport-on-Severn, Worcestershire. He originally came to Woodcote as Operations Manager in 1987. Andy Fisher was Traffic Manager, whilst Michael Bedwell had been Fleet Engineer, in charge of workshop activities since Ron Back departed in 1984. Colin Barrett resigned as a director in March 1993, leaving that role to Tony Sears, Daphne Barrett and Kim Hadwell.

AEC Reliance coaches FPX 701H and ABW 777J were chiefly used for school contract work by 1993, hence they were repainted into red and cream bus livery and were later joined by TUD 167G. As well as a further two former City of Oxford MS Leyland Leopards, 1993 saw the arrival of another former Royal Air Force bus, a 1981 Leyland Leopard with high capacity bodywork by Wadham Stringer of Waterlooville (PPJ 65W), whose products were quite common for buses and coaches used by the Forces. The following year, two pre-owned Volvo B10M coaches were taken into stock – TSV 804 had Jonckheere (Belgian) bodywork, whilst D34 ENH had an uncommon Duple 340 body.

Service A lost its off-peak journeys to Reading from 5 July 1993, although those from Woodcote to Wallingford were retained. However, these were to see further reduction in 1996. A little ground was re-gained from November 1994 when Friday service D was enlarged to take in Stadhampton and Newington once again.

Chiltern Queens celebrated its fortieth anniversary in 1995. Graham Stone and John Whitehead wrote a booklet entitled *Chiltern Queens – 40 Years of Service*, which was published by the company and a small bus rally, organised by Andy Fisher, was held at the depot on 24 September

It was in 1991 that certain of the older coaches in the fleet, which were being used mainly on school contracts, were repainted out of coach livery into red and white, with the Chiltern Queens fleetname only at the rear behind glass. AEC Reliances FPX 701H, ABW 777J and TUD 167G were repainted out of the Brunswick green and peppermint horizontal striped livery they had received back in 1984/85, while Leyland Leopard VBW 581 (formerly SFC 32P) had been in standard coach livery. FPX 701H, near the top of Alexandra Road, Reading, on the St Joseph's Convent School contract, retains its coach wheel trims. The others have lost theirs!
(All Graham Geoghegan except Chris Spencer (VBW 581))

The 1996 intake comprised just two vehicles, 2969 HJ and EBW 107Y, a twin to EBW 106Y already in stock.

(*Far left*) In December 1995, EBW 106Y, an ex-City of Oxford 1983 Leyland Tiger TRCTL11/3R fitted with a Duple 51-seat body, joined the Chiltern Queens fleet, mainly for use as a service bus.
(*Left*) 2969 HJ (previously registered EBM 443T), which arrived in April, was a Plaxton 53-seater on a 1979 Leyland Leopard chassis, so it was already 17 years old when acquired. It joined the school contract fleet and is seen here at the depot on 21 January 1997.
(*Below*) EBW 107Y, which arrived in May and seen here on 31 January 1997, looks to be at the conclusion of a good, soapy wash. (*Chris Spencer all*)

1995. On that day, an hourly bus service was operated from Reading using EUD 256K and OJO 835M, whilst coach TUD 167G made a couple of trips to Wallingford for those wishing to visit the Cholsey & Wallingford Railway. A blackboard, with Kemp's name painted on it and once used by them to advertise day trips, was presented to the company after many years of use by a local public house as a scoreboard for pub games!

The Chiltern Queens business had changed since 1987, when the fleet stood at eighteen vehicles and bus services and school contracts accounted for 70 to 75 per cent of turnover. By 1995, coaching was accounting for at least 50 per cent and most new business came from Reading and beyond, including much group travel work to London, British resorts and the near Continent.

Contracts previously operated by Horseman Coaches were won from Buckinghamshire County Council for three services to Henley College from the Stokenchurch, High Wycombe and Beaconsfield areas, starting in September 1995, outside of Chiltern Queens' traditional territory. These were registered for use by the general public as well as students attending the college. They

were designated by their contract numbers – 2225/6/7, rather than the usual letter identifiers. The contract for three Didcot town services (D1, D2 and D3) was awarded from 31 October that year, having previously been operated by Tappins Coaches of Didcot. Only a year later, the contract was lost to Thames Transit Ltd, better known as Stagecoach Oxford.

Two nine-year-old 20-seat Mercedes L608D minibuses with Alexander bodywork (D504/6 NWG) were acquired in September 1995 after being in the fleet of Lincolnshire Road Car, with one to be allocated to the Didcot town services. These were followed three months later by EBW 106Y, a Leyland Tiger from City of Oxford MS with a Duple body similar to those on the Leopards acquired previously from that source. A matching twin, EBW 107Y, arrived in May 1996. However, one more Leyland Leopard was to appear – in April 1996 – a 1979 coach with Plaxton body from Manning of Challow. It came with 'dateless' registration 2969 HJ. In autumn 1995 a Neoplan 'executive' coach had been taken on demonstration, but needless to say, there was no question of being able to afford to buy one.

The two nine-year-old Mercedes-Benz L608Ds with Alexander 20-seat bodies obtained from Lincolnshire Road Car in September 1995 were sisters **D504 NWG** and **D506 NWG**, which were ideally suited to local authority contracted bus services such as those that were rural and those, such as town services in towns like Henley and Didcot, which required small vehicles to safely negotiate residential roads.

D504 NWG is in Henley Market Place, ready to depart on service **H1**. *(Graham Geoghegan)*

D506 NWG is here on layover, parked in Richfield Avenue, Reading, before heading to Reading Station to operate service **G** to Peppard via Sonning Common.
(Graham Geoghegan)

A view, towards the end of the Chiltern Queens era, of the original depot building that had been put up by Kemp's. The photograph was taken on 5 September 1997. *(RCW Smith)*

For a short time circa March 1998, Reading Mainline Routemaster buses had to journey out to Woodcote from Reading each evening to be re-fuelled from Chiltern Queens' pumps after the fuelling arrangements next to their own depot were terminated with the departure to new premises of the haulage contractor concerned. Here, Reading Mainline 29 (ALD 948B) (formerly London Transport RM1948) quenches its thirst. (RCW Smith)

From 5 July 1996, the western end of service D was withdrawn between Long Wittenham and Brightwell. Subsequently, the Wallingford-Brightwell section was abandoned.

John Wright replaced Adam Harris as General Manager in 1996. Like the Kemps, the Wright family had previously operated buses in a different part of the country, in this case around Wrexham in North Wales. John's grandfather, Edmund Wright from Penycae, had started running buses in 1924. In 1952, on his death, the business passed to his son, Charles Wright, who was later joined by Charles' son Michael, followed by the latter's brother, John, in the late nineteen-sixties. When Charles passed away in 1979, John became the proprietor of Wrights of Wrexham and expanded the bus operations from 1986 through to the end of 1993, when the firm closed.

In due course, John Wright again considered going into business on his own account, making a proposal in late summer 1997 to take over the bus operations of Chiltern Queens, apparently by leasing a number of vehicles which would be operated under the Chiltern Queens bus service registrations. For various reasons this did not reach fruition, perhaps providing a catalyst for what was to occur in 1998.

Commercial service E from Stoke Row and Peppard Common into Reading was withdrawn on 30 August 1997.

From 13 October 1997, Chiltern Queens picked up a small package of tendered services in the Didcot area, replacing Bennett's Coaches of Chieveley. These were service 3 into the town from Harwell, Chilton and Blewbury and services D4 and D5 around Didcot town; all of these ran each weekday except Wednesday.

In the same month, Leyland Leopard RFC 12T was loaned to the Greater Reading Omnibus Co (which traded as Reading Mainline) for two months for use as a driver training vehicle. Greater Reading was owned by Michael Russell and operated several commercial services in the town from July 1994 with a fleet of iconic former London Transport AEC Routemaster buses, in competition with Reading Buses, which eventually purchased the firm in 1998. For a few weeks in the last year of ownership by Russell, fuel was purchased from Chiltern Queens, resulting in red Routemasters being seen in Long Toll!

In 1998, John Wright departed in order to establish Thames Travel – a name that would in a short space of time transform the bus-operating landscape in the south of Oxfordshire, but also reaching out to Oxford itself and much later, some of the adjoining Berkshire unitary authority areas. Wright may well have realised that there would be potential for a new player in the area and that there was some opportunity for innovation. He had been working on a scheme, with Rural Development Commission funding support and proposed a new hub-and-spoke network of services centred on Wallingford, with hourly links to Didcot, Ewelme, Goring, Woodcote and Reading as well as a service for the Wilding Road area of Wallingford.

County Council contracted service changes took effect on 12 April 1998. Chiltern Queens were unsuccessful in retaining a number of bus operations, losing out to Thames Travel, which established a base near Goring station which was soon moved to premises at Lester Way on the Hithercroft Industrial Estate in Wallingford. To launch operations, Wright acquired three Mercedes 0814D Varios, with Plaxton Beaver bodywork, as well as a Dodge S56 as back-up. The various Chiltern Queens services lost were:

3	Harwell-Didcot: to Thames Travel
13	operated Monday-Saturday, with a Wednesday journey continuing as X13 to Oxford via Long Wittenham, Clifton Hampden and Nuneham Courtenay
D4/D5	Didcot town services: to Thames Travel

Much of Chiltern Queens' 'bread-and-butter'work involved school contracts. The depot yard could be full of coaches for the middle of the day during a term time weekday, with a mass exodus after lunch. These three views (*RCW Smith*) were taken on 5 September 1997, at the start of the 1997/98 academic year.

PJH 582X shows '2225 Henley College' on its destination blind but this seems to be at variance with the computer-generated '2803' notice in the windscreen – although we are unsure where that went to!

All waiting for 'the off'!

PJH 582X nudges out of the yard.

D4/D5	operated Monday, Tuesday, Thursday, Friday and Saturday
A	Woodcote-Wallingford via Goring or Ipsden (off peak journeys) and
C	Didcot-Wallingford-Ewelme: to Thames Travel 130-133

Thames Travel also gained the contract for Sunday service X47 from Stagecoach Oxford, from Reading to Wantage via Pangbourne, Streatley, Goring Station, Aldworth, the Ilsleys and Farnborough.

New Thames Travel service 130 ran from Didcot to Wallingford via the Moretons and Brightwell, hourly, Mondays to Saturdays; 131 East Hagbourne to Wallingford via Blewbury and the Moretons (Friday); 132 Woodcote to Watlington via Crays Pond, Goring, the Stokes, Crowmarsh, Wallingford, Crowmarsh, Benson and Ewelme, Mondays to Saturdays, every one-two hours between Goring and Ewelme with three journeys extending to Woodcote and two to Watlington and 133 Ipsden-Crowmarsh-Wallingford (Friday). As well as the support from Oxfordshire County Council, funding also came from the Rural Development Commission and Thames Trains. It will be noted that the new network offered a considerable enhancement to what had been run by Chiltern Queens for many years. From 1 June 1998, a novel through ticketing arrangement was introduced, whereby a London Travelcard could be purchased from drivers on services 130 and 132, for onward travel from Goring station, where buses connected with trains.

Tony Sears notified his intention in May 1998 that he wished to retire after serving Chiltern Queens for around 42 years. His formal resignation as a director was recorded as 31 August 1998, together with that of Kim Hadwell. Tony had been living at the former Kemp residence – Greenmore – for many years and after his retirement, the property was sold. Cliff Hillman, Mrs Barrett's advisor, was appointed a director. Prior to Tony Sears' departure, he had been approached by the principal of a firm from Reading involved in Heavy Goods Vehicle driver training. This firm suggested that they could offer a contracted management service for Chiltern Queens. Despite the cost of such an arrangement, their services were commissioned. Up to that point, they had no previous experience with buses and coaches, so in due course Martin Steele, who had previously worked in the bus industry in another part of the country, was appointed as manager at Woodcote.

Chiltern Queens had withdrawn Wednesday shoppers service (F) from Woodcote to Oxford on 26 February 1996, but subsequently re-introduced it as an 'excursion' on the first Wednesday in the month, once again fitting around school contract commitments.

With money tight, some economy was needed in terms of fleet replacement and in September 1998, two 1990 Mercedes 811 26-seat buses with Alexander bodywork were purchased after use by City of Oxford MS, although they had started life in London. A third

arrived in January 1999. Also in September 1998, six coaches were re-registered with 'dateless' marks with a PIL prefix, whilst the three recently-acquired Mercedes buses were given marks prefixed XJI. From then on, some vehicle acquisitions were sourced through leasing companies, rather than being purchased outright. Another cosmetic decision taken by the new management was to brand and market the bus services as Chiltern Buses, with the first vehicles into a revised livery of red and white (rather than red and cream/ivory) being the recently-acquired Mercedes 811s and also Leyland Leopard BBW 22V.

A new contract was obtained from 12 January 1999 to operate a service designated C from Whitchurch Hill Bottom to Henley via Crays Pond, Woodcote, Checkendon, Stoke Row, Peppard and Sonning Common and Harpsden, with seven Monday-Friday journeys and five on Saturdays. It is suggested that the contract was originally awarded to Thames Travel but apparently they had insufficient drivers available. This made up for some of the ground lost previously and was another example of a country route running more frequently than it had for many years, being funded by the government's new Rural Bus Grant. It was initially run with two of the Mercedes 811s. Ten months later, commercial service G (Sonning Common-Henley) was replaced by a supported service G, with two weekday journeys running from Pangbourne to Henley, along much the same route as service C but operating into Henley via Rotherfield Greys instead of Harpsden.

A late evening journey at 22.15hrs from Reading back to Woodcote was introduced on 4 August 1999 – something that had not been provided for a considerable time. Stagecoach Oxford withdrew their service X39 (Oxford-Henley-Maidenhead-Heathrow Airport) due to staff shortage from 21 August 1999, with a replacement provided by Thames Travel from Oxford to Henley and by Courtney Coaches 139 between Henley and Maidenhead. Chiltern Queens gained a contract for service 39 between Wallingford, Dorchester-on-Thames, Clifton Hampden, Culham and Abingdon, again replacing Stagecoach Oxford facilities. Also gained by Chiltern Queens from Stagecoach Oxford, were Wednesday and Friday shoppers services 17A/17B/17C in the Cowley area of Oxford's south eastern suburbs. In geographic terms a fair distance from Woodcote, it was probably important to win whatever contracts might come the company's way. Summer 1999 also brought two new coaches on lease, being T10/20 DMB, Volvo B10Ms with Berkhof bodies.

September 1998 – Six coaches were given ageless registrations instead of their originals – and all of them were Volvo B10M-61s.

PIL 6578 was C644 SJM, a 1986 model. See this book's outside back cover – the coach still has its poppy on the front grille!
(Graham Geoghegan)

PIL 6579 was formerly D212 HFX, a 1987 model, enjoying a bath with lots of suds!
(Graham Geoghegan)

PIL 6580, formerly D34 ENH, another 1987 model, is seen here in Oxford city centre. *(Graham Geoghegan)*
The others were PIL 6576 (formerly B911 SPR); PIL 6577 (formerly C114 PUJ) and PIL 6581 (formerly E533 PRU).

PIL 6583 was another re-registration with an ageless number, this time **H788 RWJ**, which was the 1990 Scania K93CRB. This seems to have been carried out a year or so after the Volvos. Note that meanwhile someone else had **PIL 6582!!** Or was Volvo TSV 804 planned to have this number? *(Graham Geoghegan)*

Three 1990 Mercedes-Benz 811Ds with Alexander 26-seat bodies were obtained from City of Oxford, two of them, G108 PGT and G118 PGT in September 1998, and G109 PGT, in January 1999. The first two were quickly re-registered with ageless registrations **XJI 4132** and **XJI 4133** respectively, possibly before but otherwise just after entering service. G109 PGT is seen here at Reading Station. Note also the Chiltern Buses fleetname, which was also adopted around the beginning of 1999.
(Graham Geoghegan)

The photograph of **G109 PGT** (above) is rare, because the vehicle was, very soon after entering service, re-registered as **XJI 7908**, and is seen here at the same location. *(Graham Geoghegan)*

White roofs were soon adopted either on full or partial repaints. **OJO 835M** (by now referred to as 'O-Joe') appears to have received a full repaint with new fleetname transfers – but not the white **Chiltern Buses** transfers as used on the midibuses. *(Graham Geoghegan)*

And so to the 'Terrible Twins', **T10 DMB** and **T20 DMB**, Volvo B10M-62s with Berkhof 51-seat bodies (and toilets) new in July 1999. They were leased, not bought, which helps to explain the 'new image'. Leased coaches are usually supplied in 'dealer white' and an extremely attractive set of vinyl decals was applied to each vehicle, which did everything which needed to be said in marketing the coaching side of the Chiltern Queens business. For some reason, which is mentioned in the text, these two coaches seemed to be jinxed! *(Graham Geoghegan (T10 DMB); and Fair Track Ventures (T20 DMB))*

WUD 815T was another ex-City of Oxford Leyland Leopard, with Duple 49-seat body. New in 1979, it also joined the Chiltern Queens fleet in October 1990. Here, it is Watlington-bound passing through Caversham on 11th May 1991, replacing the long-established and much lamented Houses of Watlington service, which had dated back to 1912.
(Chris Spencer)

Chiltern Queens, having taken over Houses of Watlington's service to Reading, here is OJO 835M on layover in Watlington, ready to take the 13.15 departure back to Reading on 13th July 1991. *(Chris Spencer)*

A pleasant view of HCS 795N coming off Wallingford Bridge into The Street, Crowmarsh, on 20 August 1991.
(John Whitehead Colln)

This 1981 Duple-bodied Leyland Leopard, MUD 25W, was next to come from City of Oxford, in May 1993. *(Graham Geoghegan)*

And yet another one! BBW 20V was a sister to already purchased BBW 22V and came in 1993. This view is somewhat later, because the renaming of the bus services as Chiltern Buses did not take place until 1998. *(Graham Geoghegan)*

This Wright-bodied 40-seat low-floor Volvo B6BLE demonstrator, V493 NOH, was borrowed in January 2000 – and on other occasions in 2000 and 2001. Here, it is on the stand outside Reading Station in July 2001. *(Graham Geoghegan)*

Into a new era – which wasn't to last: This low-floor Volvo B6BLE with East Lancs 31-seat body, W992 BDP, was Chiltern Queens' first new service bus since 1974. As can be seen, it also came in a new livery and had an electronic destination display instead of roller blinds, this view showing it on Henley Town Service – before the livery was further enhanced!
(Graham Geoghegan)

At the end of 2000, two more Volvo B10M-62 coaches with Berkhof 51-seat bodies (and fitted with toilets) S228 KJT and S484 KJT were leased, although new in 1998 and with another operator. Their 'dealer white' livery was enhanced with the same stylish application of vinyl decals as introduced 18 months previously on T10 DMB and T20 DMB. *(John Whitehead Colln))*

Finale 2000 – 2002

The dawn of the New Millennium was, sadly, not to usher in a new era of prosperity and longevity for Chiltern Queens, although the company could claim to have operated over two centuries. The first service change came on 7 April 2000, when the school day service B from Woodcote to Didcot via Wallingford was withdrawn. This was followed by the ending of short-lived service 39 from Wallingford to Abingdon on 23 June that year.

On a brighter note, Chiltern Queens caught up with much of the rest of the bus industry when it introduced its first wheelchair-accessible low-floor vehicle. W992 BDP was a Volvo B6BLE with East Lancs 34-seat body which arrived in August 2000. It was the first brand new bus acquired, since the arrival of OJO 835M in 1974. The new Volvo came in a startling purple livery – not at all 'traditional Chiltern Queens' – being embellished with red, yellow, blue and green 'paint splashes', branding for Chiltern Buses and 'Low Floor Easy Access'. It had an electronic destination display rather than a roller blind. Immediately prior to its arrival, a similar Volvo B6BLE had been borrowed from the manufacturer, but carrying a body by Wright of Ballymena, Ireland.

Volvo coach T20 DMB was involved in a collision on the M6 Motorway on 20 November 2000, when returning with the Bracknell Bees Ice Hockey team from an away match at Ayr, resulting in some injuries.

At the end of the year 2000, two 1998 Volvo B10M/ Berkhof coaches (S228/484 KJT) were leased for Gullivers Tours work, in exchange for Volvo B10Ms E533 PRU and C114 PUJ. Volvo T20 DMB, seemingly jinxed, came to grief in France on 25 February 2001, when it overturned in icy road conditions whilst undertaking a private trip for a school near Godalming in Surrey. The accident happened near Metz, in France, whilst the party was returning from a skiing trip in the Austrian Tyrol. Three students, a teacher and both drivers were hospitalised. The coach was returned to the UK and repaired for further use. On 1 June 2001, another Chiltern Queens coach had experienced difficulties, again in France, when carrying a school party. The accompanying teachers considered that the drivers were too tired to continue and decided to offload their group of students at what was described as a closed service station south of Paris. It was reported that a replacement coach did not arrive for a further 24 hours.

Two more new Volvo B6BLE/East Lancs buses (Y313/877 KDP) arrived in March 2001, one of which was acquired with the aid of a capital grant of £24,000 from Oxfordshire County Council, in return for an agreement to use it on services C and G from Pangbourne to Henley, or an equivalent contracted service, for five years. Several vehicles left the fleet during 2001 (see Appendix 4), including the two former City of Oxford Leyland Tigers which were sold to Tourex of Oxford, thus returning to their original home ground. Two more Volvo B10Ms (M332 GFW and N498 PYS)

were taken on lease in summer 2001, followed in November by the leasing of what turned out to be the last arrival at Woodcote. This was KP51 SXU, a low-floor Dennis Dart SLF with Plaxton Mini Pointer 29-seat bodywork. The Dennis Dart was by then quite ubiquitous and numerous in UK bus fleets and is probably one of the most successful types in modern times.

The use of historic service designation A ceased on 2 April 2001, when the peak hour journeys between Woodcote and Wallingford became part of service I. A contract for a new local service in the Cowley area of Oxford – service 17 on Wednesdays and Fridays – started on 18 April and ran until 19 October. Also acquired (from White's Coaches of Berinsfield) was service 136 on 2 July from Nuffield to Reading on Mondays to Saturdays via Stoke Row, Peppard, Sonning Common and Emmer Green, followed on 5 August by transfer from Stagecoach Oxford of evening and Sunday Oxford city services 10C/10D out to Wood Farm and Cowley. The latter passed in February 2002 to City Of Oxford MS. The final contract gain was of Didcot local services D1-D3 from Thames Travel on 10 December 2001. Perhaps by way of a final fling, service I was enhanced from 19 November involving the use of the aforementioned Dennis Dart. An hourly service was offered from Reading, through Woodcote, as far as Cholsey and then every two hours onward to Wallingford.

Information received by the Vehicle Inspectorate from their French counterparts after the incidents already described, prompted a full investigation into alleged drivers' hours offences and tachograph irregularities. Apparently, coach drivers had not been taking their proper rest periods, leading to concerns about fatigue whilst driving. Evidence suggested that the law had been broken and the case was prosecuted, resulting in certain persons receiving fines.

It became more apparent in the early months of 2002 that Chiltern Queens was in rather poor shape, both in terms of financial liquidity and effective management. For various reasons, money was in short supply and losses had been allowed to accumulate. A number of staff members had left and agency drivers had been hired. Following some vehicle disposals, the fleet contained thirteen coaches and seven buses at mid-April 2002. A Dennis Dart SLF (P830 BUD) had been taken on short term lease to cover a deficiency whilst Volvo W992 BDP was being repaired after sustaining heavy front-end accident damage on 2 March. Escalating losses brought matters to a head and the company was on the point of ceasing to trade after the bank had put the firm into Administration in late March, with significant reported debts. An offer of involvement was received from Keith Horseman of Horseman Coaches Ltd, which was accepted. He obtained control of affairs with the intention of turning things around and stemming losses. The original intention, it was stated, was to keep the Chiltern Queens name for two years, but later events prompted a change of course in that respect.

W992 BDP was soon given this startling enhancement to its already eye-catching purple livery – certainly not exactly what one might expect to see trundling through the southern Chilterns – an area acclaimed as being one of outstanding natural beauty. Two more identical Volvo **B6BLEs** followed in March 2001, registered **Y313 KDP** and **Y877 KDP**.
(Philip Smith)

V246 BNV was a Plaxton-bodied 29-seat Dennis Dart SLF, hired short-term from Dawson Rentals in November 2001 and seen here in the lay-by at the top of Station Hill, Reading, just short of the usual stand outside the station, on 10 November. *(Graham Geoghegan)*

Presumably, the loan of **V246 BNV** was in anticipation of the imminent delivery of Chiltern Queens' own identical vehicle, which arrived later in the month as **KP51 SXU** – another purple 'vision'! It turned out to be the very last vehicle to be obtained by the undertaking – and it was leased rather than bought.
(Graham Geoghegan)

On 12 April 2002, the directors resigned and were replaced by Keith Horseman and other members of his family. Within a week coaching work was integrated with that of Horseman Coaches and transferred to their Reading base, whilst the bus services continued in the short term from the Woodcote premises. The number of vehicles authorised on the Chiltern Queens Operator's Licence was reduced from 25 to thirteen, three older vehicles were sold to Tourex of Oxford and two Volvo B10M coaches were returned to the leasing company.

However, Chiltern Queens had already been called to Public Inquiry before the Western Area Traffic Commissioner on 30 May, following the previous drivers' working time offences that had put doubt over the company's good repute as an operator. Keith Horseman attended and stated he had been trying to buy Chiltern Queens for five years. He was quoted in the trade press as saying, "Why she (Daphne Barrett) was not advised to sell years ago is beyond me. I was not aware that the company was due to come before a Public Inquiry". He said that when he took control it was apparent, "that the company was in a chaotic state".

The Traffic Commissioner revoked the Chiltern Queens Ltd Operator's Licence, but postponed implementation until 30 September 2002. He said he had no other option as the company had lost its reputation and suggested that if desired, any remaining vehicles should be moved onto the Horseman Coaches Ltd licence. His concern and his professional view was that the Chiltern Queens name was tarnished and its repute had gone. He urged Horseman to abandon the Chiltern Queens name as soon as possible, which prompted a change from the original planned course whereby Woodcote would become the base for Horseman's south Oxfordshire contracts and with the bus services to continue.

The contract for services 17A/B/C in Oxford passed to Heyfordian Travel on 5 July, whilst Oxfordshire County Council was given notice that Chiltern Queens would surrender their remaining bus service contracts from 7 September. They, therefore, invited new tenders. The accelerated outcome was that Didcot town services D1-D3 reverted to Thames Travel from 27 July whilst services C/G (Pangbourne-Henley), D (Stadhampton-Wallingford), H1/2/3 (Henley town services) and 136 (Nuffield-Reading) passed to Thames Travel from 2 August. The lettered services became 145/146, TB103 and 151/152/153 respectively. Thames Travel also took over the three Chiltern Queens Volvo B6BLE low-floor buses.

The remaining bus service (commercial service I) lost its Woodcote to Wallingford section of route from 12 August, when operation of it using Dennis Dart KP51 SXU transferred to the Horseman depot at Reading, leaving no activity at Woodcote. During August, three Volvo B10M coaches were sold to Tourex of Oxford – PIL 6576/8/9. Jack Passey, having officially retired in 1992, had continued to work part time and was involved in clearing-up activities at the depot, being effectively the last active employee of Chiltern Queens Ltd.

Mercedes-Benz midibus XJI 4133 found itself continuing to operate service 136 (Nuffield – Reading) (as seen here) during the wind-down period until the route was taken over by Thames Travel with effect from 3 August 2002. Note also the minor (but poignant) amendment of the fleet name. The bus also appears to have worked the remnants of service I during the wind-down, the Woodcote – Wallingford section being withdrawn from 12th August 2002, leaving just Reading – Woodcote in operation, this itself being taken over by Thames Travel running on the Chiltern Queens registration until finally withdrawn seven weeks later, on 28 September 2002. The very end of 73 years' service – Gone .. (Graham Geoghegan)

Operation of service I was also taken on by Thames Travel, from 9 September, but was still covered by the Chiltern Queens service registration. Finally, Thames Travel applied for new registrations to allow continued operation as services 140 and 142 from 1 October. The remaining Chiltern Queens coaches and Mercedes bus F344 TSC were transferred to Horseman, but most saw no further use. Dennis Dart KP51 SXU passed from Horseman to Thames Travel in November 2002.

However, Volvo B10Ms S484 KJT and T10/20 DMB remained a part of the Horseman fleet until November 2015.

Of sadness to bus enthusiasts, the staff and, of course, to the travelling public, some of whom had probably been loyal customers for many years, the friendly, respected, reliable, interesting and unique Chiltern Queens – a way of life for some – was gone. *Sic transit gloria mundi.*

After the separate sale of 'Greenmore', the Chiltern Queens depot and the parking area on the opposite side of Long Toll was sold for development with industrial units, but the actual former Kemp's garage/workshop building was more of a problem to satisfy South Oxfordshire District Council's Planning Department. *(Both John Whitehead Colln)*

Heras fencing separates the premises from the road, with the Kemp's garage/workshop, the abortive warehouse attempt beyond, and this end (extreme left) the stores building erected during the Kemp's era.

This clear view of the Kemp's garage/workshop, gives a good idea of its size and construction.

...and a final Chiltern Queens photographic tribute

RFC 12T in North Stoke, hareing back to Woodcote on a sunny 20 August 1991. *(John Whitehead)*

12th September 1991 on Peppard Common, with **WUD 815T**, Checkendon-bound, about to set off having dropped off the photographer while returning from Henley-on-Thames. *(John Whitehead)*

This is quite an interesting photograph! It shows 1976 Leyland Leopard **SFC 32P** in the depot yard next to 1962 AEC Reliance **VBW 581** on 2 September 1984. In May 1986, **SFC 32P** was re-registered with ageless or cherished mark **VBW 581** from the Reliance, which, in turn, was given **AJH 241A**. Two years later, in 1988, the latter was withdrawn and was sold in 1990. The Leopard was 'demoted' c1991 to contract work, and repainted into red livery. *(John Whitehead)*

New for the start of the 1965 coaching season and immediately following the 1965 British Coach Rally at Blackpool on 2 April, **DUD 753C**, the first Leyland Leopard to enter the fleet, was back at the seaside later the same month. *(John Whitehead)*

D34 ENH, a 1987 Volvo B10M-61, which carried an uncommon Duple 340 body with seating for 55 passengers, came second-hand in September 1994 from Country Lion, Northampton and is seen here at the depot on 23 February 1995 ready for the new coaching season. It passed to Horseman Coaches, Reading, on the collapse of Chiltern Queens in September 2002. (John Whitehead)

We recounted the disposal of 1963 AEC Reliance BMK 344A to the 63rd Reading Scout Troop in June 1984 having served Chiltern Queens since February 1970. It continued to live on Chiltern Queens premises, however – until it was stolen by vandals on 27 April 1985, who took it on a joy-ride culminating in it being driven into the River Thames at South Stoke. It is seen here parked up in the yard with service bus RCG 618, which had been withdrawn in June 1981. (John Whitehead)

OBK 602H was converted into a 28-seat 'Executive Coach' (with toilet) as early as 1978 for a perceived market which never really developed significantly, but it remained in stock until 1992. (John Whitehead)

149

Service Vehicles

This ex-military Chevrolet spent many years with Kemp's and Chiltern Queens fitted with home-built bodywork and originally with a crane. *(PM Moth)*

This tilt cab **AEC Mercury** (badged as a Leyland) succeeded the **Chevrolet. 917 BW** was Chiltern Queens' limited trade plate, which at the time allowed the wrecker to operate un-taxed. *(John Whitehead Colln)*

The latter-day Chiltern Queens service van was E263 VBW, seen here outside The Three Guineas pub at Reading Station. *(Graham Geoghegan)*

LPR 279H, which replaced the AEC, was a Guy Big J, which had spent some years beforehand as Reading Transport's wrecker. It subsequently passed into local preservation and is now incorporated in the Thames Valley & Great Western Omnibus Trust collection at Fifield, Berks. *(Keith Pauline)*

After Chiltern Queens

Ongoing development of bus services in the principal area once served by Chiltern Queens, are largely part of the story of John Wright's Thames Travel, which, no doubt, will be told fully by somebody else on a future occasion. However, a little selective summarising might be of interest.

Once Thames Travel's initial services had been introduced in April 1998, it became apparent that some of the less well-patronised journeys could be operated by a small minibus and were therefore branded as 'Taxibus'. Service TB30 ran between Wallingford and Watlington via Ewelme, whilst TB31 replaced part of service 132, running from Woodcote to Wallingford via Ipsden Turn and then on a circular route via Brightwell Baldwin, Cuxham, Chalgrove and Benson. Later, the Woodcote to Wallingford Taxibus journeys gained their own number – TB29, with this service being extended to Goring Station from Woodcote on 28 October 2002, being a belated replacement for part of erstwhile Chiltern Queens service A. By then, the Taxibus vehicles had been upgraded to a pair of 13-seat Mercedes Sprinter 411CDi minibuses.

A second operator's licence – in the name of Thames Travel (Wallingford) Ltd – came into use in May 2001, although it took several years before all operations were transferred from the entity of JE Wright trading as Thames Travel.

From 1 October 2002, Thames Travel commenced a replacement for Chiltern Queens service I. This ran from Reading to Woodcote via Chazey Heath, Cane End, Goring Heath and Crays Pond (numbered 142), returning to Reading via Checkendon, Exlade Street, Cane End and Chazey Heath (numbered 140). These arrangements proved transitional and when substantive contracts were awarded to Thames Travel by Oxfordshire County Council, the following occurred to former Chiltern Queens services from 10 February 2003:

D1/ D2/ D3:	Didcot town services re-organised and numbered 107/109
136:	Withdrawn – replaced by a diversion of Motts service M1 (Stokenchurch-Reading)
140:	Reading to Woodcote over route of service 142 (below), continuing to Henley as revised service 145 via Checkendon, Stoke Row, Sonning Common and Rotherfield Peppard, Mondays to Saturdays every two hours throughout
142:	Altered to run from Reading to Woodcote every two hours via Oxford Road, Pangbourne, Whitchurch and Crays Pond, with certain journeys to Goring Heath and Exlade Street
146:	Withdrawn and incorporated into new 145
149:	Woodcote to Reading via Crays Pond, Whitchurch Hill, Goring Heath, Cane End and Chazey Heath with one journey each way on Mondays to Fridays, replacing the original service 142
151-153:	Henley town services re-organised as services 151-154

The next upheaval came on 5 July 2004 when the contracts for services 145 and 151-4 passed to Whites Coaches, all still operating in 2016 although their future was less-assured as Oxfordshire County Council intended to withdraw all its bus service funding support due to budgetary constraints, as this is written. At the same time, service 142 was extended from Woodcote to Checkendon, whilst 140, 149 and TB29 were swept away by a significant development. Thames Travel started a new service X40, every two hours on a daily basis from RAF Benson to Reading via Wallingford, then along the B4074 road to Woodcote, Cane End and Chazey Heath. The Sunday service on this new facility was provided commercially. Some five months later the frequency was increased to hourly on Mondays to Saturdays, again on a commercial basis.

Over a period of time, patronage became such that thoughts turned to yet further enhancement. The X40 became very popular and the Sunday service was increased to hourly from 4 June 2007, but alternate journeys each day of the week no longer served Woodcote. A year later on 1 June 2008, the success story continued when the service was transformed into an Oxford-Berinsfield-Shillingford-Benson-Wallingford-Reading link, every 30 minutes on weekdays, hourly on Sundays. It was now numbered X39 (weekdays direct via the B4074) and X40 (daily via Woodcote). This effectively remains the position today and the ambitious level of service has endured. However, from the same date in 2008, the contract for service 142 was lost to Reading Buses but regained by Thames Travel on 3 June 2012. The latter's services to the Pangbourne, Goring and Streatley areas from Reading via Tilehurst relied wholly on local authority support; these included service 142 which was withdrawn from 29 September 2014 and was replaced with 143 which got no nearer to Woodcote than Whitchurch Hill, except for one school journey designated BB3 from Reading, Pangbourne, Streatley and Goring to Langtree School.

Until 2001, the Thames Travel fleet principally consisted of smaller capacity vehicles, mainly Mercedes Varios and Optare Solos, along with four Volkswagen LT55/Optare City Pacer buses purchased from Reading Buses. There then appeared over the ensuing years, a substantial number of the ubiquitous Dennis Dart SLF low floor bus, supplemented in due course by types such as Scania single-deckers with East Lancs bodywork, MAN vehicles with MCV bodywork, more Optare Solos and the Alexander Dennis Enviro E200, which was an upgrade of the Dart. There was an 80-seat Scania double-decker with East Lancs body and then three all-Scania double-

It is only intended to give here mere flavour of the scene ten or more years since the demise of Chiltern Queens with what Thames Travel have managed to achieve and we shall leave it to someone else to research and tell the fairly eventful story of that operator. At time of writing (spring 2016) there are two services linking Reading with Oxford going 'over the top' (as opposed to using the valley road through Pangbourne and Streatley) and thence via Wallingford to Oxford, and these operate all day, seven days a week, and quite frequently, with a mixture of modern single and double-deck vehicles. *(All: Gavin Francis)*

Scania-bodied 75-seater Scania N230UD 913 (OU08 HGN), is Reading-bound in Wallingford Market Place on service X39, seen here on 26 October 2012. It was new to Thames Travel in June 2008 prior to take-over by the Go Ahead Group.

Mercedes-Benz Citaro 854 (SF56 OXF) with Mercedes 42-seat body, which was transferred from City of Oxford in August 2012 seen here on service X40 Oxford-bound in Wallingford Market Place on 26 October 2012. Note the strap line for service X2!

Alexander-bodied 80-seater Scania N23OUD 210 (KF09 OXF), also transferred from City of Oxford in February 2015 is seen here due to depart on a service X39 to Reading via Wallingford and the 'Woodcote By-Pass' from St Aldates, Oxford, on 13 May 2015.

deckers in 2008. The last bus to be purchased during the company's independent ownership was an Alexander Dennis Enviro 400 double-decker in October 2010. The standard livery for the fleet became a bright green and blue, embellished by a white wavy line.

However, on 26 May 2011, the company was purchased by Go Ahead Group PLC, one of the major bus industry players in the UK, putting it under the same ownership as City of Oxford Motor Services, which had been acquired by Go Ahead from its post-National Bus era management ownership team in March 1994. Although the Thames Travel company has been kept as a separate entity with its own identity, many of the vehicles acquired since 2011 have been transferred from other companies in the Go Ahead group, including several Mercedes Benz Citaro single-deckers from City of Oxford MS, which regularly performed on service X40 through Woodcote. Thus, John Wright retired from being a bus operator for a second time, just like Harry Kemp all those years ago.

So much for the present, but back to nostalgia! Former Chiltern Queens vehicles thought to be still extant, some in a preserved state, include Dennis Lancet J3s CBW 864 and DBW 382, AEC Reliances AJH 241A (ex-VBW 581, currently owned by 'Bubbles' Sherwood's son-in-law), YNX 478, ANL 807B, TYD 122G, CYA 181J, 850 ABK and EUD 256K,

the latter two in the Oxford Bus Museum at Long Hanborough. Also preserved is D504 NWG, one of the Mercedes L608D minibuses.

In due course, the land occupied by the Chiltern Queens premises on each side of Long Toll in Woodcote, was sold. That on the south-west side of the road was developed as the Beechwood Court office complex and an adjacent Oxfordshire County Council road salt storage facility. However, the original Kemp premises on the north-east side of the road remained unused, derelict and overgrown, with the garage and other buildings falling into a dangerous state of disrepair and decay. A planning application had been refused for housing in 2009 and the site became an eyesore and a magnet for vandalism, which may have helped reduce potential opposition when an outline planning application was made by Millgate Homes in 2014 for fourteen dwellings; clearance of the site was underway by autumn of that year. Planning Permission was finally given in February 2015, as the site was now zoned for housing under the Woodcote Neighbourhood Plan.

The derelict site was the last visual reminder of Chiltern Queens in Woodcote and now that has disappeared too. Meanwhile, the company Chiltern Queens Ltd was finally formally dissolved on 4 October 2011. RIP, Chiltern Queens, but the memories live on and it is to be hoped that this book provides a worthwhile tribute.

...So what went wrong..?

Immediately following Chiltern Queens' demise, various members of the fleet found new homes. *(All: Graham Geoghegan)*

Thames Travel took on low-floor **Y313 KDP**, quickly obliterating the purple livery by spraying the vehicle 'dealer white'.

Sister vehicle **Y877 KDP** was left in purple but now carried the Thames Travel name for the 48 days that it operated service 1 on Chiltern Queens' registration, from 12th August to 28 September 2002.

'Terrible Twins' **T10 DMB** and **T20 DMB**, together with others, passed to Horseman Coaches, Reading, a few of which, including **T10 DMB** seen here, entered the Horseman fleet, the others being sold without being used.

'Greenmore' and the brick-built adjoining office were sold off separately beyond the fence; the Nissen hut, erected after the war, is on the site of the market garden.

Part of the coach parking area, and the Chiltern Queens depot building on the other side of the road from the Kemp's buildings, are seen from the road.

The Kemp's buildings became an eye-sore and dangerous through non-use and neglect, compounded by the delays brought on by difficulties with the planning process for the site's re-development. Eventually, on 11th February 2015, schemes for ten affordable housing units and four houses for sale on the open market were approved and thereafter no time was spared by building developers Millgate starting the development works. These photos by Trevor Back show the start of site clearance and groundwork in spring 2015.

With the garage/workshop demolished down to oversite slab level, the workshop pit is ready for breaking up and filling in.

An overall view of the site of the garage/workshop and pit.

This is the site of the little-used warehouse building after demolition and awaiting disposal of the arisings.

TELEPHONE :—CHECKENDON 54.

Kemp's Bus Services

(Proprietor :—H. Kemp)

WOODCOTE, READING.

PARTIES,
OUTINGS,
ETC.,
Catered for.

Buses may be
had for Private
Hire at Shortest
Notice.

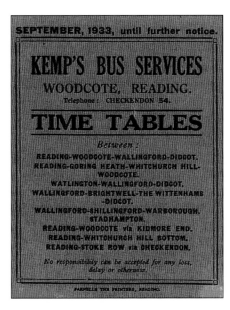

SEPTEMBER, 1933, until further notice.

KEMP'S BUS SERVICES

WOODCOTE, READING.
Telephone : CHECKENDON 54.

TIME TABLES

Between :

READING-WOODCOTE-WALLINGFORD-DIDCOT.
READING-GORING HEATH-WHITCHURCH HILL-
WOODCOTE.
WATLINGTON-WALLINGFORD-DIDCOT.
WALLINGFORD-BRIGHTWELL-THE WITTENHAMS
-DIDCOT.
WALLINGFORD-SHILLINGFORD-WARBOROUGH-
STADHAMPTON.
READING-WOODCOTE via KIDMORE END.
READING-WHITCHURCH HILL BOTTOM.
READING-STOKE ROW via CHECKENDON.

*No responsibility can be accepted for any loss,
delay or otherwise.*

PADNELLS THE PRINTERS, READING.

MARCH, 1939, until further notice.

Kemp's Bus Services

WOODCOTE READING.
Telephone : CHECKENDON 54.

TIME TABLES

BETWEEN
READING-WOODCOTE-WALLINGFORD-DIDCOT.
READING-GORING HEATH-WHITCHURCH HILL-
WOODCOTE.
WATLINGTON-WALLINGFORD-DIDCOT.
STADHAMPTON-DIDCOT, via WARBOROUGH and
THE WITTENHAMS.
READING-CHECKENDON, via KIDMORE END.
READING-WHITCHURCH HILL BOTTOM.
READING-STOKE ROW, via CHECKENDON.

No responsibility can be accepted for any loss,
delay or otherwise.

F. L. STUBBS Printer, 101, Caversham Road, Reading.

KEMP'S

MOTOR SERVICES
WOODCOTE, READING
Telephone : CHECKENDON 54

Official

TIME TABLES

MAY, 1944, *until further notice*

READING, WOODCOTE,
WALLINGFORD and DIDCOT
READING, WHITCHURCH HILL
and WOODCOTE
READING, RED LANE and
WALLINGFORD
READING, KIDMORE END and
CHECKENDON
WATLINGTON, WALLINGFORD
and BRIGHTWELL
STADHAMPTON and WALLINGFORD

*No responsibility can be accepted for any loss
or delay or otherwise*

Printed by Index Publishers (Dunstable) Ltd. Dunstable, Beds

Kemp's pre-war/wartime – driver's badge and three timetables

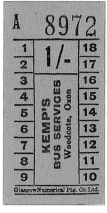

Kemp's Bus Services bell-punch and parcels tickets

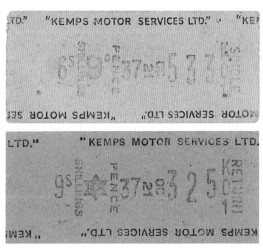

Kemp's Motor Services Ltd bell-punch and Setright tickets

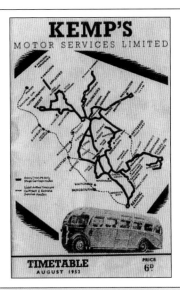

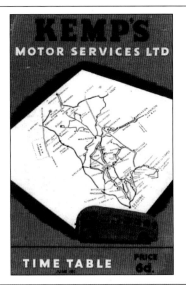

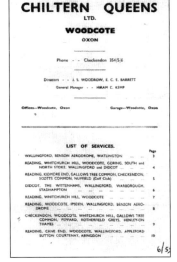

Chiltern Queens Limited

STAGE CARRIAGE ● PRIVATE HIRE ● CONTRACT HIRE ● TOURS ● EXCURSIONS
Woodcote, Reading RG8 0RP. Tel: 0491 680354 Fax: 0491 682040

Registered Office as above: Registration No. 549048 England: VAT No. 199 0053 48

Kemp's Motor Services Ltd and Chiltern Queens Ltd timetables

APPENDIX 2 – CHRONOLOGY OF THE DEVELOPMENT OF BUS SERVICES

1929-1955 – H KEMP (KEMP'S BUS SERVICES) later KEMP'S MOTOR SERVICES Ltd

Reading-Caversham-Chazey Heath-Trench Green-Nuney Green Turn-Goring Heath-Woodcote (Daily)

8/29:	Service introduced
c9/29:	Extended from Woodcote to Crays Pond-Goring-Cleeve-South Stoke-North Stoke-Mongewell-Crowmarsh-Wallingford-Brightwell-North Moreton-Didcot
By 10/34:	Some journeys extended from Didcot (White Hart/Station) to Vauxhall Camp
4/10/48:	Numbered **2**
11/6/51:	Some journeys diverted between Goring Heath and Woodcote via Whitchurch Hill and Crays Pond
19/6/55:	Transferred to Chiltern Queens Ltd

Reading-Caversham-Chazey Heath-Trench Green-Nuney Green Turn-Goring Heath-Whitchurch Hill (Daily)

17/12/29:	License granted
4/30:	Extended from Whitchurch Hill to Crays Pond-Woodcote
By 10/34:	One or two journeys each way extended from Woodcote to Ipsden (Saturdays)
4/10/48:	Numbered **6**
By 6/50:	Ipsden only served by one morning journey to Reading (Mon-Fri)
By 6/51:	Ipsden journey to Reading now Saturday only
?/53:	Ipsden-Woodcote section withdrawn
19/6/55:	Transferred to Chiltern Queens Ltd

Watlington-Britwell-Ewelme-Benson-Crowmarsh-Wallingford (Daily) and Wallingford-South Moreton-Aston Upthorpe-Aston Tirrold-Blewbury, then East Hagbourne OR Upton-West Hagbourne to Didcot (Daily)

c9/30:	Services introduced
by 3/31:	Being operated partly as a through service Watlington-Didcot
1/5/31:	Licence granted but operating between Wallingford and Didcot via Brightwell and North Moreton (in 7/31 timetable)
By 10/34:	Wallingford-Didcot section operating largely Friday, Saturday and Sunday only
By 6/36:	Whole service operating largely Friday, Saturday and Sunday only
By 3/41:	Only one journey each way west of Wallingford, to Brightwell, Saturday early evening
??:	Evening journeys to/from Wallingford via RAF Benson
By 2/47:	Service now daily Wallingford-Ewelme, extended to Watlington Fri/Sat/Sun
4/10/48:	Numbered **1**
By 6/50:	Daily between Wallingford and Watlington via either Benson village or RAF Benson
c9/51:	(certainly by 8/52: Benson village and Ewelme-Watlington section served Fri/Sat/Sun only
?/53:	Benson village served only on Sunday
19/6/55:	Transferred to Chiltern Queens Ltd

Wallingford-direct via A4130-Didcot (Daily) (Extra journeys to those provided on Reading-Didcot service)

c9/30:	Service introduced
1/5/31:	Licence application refused

Wallingford-Shillingford-Dorchester-on-Thames-Burcot-Clifton Hampden-Culham-Abingdon (Daily)

c9/30:	Service introduced
1/5/31:	Licence application to operate May-September refused-service withdrawn

Didcot-Long Wittenham-Little Wittenham-Brightwell-Wallingford (Daily)

c9/30:	Service introduced
1/5/31:	Licence granted, to operate May-September (in 7/31 timetable)
27/5/32:	Licence granted to operate throughout the year, linked to Wallingford-Stadhampton service (qv)

Chalgrove-Stadhampton-Newington-Warborough-Shillingford-Wallingford (Daily)

c9/30:	Service introduced

1/5/31:	Licence granted to operate May-September (in 7/31 timetable)
27/5/32:	Licence granted to operate throughout the year between Stadhampton and Wallingford, continuing to Brightwell-Little Wittenham-Long Wittenham-Didcot
21/4/33:	Grant of application not to run via Brightwell village
By 9/33:	Operated Friday, Saturday and Sunday only
By 10/35:	Wallingford-Didcot section suspended
By 2/36:	Operating daily Stadhampton-Wallingford-Didcot
By 6/36:	Operating Wallingford-Stadhampton only, on Friday and Saturday
??:	One journey each way Wallingford-Didcot on Sunday evening
By 8/37:	Sunday evening Wallingford-Didcot withdrawn
4/10/48:	Numbered **14**
22/11/48:	Wallingford-Brightwell-Little Wittenham-Long Wittenham-Didcot re-instated Daily
11/6/51:	Renumbered 5 and operated Stadhampton-Wallingford (Fri/Sat) and Wallingford-Didcot (Fri/Sat/Sun)
?/53:	Operated Stadhampton-Wallingford (Friday) and Wallingford-Long Wittenham (Fri/Sat/Sun)
19/6/55:	Transferred to Chiltern Queens Ltd

Reading-Caversham-Emmer Green-Chalkhouse Green-Kidmore End-Gallowstree Common-Cane End-Goring Heath-Woodcote-Checkendon (Daily)

c11/30:	Service introduced
3/7/31:	Licence granted, but service to be withdrawn between Woodcote and Checkendon
c4/34:	Withdrawn

Whitchurch Hill Bottom-Goring Heath-Nuney Green Turn-Trench Green-Chazey Heath-Caversham-Reading (Saturday) (continues to Hatch Gate and Crays Pond on return journeys from Reading). (Acquired from EG Page)

24/6/32:	Licence granted
3/7/32?:	Operation commenced
9/39:	Withdrawn

Stoke Row-Checkendon-Woodcote-Exlade Street-Cane End-Gallowstree Common-Kidmore End-Chalkhouse Green-Emmer Green-Caversham-Reading (Monday/Tuesday/Thursday/Saturday) (Acquired from WR Jackman & Son)

9/12/32:	Licence granted
20/1/33:	Application granted to operate also Wednesday and Friday
By 9/33:	Operated Saturday only
c4/34:	Revised to operate Reading-Checkendon (Daily)-Stoke Row (Saturday). Not via Woodcote, except for one Mon-Sat morning peak journey via Woodcote and Goring Heath between Checkendon and Cane End. (Incorporating service of S Hall & Son)
9/39:	Withdrawn between Checkendon and Stoke Row
27/9/48:	Numbered **3**. Extended from Checkendon to Scots Common and Nuffield and one Sunday evening journey further extended to RAF Benson
By 6/50:	Extended from Nuffield to Turners Court (Colony)
By 6/51:	Turners Court journeys were one each way Tue/Thur/Sat and two on Sunday
By 8/52 (c9/51?):	Turners Court journeys were one each way on Saturday and two on Sunday
?/53:	Withdrawn between Nuffield and Turners Court
19/6/55:	Transferred to Chiltern Queens Ltd

Reading-Caversham-Chazey Heath-Trench Green-Nuney Green Turn-Goring Heath-Woodcote-Red Lane-Ipsden Turn-White House-Mongewell-Crowmarsh-Wallingford (Saturday and Sunday)

By 5/44 (1943?):	Service introduced
By 2/47:	One evening journey each way extended from Wallingford to Crowmarsh-RAF Benson
4/10/48:	Numbered **12**. Operating Reading-RAF Benson (Daily)
19/6/55:	Transferred to Chiltern Queens Ltd

Checkendon-Woodcote-Crays Pond-Hatch Gate-Whitchurch Hill Bottom-Goring Heath-Cane End-Gallowstree Common-Peppard-Rotherfield Greys-Henley-on-Thames (Thursday). Indirect replacement for service of WR Jackman & Son.

| After 5/44 but before 2/47: | Service introduced |
| 4/10/48: | Numbered **13** |

| 3/3/50: | Application granted to divert via Kidmore End Turn and Sonning Common between Gallowstree Common and Peppard |
| 19/6/55: | Transferred to Chiltern Queens Ltd |

21. Henley-on-Thames (Market Place)-Henley Station-Western Avenue-Harpsden (Monday-Saturday)

| 1/6/50: | Service introduced |

By 8/52? (granted 12/52):Acquired by Spiers Coaches, Henley-on-Thames

22. Henley-on-Thames (Market Place)-Gainsborough Hill Estate-Wootton Estate-Rotherfield Greys Road (Monday-Saturday)

| 1/6/50: | Service introduced |

By 8/52? (granted 12/52):Acquired by Spiers Coaches, Henley-on-Thames

19. Reading-Caversham-Chazey Heath-Cane End-Exlade Street-Woodcote-Ipsden Turn-White House-Crowmarsh-Wallingford-Brightwell-Long Wittenham Turn-Appleford-Sutton Courtenay-Drayton-Abingdon (Daily)

1/9/50:	Service introduced
By 6/51:	Extended from Abingdon to RAF Abingdon (Thursday late evening/Saturday/Sunday evening)
By 8/52:	Thursday late evening extension to RAF Abingdon withdrawn. Certain journeys withdrawn between Reading and Wallingford, requiring a connection by service 12
?/53:	Journeys to RAF Abingdon operated Saturday and Sunday evenings
19/6/55:	Transferred to Chiltern Queens Ltd

1955-2002 – CHILTERN QUEENS Ltd

SERVICE 1 (Watlington-Britwell Salome (Fri/Sat/Sun)-Ewelme-RAF Benson-Crowmarsh-Wallingford (Daily))

| 19/6/55: | Taken over from Kemp's Motor Services Ltd |
| 22/12/55: | Withdrawn and incorporated in Service B |

SERVICE 5 (Stadhampton-Newington-Warborough-Shillingford (Friday)-Wallingford-Brightwell-Little Wittenham-Long Wittenham-Didcot (Daily))

| 19/6/55: | Taken over from Kemp's Motor Services Ltd |
| 22/12/55: | Withdrawn and partly incorporated in Service C. |

SERVICE 6 (Reading-Caversham-Chazey Heath-Trench Green-Nuney Green Turn-Goring Heath-Crays Pond-Woodcote (Daily))

| 19/6/55: | Taken over from Kemp's Motor Services Ltd |
| 22/12/55: | Withdrawn and incorporated in Service A |

SERVICE A (Reading-Caversham-Chazey Heath-Trench Green-Nuney Green Turn-Goring Heath-Whitchurch Hill-Crays Pond-Woodcote-Crays Pond-Goring-Cleeve Crossroads-South Stoke-North Stoke-Mongewell-Crowmarsh-Wallingford-Brightwell-North Moreton-Didcot (Daily))

19/6/55:	Service 2 taken over from Kemp's Motor Services Ltd
22/12/55:	Re-designated Service A, and revised to operate Reading-Caversham-Chazey Heath-Trench Green-Nuney Green Turn-Goring Heath-Woodcote-Ipsden Turn-Ipsden (White House)-Mongewell-Crowmarsh-Wallingford-Brightwell-North Moreton-Didcot (Daily)
16/6/68:	Withdrawn on Sunday
2/1/79:	Diverted via Cane End and Abbotsfield Crossroads to Woodcote, instead of via Trench Green, Nuney Green Turn and Goring Heath
4/1/82:	Some journeys diverted between North Moreton and Didcot via South Moreton; Service reduced to two Reading-Didcot through journeys and various short workings
15/7/83:	One journey each way on Friday diverted between South Moreton and Didcot via Aston Upthorpe, Aston Tirrold, Blewbury and East Hagbourne (replacing City of Oxford Service 323)
27/10/86:	Revised to operate three basic patterns, viz.: i) Wallingford-Crowmarsh-Mongewell-Ipsden (White House)-Ipsden Turn-Woodcote-Abbotsfield Crossroads-Cane End-Chazey Heath-Caversham-Reading (Monday-Friday peak hours); ii) Wallingford-Crowmarsh-Mongewell-North Stoke-South Stoke-Cleeve Crossroads-Goring-Crays Pond-Woodcote-Crays Pond-Whitchurch Hill-Abbotsfield Crossroads, then as i) to Reading (Monday-Saturday); iii) Woodcote-Crays Pond-Goring-Cleeve Crossroads-South Stoke-North Stoke-Ipsden (White House)-Mongewell-Crowmarsh-Wallingford (Monday-Saturday). Mainly under contract to Oxfordshire County Council.

25/4/88:	Variant ii) operated via Penny Royal instead of via Whitchurch Hill between Crays Pond and Abbotsfield Crossroads
15/5/89:	Variant ii) diverted via Tokers Green between Cane End and Chazey Heath
27/4/92:	Variant ii) withdrawn
19/5/95:	Variant iii) diverted on Friday via Ipsden village
1/7/96:	Variant i) diverted between Woodcote and Cane End via Crays Pond, Whitchurch Hill and Goring Heath. Operated Monday-Saturday peak hours, but morning journey to Reading operated as part of Service I. Variant iii) morning off-peak journeys withdrawn on Monday and Tuesday
12/4/98:	Variant iii) withdrawn-to Thames Travel Service 132.
2/4/01:	Remainder became part of Service I

SERVICE B (RAF Benson-Crowmarsh-Wallingford-Crowmarsh-Mongewell-Ipsden (White House)-Ipsden Turn-Woodcote-Goring Heath-Nuney Green Turn-Trench Green-Chazey Heath-Caversham-Reading (Daily))

19/6/55:	Service 12 taken over from Kemp's Motor Services Ltd
22/12/55:	Re-designated Service B and revised to operate Watlington-Britwell Salome-Ewelme-RAF Benson-Crowmarsh-Wallingford-Crowmarsh-Mongewell-North Stoke-South Stoke-Cleeve Crossroads-Goring-Crays Pond-Whitchurch Hill-Goring Heath-Nuney Green Turn-Trench Green-Chazey Heath-Caversham-Reading (Daily). Some journeys diverted at Crays Pond to/from Woodcote.
??:	Withdrawn on Sunday Watlington-Ewelme
16/6/68:	Withdrawn on Sunday
By 1971:	Only one journey each way over Watlington-Ewelme section
23/2/81:	Withdrawn between Watlington and Ewelme
5/4/86:	One Reading journey each way on Friday diverted between Whitchurch Turn and Caversham via Cane End, Gallowstree Common, Kidmore End, Chalkhouse Green and Emmer Green
25/10/86:	Withdrawn

SERVICE C (Reading-Caversham-Chazey Heath-Cane End-Exlade Street-Woodcote-Ipsden (White House)-Mongewell-Crowmarsh-Wallingford-Brightwell-Long Wittenham Turn-Appleford-Sutton Courtenay-Drayton-Abingdon (Daily)-RAF Abingdon (Sat/Sun))

19/6/55:	Service 19 taken over from Kemp's Motor Services Ltd
22/12/55:	Re-designated Service C and revised to operate Stadhampton-Newington-Warborough-Shillingford-Wallingford-Brightwell-Little Wittenham-Long Wittenham-Appleford-Sutton Courtenay-Drayton-Abingdon-RAF Abingdon (Daily). One Saturday journey from RAF Abingdon to Reading and one Sunday journey from Reading to RAF Abingdon remained on original route and still numbered 19.
By 2/56:	Service 19 journeys withdrawn
6/58:	Diverted at Long Wittenham to Didcot instead of to RAF Abingdon and diverted via Sinodun Road between Wallingford and Brightwell. Stadhampton to Warborough section only operated on Friday. Withdrawn on Sunday
By 8/59 (granted 8/6/59):	Reduced to operate on Friday only
21/2/69:	Withdrawn between Stadhampton and Warborough
4/1/82:	Withdrawn between Long Wittenham and Didcot
31/10/86:	Re-designated Service D and operated Long Wittenham-Little Wittenham-Brightwell-Wallingford and Warborough-Shillingford-Wittenham Close-Wallingford (Friday). Under contract to Oxfordshire County Council
4/11/94:	Extended from Warborough to Newington and Stadhampton
5/7/96:	Withdrawn between Long Wittenham and Brightwell
By 1/01:	Brightwell-Wallingford section withdrawn
2/8/02:	Withdrawn-to Thames Travel Service TB103

SERVICE D (Nuffield-Scots Common-Checkendon-Exlade Street-Cane End-Gallowstree Common-Kidmore End-Chalkhouse Green-Emmer Green-Caversham-Reading (Daily))

19/6/55:	Service 3 taken over from Kemp's Motor Services Ltd
22/12/55:	Re-designated Service D and revised to operate Nuffield (Thursday)-Scots Common-Checkendon-Exlade Street-Cane End-Gallowstree Common-Kidmore End-Chalkhouse Green-Emmer Green-Caversham-Reading (Daily)
By 2/56:	Nuffield served only by one late evening journey each way
By 5/58:	Nuffield served by one morning journey Monday-Saturday and one late evening journey on Saturday each way

16/10/61:	Withdrawn between Nuffield and Checkendon and withdrawn on Sunday
22/4/74:	Temporarily transferred to City of Oxford MS, except one early morning journey from Checkendon still operated by Chiltern Queens
1/6/76:	Chiltern Queens resumed main service. Extended to run from/to Woodcote. 7.18am journey Checkendon to Reading in school term time believed to have been operated for a period by Tappins Coaches, Didcot, but withdrawn c1/77
11/6/84:	Withdrawn on Monday-Friday mornings (replaced by a feeder service from Checkendon to Woodcote to connect with Service B to/from Reading) and on Saturday
1/4/85:	Revised to operate one morning return journey to Reading on Mon/Tue/Wed/Thur, plus one Mon-Fri evening peak journey from Reading
1/4/86:	Friday morning service provided by means of a diversion on Service B
25/10/86:	Withdrawn due to Davron Travel having registered a new commercial service

SERVICE 13 (Checkendon-Woodcote-Crays Pond-Whitchurch Hill-Goring Heath-Cane End-Gallowstree Common-Kidmore End Turn-Sonning Common-Rotherfield Peppard-Greys Green-Rotherfield Greys-Henley (Thursday))

19/6/55:	Taken over from Kemp's Motor Services Ltd
10/4/84:	Introduced also on Tuesday between Gallowstree Common and Henley
4/4/85:	Revised to operate from Checkendon to Henley on Thursday/Friday.
5/4/86:	Diverted on Friday between Rotherfield Greys and Henley via Harpsden
27/10/86:	Re-designated Service **G** and not via Harpsden. Under contract to Oxfordshire County Council
15/8/88:	Withdrawn on Friday
30/4/92:	Contract lost to Horseman Coaches Service 57, but Chiltern Queens continued commercially from Sonning Common (Grove Road/Peppard Road) to Henley on Thursday
1/11/99:	Commercial service withdrawn and replaced by new Service G under contract to Oxfordshire County Council, operated Pangbourne-Whitchurch-Whitchurch Hill-Crays Pond-Woodcote-Checkendon-Stoke Row-Peppard Common-Rotherfield Peppard-Greys Green-Rotherfield Greys-Henley (Mon-Sat) (two journeys)
5/3/01:	Additional journeys transferred from Service C (below). Diverted via Manor Road in Whitchurch.
2/8/02:	Withdrawn-to Thames Travel Service 146

Mapledurham-Lilley Farm-Reading (Saturday).

8/1/64 (licence granted but may have commenced 12/63):	Contract basis-no fares collected on vehicle
28/2/67:	Licence expired, although ceased to operate considerably earlier

SERVICE E (Woodcote-Crays Pond-Goring-Streatley-Moulsford-Cholsey-Wallingford, with connection to/from Didcot Girls School by Service A. Afternoon journey on Monday commenced at Didcot Girls School via Didcot-North Moreton-Brightwell. (Schooldays-school students only beyond Goring Station))

4/9/84:	Service commenced.
27/10/86:	Re-designated Service **B** and operated Monday-Saturday peak hours between Woodcote and Didcot (and to Didcot Girls School on school days only), partly under contract to Oxfordshire County Council
1/7/96:	Operated only on school days. Contracted journeys withdrawn
7/4/00:	Withdrawn

SERVICE F (Woodcote-Crays Pond-Whitchurch Hill-Whitchurch-Pangbourne (Tuesday))-to replace Pangbourne Coaches service

2/4/85:	Service commenced
28/10/86:	Re-designated Service **E** under contract to Oxfordshire County Council
21/4/92:	Withdrawn-to Horseman Coaches Service 58

SERVICE G (Woodcote-Crays Pond-Goring-Streatley-Moulsford-Cholsey-Wallingford-Brightwell-North Moreton-Long Wittenham-Clifton Hampden-Courtier's Green-Oxford (Wednesday))

20/11/85:	Service commenced
29/10/86:	Re-designated Service **F**. Under contract to Oxfordshire County Council
27/4/88:	Diverted between Goring and Wallingford via Cleeve Cross Roads, South Stoke, North Stoke, Mongewell and Crowmarsh
29/4/92:	Re-designated Service **K**
5/7/93:	Re-designated Service **F**
26/2/96:	Withdrawn

| By 7/98: | Reinstated (as an unregistered Excursion?) on 1st Wednesday of each month and certain Wednesdays before Christmas |
| 3/11/99: | Withdrawn |

SERVICE C (Ewelme-RAF Benson-Crowmarsh-Wallingford-Brightwell-North Moreton-South Moreton-Didcot (Monday-Saturday) with one journey each way (Friday) diverted between South Moreton and Didcot via Aston Upthorpe, Aston Tirrold, Blewbury and East Hagbourne). Under contract to Oxfordshire County Council

| 27/10/86: | Service commenced |
| 10/4/98: | Withdrawn-to Thames Travel, Services 130/132 |

SERVICE H (Watlington-Howe Hill-Cookley Green-Park Corner-Nettlebed-Highmoor Cross-Satwell-Greys Green-Rotherfield Peppard-Sonning Common-Emmer Green-Caversham-Reading (Monday-Saturday)). Under contract to Oxfordshire County Council to replace House's of Watlington service

| 1/9/87: | Service commenced |
| 27/7/91: | Withdrawn-to Motts Travel, Service M1 |

SERVICE I (Maidensgrove-Russells Water-Cookley Green-Park Corner-Nettlebed (Tuesday/Saturday) or Nuffield-Stoke Row (Thursday)-Highmoor Cross-Satwell-Greys Green-Rotherfield Greys-Henley (Tuesday/Thursday/Saturday)). Under contract to Oxfordshire County Council to replace House's of Watlington service

1/9/87:	Service commenced
13/4/88:	Withdrawn between Maidensgrove and Russells Water.
18/8/88:	Diverted via Nettlebed between Park Corner and Nuffield on Thursday
27/7/91:	Withdrawn-to Motts Travel, Service M36

SERVICE H (Rotherfield Peppard-Sonning Common-Kidmore End Turn-Emmer Green-Caversham-Reading (Monday-Saturday)). Operated commercially in competition with Reading Buses Service 137

29/7/91:	Service commenced
27/4/92:	Re-designated Service J. Extended to run from/to Stoke Row (Monday-Friday peak hours)
5/7/93:	Re-designated Service E
4/10/93:	One journey each way extended from Reading Station to Kings Meadow Tesco
1/7/96:	Peak hour journeys also operated on Saturday and in the evening extended from Stoke Row to Checkendon and Exlade Street
4/9/96:	Withdrawn between Rotherfield Peppard and Stoke Row/Exlade Street
30/8/97:	Withdrawn

SERVICE I (Reading-Caversham-Chazey Heath-Cane End-Goring Heath-Whitchurch Hill-Crays Pond-Woodcote-Checkendon-Exlade Street-Cane End-Chazey Heath-Caversham-Reading (Monday-Saturday)). Service acquired from Davron Travel

29/7/91:	Service commenced
4/10/93:	One journey each way extended from Reading Station to Kings Meadow Tesco
4/8/99:	Friday and Saturday evening journeys added (Monday-Saturday evenings during December 1999)
2/4/01:	Woodcote to Wallingford peak journeys on Service A re-designated Service I, but diverted via Crays Pond, Goring, Streatley, Moulsford and Cholsey
12/8/02:	Woodcote to Wallingford section withdrawn and operation transferred to Horseman Coaches depot at Reading
9/9/02:	Taken over by Thames Travel, running on Chiltern Queens Registration
28/9/02:	Withdrawn-to Thames Travel, Services 140/142

HENLEY TOWN SERVICES H1/H2/H3/H5 (Monday-Saturday): H1 Greys Road with some journeys via Ancastle Green: H2 Vicarage Road/Harpsden Road: H3 Abrahams Estate: H5 (extension of H1 to Harpsden Golf Club, two journeys). Acquired from The Bee Line under contract to Oxfordshire County Council

27/4/92:	Services commenced
14/5/95:	H5 withdrawn
22/1/96:	H2 diverted via Henley Tesco
5/3/01:	H1 not via Ancastle Green
3/8/02:	Withdrawn-to Thames Travel, Services 151-153

HENLEY COLLEGE SERVICES 2225 (Stokenchurch-Lane End-Marlow Bottom-Marlow-Henley College); 2226 (High Wycombe-Sands-Booker-Marlow-Henley College), 2227 (High Wycombe-Loudwater-Beaconsfield-Wooburn Green-Flackwell Heath-Bourne End-Little Marlow-Marlow-Henley College); 2228 (see below) (College Days)). Under contract to Buckinghamshire County Council

?/9/95:   Services 2225, 2226 and 2227 commenced

?/9/96:   Service 2226 revised to commence from Naphill and operated via Downley to Sands. Service 2228 (Widmer End-Hazlemere-High Wycombe-Cressex-Marlow-Henley College) commenced.

?/7/02:   All four services withdrawn

DIDCOT TOWN SERVICES D1/D2/D3 (Monday-Saturday):D1 Didcot Parkway Station-Broadway-Tesco-Tamar Way-Trent Road-Mersey Way-Avon Way (Ladygrove Health Centre): D2 Avon Way (Ladygrove Health Centre) as D1 to Didcot Parkway Station, then Milton Park (peak hours): D3 Didcot Parkway Station-Foxhall Road-Queensway-Newlands Avenue (Family Centre), one journey. Oxfordshire County Council contract taken over from Tappins Coaches, Didcot.

31/10/95:   Services commenced

19/10/96:   Withdrawn-to Stagecoach (Thames Transit)

SERVICE 3 (Harwell AERE-Chilton-Upton-Blewbury-East Hagbourne-Didcot (Monday/Tuesday/Thursday/Friday/Saturday)). Oxfordshire County Council contract taken over from Bennett's Coaches

13/10/97:   Service commenced

10/4/98:   Withdrawn-to Thames Travel, service 13

DIDCOT TOWN SERVICES D4/D5 (Monday/Tuesday/Thursday/Friday/Saturday):D4 Didcot Parkway Station-Broadway-Mereland Road-Lloyd Road-Queensway-Newlands Avenue-Fairacres Road-Broadway-Didcot Parkway Station: D5 Didcot Parkway Station-Broadway-Meadow Way-Didcot Hospital-Slade Road-Freeman Road-The Oval-Lydalls Road-Broadway-Didcot Parkway Station. Oxfordshire County Council contract taken over from Bennett's Coaches

13/10/97:   Services commenced

10/4/98:   Withdrawn-to Thames Travel, services D4/D5

SERVICE C (Whitchurch Hill-Crays Pond-Woodcote-Checkendon-Stoke Row-Rotherfield Peppard-Sonning Common-Hunts Green-Harpsden-Henley (Monday-Saturday)) Under contract to Oxfordshire County Council

12/1/99:   Service commenced

12/4/99:   Diverted in Sonning Common via Woodlands Road

1/11/99:   One journey extended from Whitchurch Hill to Whitchurch and Pangbourne on Monday-Friday. Diversion in Sonning Common via Woodlands Road withdrawn.

5/3/01:   Reduced to operate Woodcote to Henley (peak hours only)

3/8/02:   Withdrawn-to Thames Travel, service 145

SERVICE 39 (Wallingford-Shillingford-Dorchester-Clifton Hampden-Burcot-Culham-Abingdon (Monday-Saturday). (One journey starts from Crowmarsh; Some journeys operate from Wallingford to Shillingford via Crowmarsh and Benson and from Dorchester to Burcot via Berinsfield)) Under contract to Oxfordshire County Council. Partial replacement for Stagecoach (Thames Transit) service 39

21/8/99:   Service commenced

23/6/00:   Withdrawn

OXFORD CITY SERVICES 17A/17B/17C (Wednesday/Friday): 17A Boundary Brook Road-Iffley-Cowley Centre (Templars Square): 17B Lye Valley Estate-Wood Farm Road-The Slade-Fletcher Road-Fernhill Road-Cowley Centre (Templars Square): 17C Southfields Park-Cowley Road-Oxford. Taken over from Stagecoach (Thames Transit) under contract to Oxfordshire County Council

23/8/99:   Services commenced

18/4/01:   Service 17A extended to start at Herschel Crescent via Bartholomew Road and Henley Avenue; Service 17C extended to Cowley Centre, Bartholomew Road and Herschel Crescent on return from Oxford

22/10/01:   Service 17A extended to start at Cowley Centre before Herschel Crescent and extended from terminus at Cowley Centre to Cowley Retail Park (Tesco); Service 17C curtailed to terminate at Cowley Centre on return from Oxford

5/7/02:   Withdrawn-to Heyfordian Travel

SERVICE 17 (Donnington Health Centre-Boundary Brook Road-Cowley Centre-Herschel Crescent-Beauchamp Lane-Cowley Centre (Templars Square) (Wednesday/Friday)). Under contract to Oxfordshire County Council

18/4/01:   Service commenced
19/10/01:   Withdrawn

SERVICE 136 (Nuffield-Stoke Row-Rotherfield Peppard-Sonning Common-Gallowstree Common-Kidmore End-Chalkhouse Green-Emmer Green-Caversham-Reading-Kingsmeadow (Tesco) (Monday-Saturday). One journey each way). Taken over from White's Coaches under contract to Oxfordshire County Council

2/7/01:   Service commenced
3/8/02:   Withdrawn-to Thames Travel, service 136

OXFORD CITY SERVICES 10C/10D (Oxford Station-City Centre-Banbury Road-John Radcliffe Hospital-Wood Farm-Cowley Centre-City Centre-Oxford Station (Evening/Sunday-10C hourly clockwise and 10D hourly anti-clockwise)). Taken over from Stagecoach (Thames Transit) under contract to Oxfordshire County Council

5/8/01:   Services commenced
9/2/02:   Withdrawn-to City of Oxford

DIDCOT TOWN SERVICES D1/D2/D3 (Monday-Saturday): D1 Didcot Parkway Station-Broadway-Tesco-Tamar Way-Trent Road-Avon Way (Ladygrove Health Centre): D2 Avon Way (Ladygrove Health Centre)-Trent Road-Tamar Way-Broadway-Didcot Parkway Station-Milton Park (peak hours): D3 Didcot Parkway Station-Broadway-Mereland Road-Lloyd Road-Queensway-Meadow Way-Didcot Hospital-Slade Road-Freeman Road-Broadway-Didcot Parkway Station. Taken over from Thames Travel under contract to Oxfordshire County Council

29/10/01:   Services commenced
10/12/01:   Service D1 diverted on return from Avon Way via Mersey Way
27/7/02:   Withdrawn-to Thames Travel

Wallingford Market Place in the mid-1950s, with former Kemp's utility Bedford OWB BBW 701. *(Commercial post card)*

Market Place, Wallingford

Reg. No	Chassis Type	Body Manufacturer & Type	Year New	Immediate Previous Operator	Date into Kemp fleet	Date Out	Disposal where known or subsequent owner	Notes
XB 8347	Daimler CB	United B--F	1920	United Automobile Services	7/29	/31	?	
PW 1935	Daimler CB	United B26F	1924	United Automobile Services	7/29	c9/31	?	
PW 3324	Daimler CB	United B26F	1925	United Automobile Services	c9/29	6/33	Ducker, Little Stoke Manor Farm (shed)	
WT 9156	Karrier JH	? B26 (?)	1925	Harrogate & District Road Car	/29	/31	Caravan, Purley on Thames	
PW 121	Daimler CB	United B20F (?)	1923	United Automobile Services	8/30	7/32	Smith, Paddington (Scrap)	
PW 127	Daimler CB	United B24F	1923	United Automobile Services	8/30	9/31	Barkus, Reading (Scrap)	
WT 5891	Reo Speedwagon FB	? C14	1924	West Yorkshire Road Car	by 9/30?	9/32	?	Definitely owned by 7/31
?	Chevrolet	? 14	?	?	/31	/32	?	Possibly retained out of service until c1933/4
MY 5191	Ford AA	? B20F	1930	?	/31	/33 (?)	Adderley, Abingdon (Goods) by 1935	
UD 4652	Bedford WLB	Strachan B20F	1931	New	9/31	/44	?	Seats removed and used for Goods 2/43
UD 4656	Bedford WLB	Reall B20F	1931	New	9/31	/41(?)	Goode, London E9 (Goods)	
UD 4678	Bedford WLB	Strachan B20F	1931	New	9/31	/41	Eugene, London SW17 (Goods)	
UD 4863	Commer Centaur B40	Strachan B20F	1932	New	by 2/32	/44 (?)	?	
XG 267	BAT Cruiser	? C20	1930	United Automobile Services	/32	9/32	Andrews, Bristol	
PY 9131	Reo	? B20	1928	United Automobile Services	/32	9/34	?	
TO 7230	Maudslay ML4B	Vickers B26F	1928	Nottingham City Transport	9/32	by /38	?	
TO 7231	Maudslay ML4B	Vickers B26F	1928	Nottingham City Transport	9/32	by /38	?	
RD 4378	Ford AA	? B--F	1933	New	3/33	?	?	Not definitely confirmed as a bus
UP 2082	Gilford 166SD	Duple C24D	1928	Majestic Coaches, Ebchester	c /34	9/37(?)	Hardy, London SW2	In stock with supplying dealer 11/33
UP 2189	Gilford 166SD	Duple C24D	1929	Majestic Coaches, Ebchester	c /34	12/37	?	In stock with supplying dealer 11/33
JC 1288	Gilford 168SD	Vickers B26F	1933	Crosville MS	3/35	by /39	Gibb & Partners, London W1	
?	Gilford	? 26	?	?	?	by 9/39	?	Existence of this vehicle uncertain
UL 4418	Leyland Lioness PLC1	Birch C24F	1929	Birch Bros, London NW5	5/37	7/39	?	
UL 4419	Leyland Lioness PLC1	Birch C24F	1929	Birch Bros, London NW5	5/37	7/39	? Lorry	
UD 9431	Dennis Lancet II	Dennis C39F	1938	New	3/38	12/53	Ardler Coachworks, Reading	
VX 9906	Commer Invader 6TK	? B20F	1931	Fox & Hart, Hounslow	/38	/41	ARP Unit, Rayleigh	
PL 603	Commer Invader 6TK	? C20F	1930	Shaw & Duval, Surbiton	12/38	7/39	Hardy, London SW2	
JG 1xxx(?)	Morris Commercial Viceroy	? C20F	(?)	(?)	?	/41	?	Not positively identified – see text
JG 2835	Morris Commercial RP	East Kent B20F	1933	East Kent Road Car	/39	/45	?	
EXK 599	Bedford WTB	Duple C25F	1938	White Heather, Southsea	10/40	6/55	Chiltern Queens, Woodcote	Re-registered DUD 784 6/49
AYA 170	Dennis Ace	Dennis B20F	1934	White Heather, Southsea	10/40	/42	Gradually scrapped at Woodcote	
UD 5469	Bedford WLB	Duple C20F	1933	?	/41	10/44 (?)	Showman ?	With W Smith, Great Milton until c3/38
DKP 410	Dennis Arrow Minor	Dennis C25F	1937	Crown Coaches, Tongham	/41	6/55	Chiltern Queens, Woodcote	Re-seated to C26F c-/41
EUO 187	Commer PLNF5	Heaver C26F	1938	Burfitt, Ilfracombe	7/41	10/48	Turner & Butcher, Kenninghall	
BBW 274	Bedford OWB	Mulliner B32F	1942	New	10/42	9/48	Huntley, East Oakley	
BBW 268	Bedford OWB	Duple B32F	1942	New	11/42	6/47	Armitage, Flockton	
BBW 331	Bedford OWB	Duple B32F	1943	New	1/43	12/48	West Bros, Bray	
BBW 701	Bedford OWB	Duple B32F	1943	New	12/43	6/55	Chiltern Queens, Woodcote	B30F 1949 and B28F 1950
BBW 702	Bedford OWB	Duple B32F	1943	New	12/43	6/55	Chiltern Queens, Woodcote	B30F 1949 and B28F 1950
BBW 950	Bedford OWB	Duple B32F	1944	New	10/44	6/55	Chiltern Queens, Woodcote	B30F 1949 and B28F 1950
WN 6224	Dennis Lancet	Weymann B32F	1934	Clarke, Rubery	8/46	c9/52	Norris House School, Woodcote	Body recorded also as by DJ Davies
CBW 522	Bedford OB	Duple B32F	1947	New	2/47	6/55	Chiltern Queens, Woodcote	
CBW 864	Dennis Lancet J3	Whitson C35F	1947	New	4/47	6/55	Chiltern Queens, Woodcote	
CUD 286	Commer Commando	? C32F	1947	New	6/47	4/50(?)	Turner & Butcher, Kenninghall	Body possibly by Burlingham or SMT
OU 5721	Commer Invader 6TK	Abbott C20F	1930	Gregory, Hook	11/47	/50(?)	?	
WJ 4392(?)	Commer Centaur B40	?	1932	Gregory, Hook	12/47	12/47	Sold for scrap	Acquired only for spare parts
BRD 922	AEC Regal	LPTB B32F	1938	Smith, Reading	5/48	6/55	Chiltern Queens, Woodcote	Given coach seats. Originally registered EYK 229

Reg. No	Chassis Type	Body Manufacturer & Type	Year New	Immediate Previous Operator	Date into Kemp fleet	Date Out	Disposal where known or subsequent owner	Notes
VD 3424	Leyland Lion LT5A	Leyland B32R	1934	Central SMT	6/48	9/50	Deacon, Dorchester On Thames (Scrap)	
WV 1545	Dennis Lancet	Heaver C32F	1933	King & Donovan, Yattendon	7/48	2/51	?	
DBW 66	TSM K6LA7	Vincent C33F	1948	New	8/48	6/55	Chiltern Queens, Woodcote	
JO 7875	AEC Regent	Park Royal H28/24R	1933	City of Oxford MS	8/48	1/51	Deacon, Dorchester On Thames (Scrap)	Acquired for spare parts
JO 7876	AEC Regent	Park Royal H28/24R	1933	City of Oxford MS	9/48	12/50	Deacon, Dorchester On Thames (Scrap)	
DBW 67	Bedford OB	Mulliner B28F	1948	New	9/48	c3/51	Deacon, Dorchester On Thames (Dealer)	
DBW 382	Dennis Lancet J3	Vincent C33F	1949	New	11/48	6/55	Chiltern Queens, Woodcote	
VV 1164	Dennis Lancet	Grose B26F	1932	Northampton Transport	1/49	11/50	North, Horsley Woodhouse, Derbys	normal control model; only engine removed for spares before disposal; converted to forward control, re-engined, re-bodied and re-registered by new owner
DUD 401	TSM K6LM7	Dutfield C33F	1949	New	5/49	6/55	Chiltern Queens, Woodcote	
EOT 48	Bedford OWB	Duple B32F	1945	Gregory, Hook	8/49	6/55	Chiltern Queens, Woodcote	Re-seated B28F in 2/50
EBW 838	Commer Avenger	Dutfield C37F	1950	New	5/50	6/55	Chiltern Queens, Woodcote	Chassis delivered 1948, then stored
EFC 300	Leyland Cub KPZ2	Park Royal B20F	1937	City of Oxford MS	9/50	6/55	Chiltern Queens, Woodcote	B24F before entering service. Withdrawn 1/55
CFC 784	AEC Regent	Weymann L26/26R	1936	City of Oxford MS	3/51	6/55	Chiltern Queens, Woodcote	
CFC 785	AEC Regent	Weymann L26/26R	1936	City of Oxford MS	3/51	8/54	Scrap Dealer, Crays Pond	Withdrawn 3/53
CFC 793	AEC Regent	Weymann L26/26R	1936	City of Oxford MS	3/51	8/54	Scrap Dealer, Woodcote	Used for spare parts
CFC 794	AEC Regent	Weymann L26/26R	1936	City of Oxford MS	3/51	8/54	Scrap Dealer, Woodcote	Used for spare parts
CFC 786	AEC Regent	Weymann L26/26R	1936	City of Oxford MS	5/51	6/55	Chiltern Queens, Woodcote	Withdrawn 3/55
CFC 787	AEC Regent	Weymann L26/26R	1936	City of Oxford MS	5/51	8/54	Jackson (Breaker), Reading	
CWL 654	AEC Regent	Park Royal L26/26R	1936	City of Oxford MS	10/51	8/54	Scrap Dealer, Crays Pond 8/54	Withdrawn 12/51
EFC 291	AEC Regal	Weymann B32F	1937	City of Oxford MS	10/51	6/55	Chiltern Queens, Woodcote	Withdrawn 4/55
DLU 157	AEC Regent	LPTB L27/26R	1937	Hants & Sussex, Emsworth	8/54	6/55	Chiltern Queens, Woodcote	
DYL 860	AEC Regent	LPTB L27/26R	1937	Hants & Sussex, Emsworth	9/54	6/55	Chiltern Queens, Woodcote	
DGX 346	AEC Regent	LPTB H30/26R	1937	London Transport	2/55	6/55	Chiltern Queens, Woodcote	Not operated

Explanation Of Codes Used For The Bodywork Layout Of Vehicles

Bus enthusiasts use a three part code in fleet listings to describe the basic layout and seating capacity of a particular vehicle. The elements of this code that apply to the lists in this book are as follows:

First element (alphabetic): Any one of the following:

B Single-deck bus

C Single-deck coach

DP Single-deck dual-purpose vehicle

FC Full-fronted single-deck coach

H Conventional height double-deck bus

L Low height double-deck bus

M Minibus

Second element (numeric): The passenger seating capacity of the vehicle. A single figure is shown for single-deckers, while double-deckers are shown with the upper-deck capacity over that of the lower-deck.

Third element (alphabetic): Any one of the following:

C Centre entrance

D Dual entrance

F Front or forward entrance

R Rear entrance (with open platform on double-deck vehicles)

Note: A suffix t indicates that a toilet compartment is incorporated.

For example, B32F indicates a 32-seat single-deck service bus with a front entrance, while a double-deck bus shown as H30/26R indicates a double-decker of conventional height, with 30 seats upstairs and 26 seats on the lower-deck and with a rear platform.

Normal control refers to a vehicle in which the driver sits behind the front axle. On a forward control vehicle the driver sits above or ahead of the front axle, the steering linkage being 'cranked' rather than straight.

APPENDIX 4 – CHILTERN QUEENS FLEET LIST

Reg. No.	Chassis Type	Body Manufacturer & Type	Year New	Immediate Previous Operator	Into CQ fleet	Date w'drawn	Initial Disposal	Notes
CFC 784	AEC Regent	Weymann L26/26R	1936	Kemp's MS, Woodcote	6/55	3/56	Deacon, Dorchester on Thames (scrap) 4/57	
CFC 786	AEC Regent	Weymann L26/26R	1936	Kemp's MS, Woodcote	6/55	n/a	Scrapped at Woodcote /55	Not operated
DGX 346	AEC Regent	LPTB H30/26R	1937	Kemp's MS, Woodcote	6/55	n/a	Remains dumped rear of depot /56	Not operated
DLU 157	AEC Regent	LPTB L27/26R	1937	Kemp's MS, Woodcote	6/55	9/58	Unknown scrap dealer	
DYL 860	AEC Regent	LPTB L27/26R	1937	Kemp's MS, Woodcote	6/55	4/57	Deacon, Dorchester on Thames (scrap) 5/57	
EFC 291	AEC Regal	Weymann B32F	1937	Kemp's MS, Woodcote	6/55	n/a	Unknown scrap dealer	Not operated
BRD 922	AEC Regal	LPTB DP32F	1938	Kemp's MS, Woodcote	6/55	12/57	Scrapped at Woodcote by 8/59	
EFC 300	Leyland Cub KPZ2	Park Royal B24F	1938	Kemp's MS, Woodcote	6/55	n/a	Unknown scrap dealer /56	Not operated
DKP 410	Dennis Arrow Minor	Dennis C25F	1937	Kemp's MS, Woodcote	6/55	n/a	Sold 7/55, later Walden, Epping 8/57	Not operated
DUD 784	Bedford WTB	Duple C26F	1938	Kemp's MS, Woodcote	6/55	7/58	Scrapped at Woodcote /60	Latterly used as a crew bus
BBW 701	Bedford OWB	Duple B28F	1943	Kemp's MS, Woodcote	6/55	3/61	Main (dealer), Benson 3/66	Used as a crew bus from 3/61
BBW 702	Bedford OWB	Duple B28F	1943	Kemp's MS, Woodcote	6/55	7/55	Unknown scrap dealer 8/56	
BBW 950	Bedford OWB	Duple B28F	1944	Kemp's MS, Woodcote	6/55	10/58	Scrapped at Woodcote by 8/59	
EOT 48	Bedford OWB	Duple B28F	1945	Kemp's MS, Woodcote	6/55	10/55	Unknown scrap dealer by 3/56	
CBW 522	Bedford OB	Duple B32F	1947	Kemp's MS, Woodcote	6/55	7/57	Scrapped at Woodcote by 8/59	
CBW 864	Dennis Lancet J3	Whitson C35F	1947	Kemp's MS, Woodcote	6/55	10/71	Ryan, Hanworth (Preserved) 6/81	Rebodied Plaxton FC37F 7/60
DBW 66	TSM K6LA7	Vincent C33F	1948	Kemp's MS, Woodcote	6/55	9/63	Thomas (Showman), Reading 5/64	
DBW 382	Dennis Lancet J3	Vincent C33F	1948	Kemp's MS, Woodcote	6/55	/69	West Surrey Preservation Group 9/79	Rebodied Plaxton FC37F 7/58
DUD 401	TSM K6LM7	Dutfield C33F	1949	Kemp's MS, Woodcote	6/55	11/64	Main (Dealer), Benson 3/66	Rebuilt by Chiltern Queens 7/59
EBW 838	Commer Avenger	Dutfield C37F	1950	Kemp's MS, Woodcote	6/55	10/58	Scrapped at Woodcote by 4/61	
HRK 901	Leyland Comet CPO1	Strachan C33F	1950	Homeland, Croydon	7/55	10/64	Main (dealer), Benson 3/66	
HRK 906	Leyland Comet CPO1	Strachan C37F	1950	Homeland, Croydon	7/55	5/63	Main (dealer), Benson 3/66	
LPF 250	Maudslay Marathon III	Whitson C33F	1947	Majestic, London E10	7/55	11/64	Thomas (Dealer), Reading 11/64	
LPH 429	Maudslay Marathon III	Whitson C33F	1947	Majestic, London E10	7/55	11/65	Main (dealer), Benson 3/66	Rebuilt by Chiltern Queens FC33F 2/61
LPK 200	Maudslay Marathon III	Westnor C33F	1947	Majestic, London E10	7/55	10/60	Scrapped at Woodcote /61	
LMO 743	AEC Reliance MU3RV	Duple Midland B44F	1955	New	10/55	7/75	Scrap Dealer, Colnbrook c6/81	
LMO 744	AEC Reliance MU3RV	Duple Midland B44F	1955	New	10/55	2/76	Scrap Dealer, Colnbrook c6/81	
LMO 745	AEC Reliance MU3RV	Duple Midland B44F	1955	New	10/55	11/76	Scrap Dealer, Colnbrook c6/81	
JWL 729	Guy Arab II	Roe L27/28R	1943	City of Oxford MS	2/57	2/58	Scrapped at Woodcote by 8/59	Withdrawal also given as 6/58
JWL 731	Guy Arab II	Roe L27/28R	1943	City of Oxford MS	3/57	6/58	Scrapped at Woodcote by 8/59	
JWL 858	Guy Arab II	Roe L27/28R	1944	City of Oxford MS	6/57	11/59	Jeremy (Dealer), London E1 3/61	
NPC 727	Guy Vixen	Wadham FC29F	1949	Whites, Camberley	12/57	8/64	Brompton Sanatorium 11/64	
NPE 61	Guy Vixen	Wadham FC29F	1949	Whites, Camberley	12/57	6/64	Main (dealer), Benson 3/66	
MUD 975	AEC Reliance 2MU3RA	Duple C43C	1958	New	6/58	9/80	Fowler 3F Society /81	
NBW 407	AEC Reliance 2MU3RA	Plaxton B45F	1958	New	8/58	9/80	Scrap Dealer, Colnbrook c6/81	
NPA 461	Albion Victor FT3AB	Whitson C31F	1949	Whites, Camberley	9/58	5/65	Main (dealer), Benson 3/66	
NPF 552	TSM K6LM7	Dutfield C33F	1949	Whites, Camberley	9/58	7/59	Smith (Breaker), Woodcote by 5/60	
EEA 8	Austin CXB	Mann Egerton C29F	1948	Taylor, Carterton	11/58	5/61	Scrapped at Woodcote 10/61	
SPD 207	Dennis Falcon L6	Gurney Nutting DP30F	1952	Yellow Bus, Stoughton	1/59	5/67	Passey (Dealer), Benson 1/69	
KGU 599	Dennis Lancet J3	Burlingham C35F	1949	Whites, Camberley	7/59	4/62	Passey (Dealer), Benson 1/68	
NPA 462	Albion Victor FT3AB	Whitson C31F	1949	Whites, Camberley	7/59	3/67	Passey (Dealer), Benson by 9/69	
SBW 562	Bedford CALV	Martin Walter M11	1960	New	10/60	10/71	Scrapped	Non-PSV from 3/71
HRU 755	Dennis Lancet J3	Plaxton C33F	1949	Hoare, Chickerell	4/61	3/67	Passey (Dealer), Benson 1/69	
704 JMB	Ford Thames 570E	Burlingham C41F	1960	Super, Upminster	6/61	7/72	Sold c9/75	
OTD 948	Dennis Lancet J10	Yeates FC35F	1952	Todd, Whitchurch	3/62	8/65	Passey (Dealer), Benson 1/68	
FUT 452	Dennis Lancet J3	Duple C35F	1949	Todd, Whitchurch	3/62	n/a	Broken for spares	Not operated
VBW 581	AEC Reliance 4MU3RA	Plaxton C51F	1962	New	5/62	/88	Somerbus (Dealer), Paulton 9/90, then to Graveling, Peterborough (Preserved)	Re-registered AJH 241A in 5/86
530 BPG	Dennis Pelican PU2	Duple Midland B44F	1956	Daisy, Broughton	9/62	10/70	Chassis scrapped at Woodcote 5/77	Body rebuilt and placed on YNX 478 5/72
XBW 242	AEC Reliance 4MU3RA	Plaxton C51F	1963	New	4/63	by 3/89	Jacobs, Saltash 3/91	Re-registered AJH 163A in 6/85
NWF 286	AEC Reliance MU3RV	Plaxton C41C	1954	Harding, Birkenhead	6/64	6/73	Scrapped at Woodcote 5/77	
850 ABK	AEC Reliance 2MU3RA	Duple C43F	1962	Don, Southsea	6/64	by 5/89	Bayliss, Oxford (Preserved) 5/89	
LLU 420	AEC Regal III	Gurney Nutting FC35F	1951	Thomas (Dealer), Reading	11/64	1/67	Scrapped at Woodcote 3/67	
JCX 756	AEC Reliance MU3RV	Plaxton C41C	1955	Payne, Bedworth	11/64	3/70	Scrapped at Woodcote 10/70	
DUD 753C	Leyland Leopard PSU3/3R	Plaxton C51F	1965	New	1/65	6/89	Luckett, Watford 9/90	

Reg. No.	Chassis Type	Body Manufacturer & Type	Year New	Immediate Previous Operator	Into CQ fleet	Date w'drawn	Initial Disposal	Notes
LNV 303	AEC Reliance MU3RV	Duple C41C	1955	York Bros, Cogenhoe	3/65	7/73	Scrapped at Woodcote 5/77	
LDL 896	AEC Reliance MU3RV	Yeates C41C	1955	Shotter, Brighstone	6/65	7/73	Scrapped at Woodcote by 12/74	
UUG 39	AEC Reliance MU3RV	Plaxton C41C	1955	George, Huddersfield	2/66	5/71	Scrapped at Woodcote 5/77	
UUG 37	AEC Reliance MU3RV	Plaxton C41C	1955	Hill, Tredegar	7/66	5/69	Scrapped at Woodcote 5/77	
KBV 778	AEC Reliance MU3RV	Plaxton C41C	1958	Ribblesdale, Blackburn	1/67	5/75	Music Group, London by 7/81	
OUN 628	Bedford SBG (oil)	Duple C41F	1957	Williams, Ponciau	4/67	5/73	Reed, Maidenhead 5/74	
135 KD	AEC Reliance 2MU3RV	Burlingham C41F	1962	Westercroft, Bradford	4/67	12/79	Mobile home 6/81	
26 MTF	AEC Reliance 2MU3RV	Yeates C41F	1960	Pearson, Rochdale	8/67	12/77	Smith (Breaker), Woodcote by 7/81	
VBD 78	AEC Reliance 2MU3RV	Duple C41F	1960	York Bros, Cogenhoe	2/68	2/78	Smith (Breaker), Woodcote by 7/81	
JNR 298	AEC Regal IV	Willowbrook DP43F	1953	Robinson, Burbage	2/68	12/71	Brown, Hounslow (Preserved) 2/72	
TUD 167G	AEC Reliance 6U3ZR	Plaxton C57F	1968	New	4/69	by 8/95	The Film Producing Unit, Bracknell /96	
YNX 478	AEC Reliance MU3RA	Duple C41F	1958	Marsh, Harvington	1/70	7/88	Oxford Bus Museum (Preserved) 4/89	Rebodied Duple Midland B44F from 530 BPG 5/72, licensed 1/73
BMK 344A	AEC Reliance 2MU3RA	Duple C45F	1963	Ivory, Tetbury	2/70	6/84	63rd Reading Scout Group 6/84	
RCG 618	AEC Reliance MU3RV	Weymann B43F	1957	Aldershot & District	12/70	6/81	Caravan, Oxford by 7/87	
591 STT	AEC Reliance 2MU4RA	Duple C45F	1964	Spiers, Henley	4/71	6/85	63rd Reading Scout Group 8/85	Sold with registration JTF 825B
ABW 777J	AEC Reliance 6U3ZR	Plaxton C53F	1971	New	4/71	by 8/95	The Film Producing Unit, Bracknell /96	
WVA 453	AEC Reliance 2MU3RA	Willowbrook B45F	1960	OK, Bishop Auckland	12/71	7/78	Scrapped at Woodcote by 6/81	
FPX 701H	AEC Reliance 6U3ZR	Plaxton C51F	1970	Byng, Portsmouth	3/72	12/94	Reeves, Woodley 12/94 (Non-PSV)	
OBK 602H	AEC Reliance 6MU4R	Plaxton C45F	1970	Byng, Portsmouth	3/72	by 7/92	Richardson, Pangbourne (Caravan) /92	'Executive' configuration C28Ft /78
EUD 256K	AEC Reliance 6MU4R	Plaxton B47F	1972	New	3/72	/96	Oxford Bus Museum (Preserved) 8/97	
SOU 440	AEC Reliance MU3RV	Weymann B41F	1958	Thames Valley & Aldershot OC	5/73	5/77	Unknown scrap dealer 5/77	
XWD 3	AEC Reliance MU3RA	Duple C41F	1958	Spencer, High Wycombe	6/73	n/a	Broken for spares	Not operated
2922 DK	AEC Reliance 4U3RA	Harrington C45F	1962	Spencer, High Wycombe	6/73	n/a	Not traced	Not operated
YBD 506	Bedford SB1	Duple C41F	1961	Spencer, High Wycombe	6/73	n/a	Grove Coaches, Furlong (?)	Not operated
OJO 835M	Leyland Leopard PSU3B/4R	Plaxton B55F	1974	New	2/74	by 10/98	Exported to Cameroon 10/98	
474 FCG	AEC Reliance 4MU4RA	Park Royal DP49F	1963	Spiers, Henley	2/75	by 9/90	Somerbus (Dealer), Paulton 9/90, then to Jeal, Crawley	B53F configuration 3/75
478 FCG	AEC Reliance 4MU4RA	Park Royal DP49F	1963	Spiers, Henley	8/75	10/82	Body scrapped at Woodcote /85	B53F configuration 3/77
471 FCG	AEC Reliance 4MU4RA	Park Royal DP49F	1963	Spiers, Henley	9/75	n/a	Scrapped at Woodcote 5/77	Not operated
SFC 32P	Leyland Leopard PSU5A/4R	Plaxton C57F	1976	New	4/76	/99	Scrap Dealer, Dorchester-on-Thames by 4/00	Re-registered VBW 581 5/86
ANL 807B	AEC Reliance 2MU3RA	Plaxton C41F	1964	Liley, Basingstoke	5/77	by 7/93	Graveling, Peterborough (Preserved) 7/93	
GMC 747J	Mercedes Benz O302	Mercedes C45F	1971	Worldwide, London SE5	5/78	/88	Murphy, Rowlands Gill 2/89	Re-registered XBW 242 6/85
PJH 582X	Leyland Leopard PSU3E/4R	Plaxton C53F	1979	New	2/79	4/02	Tourex, Oxford 4/02	Entered service 5/82
UUD 623T	Leyland Leopard PSU3E/4R	Plaxton C53F	1979	New	3/79	9/02	Horseman, Reading 9/02	Entered service 7/81, re-registered 591 STT 8/85
TYD 122G	AEC Reliance 6MU3R	Willowbrook B45F	1969	Tillingbourne, Gomshall	9/80	by 7/92	Huckle, Edgbaston (Preserved) 7/92	
TJO 54K	AEC Reliance 6MU4R	Marshall DP49F	1972	City of Oxford MS	12/80	9/90	Luckett, Watford 9/90	B53F configuration 4/87
TJO 55K	AEC Reliance 6MU4R	Marshall DP49F	1972	City of Oxford MS	12/80	9/90	James, Easton Grey 9/90	B53F configuration 5/87
LUA 244V	Volvo B58-61	Plaxton C51F	1980	Parry, Leominster	8/85	5/94	Vale, Great Kingshill (Dealer) 5/94, then to Barfoot, West End 11/94	
C644 SJM	Volvo B10M-61	Plaxton C53F	1986	New	5/86	8/02	Tourex, Oxford 8/02	Re-registered PIL 6578 9/98
B911 SPR	Volvo B10M-61	Plaxton C53F	1985	Excelsior, Bournemouth	12/86	9/02	Tourex, Oxford 9/02	Re-registered PIL 6576 9/98
HCS 795N	Leyland Leopard PSU3/3R	Alexander B53F	1975	Clydeside	11/87	by 4/94	Appleby, Hull 12/94	
E533 PRU	Volvo B10M-61	Plaxton C48Ft	1987	New	12/87	1/01	Berkhof, Basingstoke (Dealer) 1/01	Re-registered PIL 6581 9/98
CYA 181J	AEC Reliance 6MU3R	Plaxton B47F	1970	Brutonian, Bruton	2/88	6/92	Hearson, Newcastle Under Lyme 6/92	
BMO 891T	AEC Reliance 6U3ZR	Marshall B54F	1979	MoD (RAF)	10/88	5/94	Thomas, West Ewell (Dealer), then to Palmer, Blackwater	Originally carried military registration 48AC82
D262 HFX	Volvo B10M-61	Plaxton C53F	1987	Excelsior, Bournemouth	12/88	4/02	Tourex, Oxford 8/02	Re-registered PIL 6579 9/98
RFC 10T	Leyland Leopard PSU3E/4R	Duple C49F	1978	City of Oxford MS	5/89	by 9/98	Stock Car Transporter, Reading 9/98	
RFC 12T	Leyland Leopard PSU3E/4R	Duple C49F	1978	City of Oxford MS	10/90	by 10/98	Used for spares 10/98, then Scrap Dealer, Dorchester on Thames by 4/00	
WUD 815T	Leyland Leopard PSU3E/4R	Duple C49F	1979	City of Oxford MS	10/90	by 12/01	Unknown owner, Wallingford by 12/01	
H788 RWJ	Scania K93CRB	Plaxton C55F	1990	New	10/90	4/02	Horseman, Reading 9/02	Re-registered PIL 6583 1999
B915 CMR	MAN SR280	MAN C53F	1984	Lee & Back, Caversham	7/91	3/93	Boorman, Sandy 4/93	

172

Reg. No.	Chassis Type	Body Manufacturer & Type	Year New	Immediate Previous Operator	Into CQ fleet	Date w'drawn	Initial Disposal	Notes
F986 TTF	Mercedes Benz 811D	Optare B33F	1989	Lee & Back, Caversham	7/91	7/01	Boults (Dealer), Manchester 7/01	
YFC 18V	Leyland Leopard PSU3E/4R	Duple C49F	1979	City of Oxford MS	11/91	by 4/00	Scrap Dealer, Dorchester on Thames by 4/00	
F344 TSC	Mercedes Benz 811D	Alexander DP29F	1988	Bowen, Bridgnorth	3/92	9/02	Horseman, Reading 9/02	
BBW 22V	Leyland Leopard PSU3E/4R	Duple C49F	1979	City of Oxford MS	11/92	2/99	Weaver, Newbury 2/99	
C114 PUJ	Volvo B10M-61	Caetano C49Ft	1986	Hughes, Llanfair Caereinion	3/93	12/00	Berkhof, Basingstoke (Dealer) 12/00	Previously registered C690 CDS & SEL 4X. Re-registered PIL 6577 9/98
MUD 25W	Leyland Leopard PSU3F/4R	Duple C49F	1981	City of Oxford MS	5/93	4/02	Tourex, Oxford 4/02	
BBW 20V	Leyland Leopard PSU3E/4R	Duple C49F	1979	City of Oxford MS	by 8/93	by 12/01	Berinsfield Car Breakers by 12/01	
PPJ 65W	Leyland Leopard PSU5C/4R	Wadham Stringer B54F	1981	MoD (RAF)	11/93	4/02	Tourex, Oxford 4/02	Originally carried military registration 50AC08
TSV 804	Volvo B10M-61	Jonckheere C48F	1986	Gunton, Ongar	9/94	11/00	Not traced	Previously registered C28 GNK C49Ft configuration /96
D34 ENH	Volvo B10M-61	Duple C55F	1987	Country Lion, Northampton	9/94	4/02	Horseman, Reading 9/02	Re-registered PIL 6580 9/98
D504 NWG	Mercedes Benz L608D	Alexander B20F	1986	Lincolnshire Road Car	9/95	7/02	McCaffery (Preserved) 7/02	
D506 NWG	Mercedes Benz L608D	Alexander B20F	1986	Lincolnshire Road Car	9/95	/99	Caravan, South Stoke /99	
EBW 106Y	Leyland Tiger TRCTL11/3R	Duple C51F	1983	City of Oxford MS	12/95	by 12/01	Tourex, Oxford by 12/01	
2969 HJ	Leyland Leopard PSU3E/4R	Plaxton C53F	1979	Manning, Challow	4/96	by 1/01	Scrapped by 9/02	Previously registered EBM 443T
EBW 107Y	Leyland Tiger TRCTL11/3R	Duple C50F	1983	City of Oxford MS	5/96	by 12/01	Tourex, Oxford by 12/01	
G108 PGT	Mercedes Benz 811D	Alexander B26F	1990	City of Oxford MS	9/98	/00	Lister (Dealer), Bolton /00, then to Iqbal, Accrington 10/00	Re-registered XJI 4132 in 10/98
G118 PGT	Mercedes Benz 811D	Alexander B26F	1990	City of Oxford MS	9/98	9/02	Believed sold for scrap 9/02	Re-registered XJI 4133 in 10/98
G109 PGT	Mercedes Benz 811D	Alexander B26F	1990	City of Oxford MS	1/99	/00	Lister (Dealer), Bolton /00, then to Iqbal, Accrington 10/00	Re-registered XJI 7908 in -/99
T10 DMB	Volvo B10M-62	Berkhof C51Ft	1999	New	7/99	4/02	Horseman, Reading 4/02	
T20 DMB	Volvo B10M-62	Berkhof C51Ft	1999	New	7/99	4/02	Horseman, Reading 4/02	
W992 BDP	Volvo B6BLE	East Lancs B31F	2000	New	8/00	8/02	Thames Travel, Wallingford 8/02	
S228 KJT	Volvo B10M-62	Berkhof C51Ft	1998	Buddens, Romsey	12/00	4/02	Horseman, Reading 9/02	
S484 KJT	Volvo B10M-62	Berkhof C51Ft	1998	Buddens, Romsey	12/00	4/02	Horseman, Reading 9/02	
Y313 KDP	Volvo B6BLE	East Lancs B36F	2001	New	3/01	8/02	Thames Travel, Wallingford 8/02	
Y877 KDP	Volvo B6BLE	East Lancs B31F	2001	New	3/01	8/02	Thames Travel, Wallingford 8/02	
M332 GFW	Volvo B10M-62	Caetano C49Ft	1995	Jones, Newtown	by 8/01	4/02	Returned to Dawsonrentals 4/02, then to Norfolk County Council	
N498 PYS	Volvo B10M-62	Van Hool C50F	1996	Rich, Croydon	by 8/01	4/02	Returned to Dawsonrentals 4/02, then to Truronian, Truro	Originally registered LSK 824
KP51 SXU	Dennis Dart SLF	Plaxton B29F	2001	New	11/01	9/02	Horseman, Reading 10/02, then to Thames Travel, Wallingford 11/02	

Temporarily with Chiltern Queens

Reg. No.	Chassis Type	Body Manufacturer & Type	Year New	Immediate Previous Operator	Into CQ fleet	Date w'drawn	Initial Disposal	Notes
V493 NOH	Volvo B6BLE	Wright B40F	1999	Volvo Demonstrator	1/00	5/01	On Loan in 1/00, 8/00 and 4/01 to 5/01	
N222 LFR	MAN NL222FR	East Lancs B43F	1998	Mayne, Clayton	7/01	9/01	Short term hire	
V246 BNV	Dennis Dart SLF	Plaxton B29F	1999	Daybird Roadline, Killamarsh	11/01	11/01	Short term hire from Dawsonrentals	
P830 BUD	Dennis Dart SLF	Marshall B38F	1997	Accord Southern, Chichester	3/02	by 4/02	Short term hire from Dawsonrentals	

APPENDIX 5 – MANAGEMENT AND STAFF

The following are the names as can now be remembered by Tony Sears, John Davies, Michael Allen and others, from different periods of time, of individuals who were employers and employees of the two businesses. These are the people who, in their various ways, did their best to provide rural southern Oxfordshire, and part of Berkshire, with the bus services that opened up the area to bring connection to the outside world. Many were well-known local characters . .!

KEMP'S BUS SERVICES and KEMP'S MOTOR SERVICES Ltd

Management & Inspection
Harry Kemp (Proprietor and Manager)
Hiram 'John' Kemp (Managing Director)
Ethel Green (Company Secretary from 1945)
John Highe (Inspector and later Traffic Manager)
John Holder (Inspector)
Albert Jones (Inspector)
Tony Sears (Traffic Man. & Chief Engineer, 1954/5)

Office
Brenda Allen
Daphne Gutteridge
Kath Gutteridge
Pat McAra
Hilda McAra
Bill Passey (Inspector & Cashier)
Mary Passey (Mary Baldwin from 1951)

Workshop & Garage (some also drivers)

Ernie Brant (Garage Foreman)
Pete Burridge (Tyre Fitter)
John Davies (Yard Boy)
John Gutteridge
??? Jefferies (Garage Foreman replaced Ernie Brant)
Ted New (Cleaner)
Jack Passey
Peter Pearce (Yard Boy)
Tony Sears
Charlie Sharp (Upholsterer)
Eric Tappern (Workshop Technician)
George Vaughan (Gardener)
Ben Warner (Carpenter)

Drivers
Stan Beasley
Bob Birch
Les Booker
Bill China
Ken Clarke
Tommy Coles
'The Duchess'
Ted Fisher
George Goodenough
George Jarman
Charlie Lee
Cyril 'Tiger' Lilley
Cyril Minchin
Lou Novell
George Painter
Jim Pearce
Fred Prior
Harry Richards
Percy Sherwood
Roland 'Bubbles' Sherwood
Fred Smith
George Staines
Esme Swain
Frank 'Rusty' Thatcher
Tex Westland
Albert Wild
Bill Wise

Conductors
Cyril Baldwin (also Garage)
Alfie Smith
Bob Waite

CHILTERN QUEENS Ltd
Management & Inspection
Hiram 'John' Kemp (General Manager 1955-56)
Tony Sears (General Manager; Man. Dir. 1956-98)
John Holder (Traffic Manager 1955-56)
??? Cramp (Traffic Manager)
Cyril Minchin (Traffic Manager)
Adam Harris (Operations Manager; Gen. Man.)
Andy Fisher (Traffic Manager)
John Wright (General Manager)
Martin Steele (Manager)

Office
John Arbuckle (part-time Accountant)
Daphne Aylett
Mary Baldwin
Barbara Hutchins
Pat McAra
Hilda McAra
Valerie Moodie (nee Sherwood)
Anne Fowler (nee Skinner)
Miriam Smith

Workshop & Garage (some also drivers)
Wayne Ball
Ron Back (Workshop Foreman/Chief Engineer)
Michael Bedwell (Chief Engineer)
Ken Breakespear (Fitter)
Pete Burridge (Tyre Fitter)
Clive George (Upholstery Trimmer)
Robert Laver (Fitter)
Ted New (Cleaner)
Jack Passey (Workshop Technician)
Len Sears (Chief Engineer)
Garry Skinner (Fitter)
Tommy Thatcher (Apprentice)
Ben Warner (Carpenter)

Drivers (some part-time)
Bert Allen
Michael Allen
John Allum
Trevor Back
Fred Ball
Ray Barnett
John Beechey
Bob Butler
Bill China
Harry Collings
Geoff Cook
Ken Clarke
Fred Coles
Mick Davis
Brian Critchfield
Michael 'Dan' Dare

Ian Denison
Reg Dore
Dennis Eldridge
Walter Good
George Goodenough
Dick Gordon
Nigel Haniford
John Hannington
Gerry Higgs
Frank Hoskins
Kevin King
Steve King
Ray Lander
Charlie Lee
David Lee
Gordon Lee
Chris Lewington
Cyril 'Tiger' Lilley
Ian Lucas
Arnold 'Spike' Millican
Terry Newman
Linda Ould
George Painter
Jim Pearce
Bill Pearson
Kim Pembroke
Nelson Prior
Ray Prior
Brian Rawlins
Dave Read
Rev. John Shearer
Percy Sherwood
Roland 'Bubbles' Sherwood
Philip Smith
Des Spokes
Mike Spratley
Pete Stevens
Mick Stock
Fred Stone
Nick Swift
Alan Tull
Pete Turner
Bill Wheeler
Bill Wise

Conductors
Charlie Carter
Ted Horne
Tom Nash
Jack Spokes

Staff outing

1. Mrs. China
2. Ellen Webb (not a CQ employee)
3. Mrs. Fanny Sherwood
4. Cyril Lilley's daughter
5. Tony Sears' daughter Sherry
6. Pat McAra
7. Mrs. Rosa Passey
8. Mrs. Warner
9. Bill Passey
10. Charlie Lee
11. Benny Warner
12. Jack Passey
13. Mrs. Joyce Back
14. Cyril Minchin
15. Valerie Sherwood
16. "Bubbles" Sherwood
17. Michael Allen
18. Bill China
19. Daphne Aylett
20. Ron Back

A 1959 Chiltern Queens' staff and family outing to Bognor Regis used MUD 975. Bill China was driving. *(Jack Passey Colln)*

SELECTED BIBLIOGRAPHY

Having consulted the following to varying degrees, we are indebted to the authors, editors and publishers.

Books
Jordan, V, *Portrait of a South Chiltern Village* (Windmill Enterprises 1996)
Lacey, P, *Thames Valley – The British Years 1915-1920* (Paul Lacey 1990)
Lacey, P, *A History of the Thames Valley Traction Co Ltd 1920-1930* (Paul Lacey 1995)
Stone, G & Whitehead, J, *Chiltern Queens 40 Years of Service* (Chiltern Queens Ltd 1995)
The Publications Committee, *Goring & Streatley Golf Club, The First Hundred Years 1895-1995* (Goring & Streatley Golf Club 1995)

Magazine & Trade Press Articles
Anon, *West Chilterns* (Modern Transport 1940)
Anon, *Chiltern Queens 'O' Licence Revoked* (Coach & Bus Week Summer 2002)
Dare, MJC, *The Renaissance* (Buses Illustrated, Ian Allan 1963)
Millar, A, *Happy Anniversary* (Coach & Bus Week May 1995)
Taylor, J, *Chiltern Queens* (Buses Extra 75, Ian Allan 1991)
Zarywacz, R, *Queen of the Chilterns* (Bus & Coach Preservation April 2001)

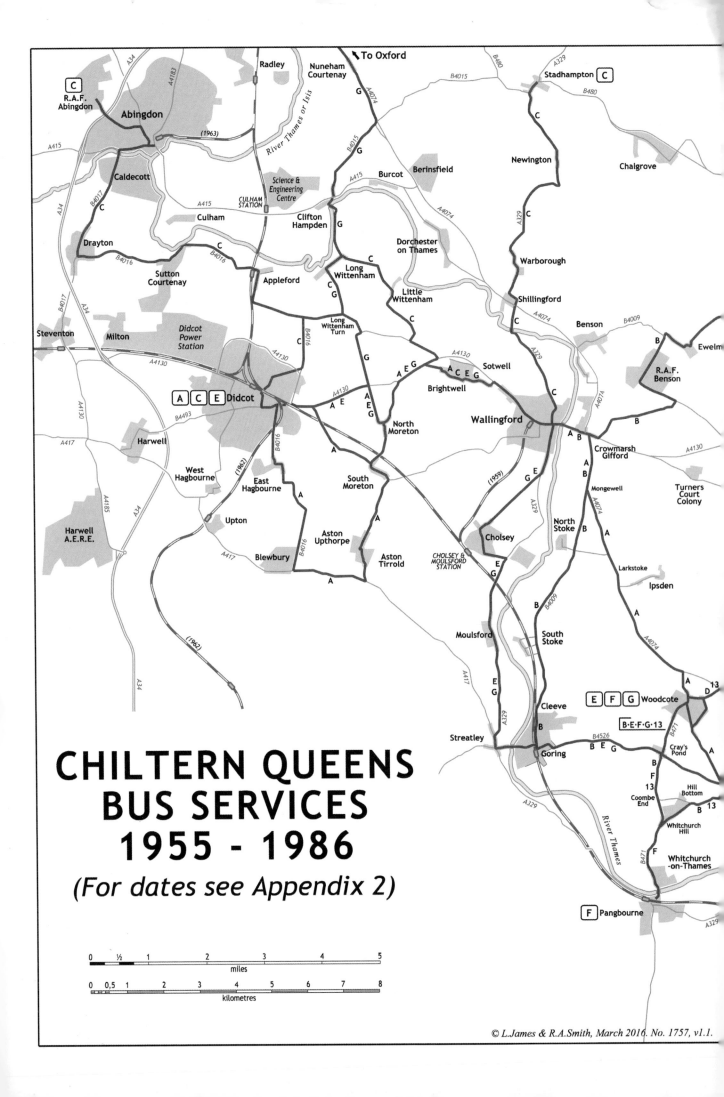

CHILTERN QUEENS BUS SERVICES 1955 - 1986

(For dates see Appendix 2)